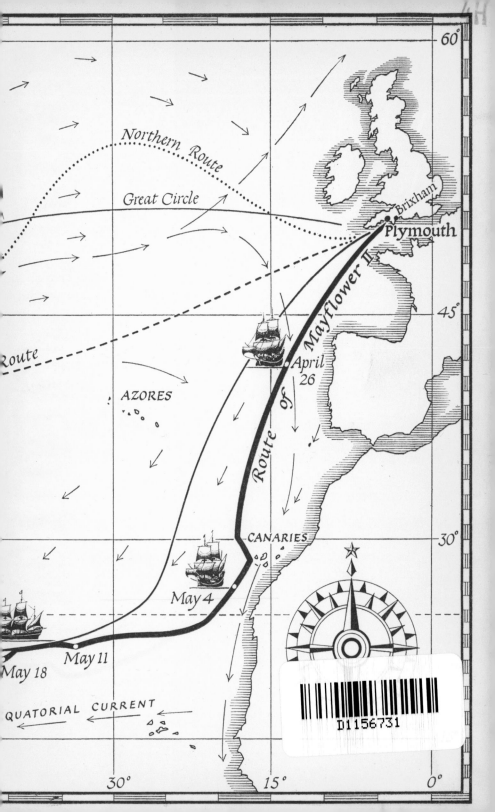

60°

Northern Route

Great Circle

Brixham

Plymouth

Mayflower II

45°

Route

AZORES

April
26

Route of

CANARIES

30°

May 4

May 11

May 18

QUATORIAL CURRENT

30°   15°   0°

The Second *Mayflower* Adventure

To Mayor Tucker,

Warwick Charlton

St Louis, 26th May 1958

The Second
Mayflower Adventure

by
WARWICK CHARLTON

With Illustrations

Boston · Little, Brown and Company · *Toronto*

LIBRARY OF CONGRESS CATALOG CARD NO. 57-13268

FIRST EDITION

This book is gratefully dedicated to
Henry Hornblower II
President, Plimoth Plantation

The author wishes to thank the editors of *The American Neptune* and William A. Baker for permission to use the material in the Appendix: "Design for *Mayflower*." Copyright 1954 by The American Neptune Incorporated.

Excerpts from *Of Plymouth Plantation 1620–1647* by William Bradford, edited by Samuel Eliot Morison, are used by permission of Alfred A. Knopf Incorporated.

Published simultaneously in Canada
by Little, Brown & Company (Canada) Limited

PRINTED IN THE UNITED STATES OF AMERICA

Contents

*(Illustrations appear between pages 90 and 91
and pages 186 and 187.)*

PART ONE
Prelude to a Voyage

All great and honourable actions are accompanied with great difficulties and must be both enterprised and overcome with answerable courages. The dangers were great, but not desperate. The difficulties were many, but not invincible.

Governor William Bradford, *Of Plymouth Plantation*

I

The Beginning

THE *Mayflower* has become a symbol. A small, ill-equipped
merchant vessel of some 180 tons which in 1620 bore a group of
English Protestants from England to America has achieved a
place in the cherished traditions of both countries. Between two
people "divided," as we are so often reminded by the politicians,
the anthologists and the after-dinner speakers, "by a common
language," a leaky, storm-battered ship, manned by a none too
savory crew, remains a permanent link revered by both. Her
voyage, the very crossing of the Atlantic itself symbolic, is accepted as the first meeting point and the point of departure of
the histories of the two English-speaking peoples. Ahead lay their
separate destinies, meeting at times in enmity, but more and more
in friendship and understanding. Behind lay a common heritage,
and it was *Mayflower* that took the accumulated, sifted wisdom
of the Old World to the New.

This I see and understand now. But my part in the story of
the second *Mayflower* does not begin at that point. There was
at first no thought of the reaffirmation of the ties laid by the
Pilgrim Fathers; no clear redefinition of the ideals they embodied
in their Compact and in their emigration to America.

Like many Englishmen of my generation, the war had brought
me into close contact with many Americans. Together we had
fought, worked, argued, laughed and lived. Together we had un-
consciously proved, and realized, that it was not the common
language that raised the barriers, but the ordinary weaknesses of
men and the vastness of the Atlantic Ocean. Together we had

reached in stumbling words the agreement that the understanding we had found in war should not be allowed to crumble in peace, when "Anglo-American relations" would be the nominated phrase for what was unconscious and unaffected friendship in more anxious times.

We had agreed in war, but in the uneasy days that followed, the tangible reaffirmations of friendship and mutual respect and understanding became more and more official phrases, press conferences and newspaper platitudes. Something more permanent yet less official was needed; some measure or plan that would perhaps link the hearts and minds of the peoples and not merely the governmental parties; something that would give a sense of community feeling to both the English and the Americans, and would stand apart from politics and international crises.

And it all began quite simply.

On a stage of a journey home from Singapore I came across the journal of William Bradford, who sailed to America in *Mayflower* and was elected governor of the little colony of Pilgrim Fathers at Plymouth. More out of curiosity than interest I had taken the book to my cabin, and idly, for I was hot and uncomfortable, and my one desire was to be back in England again, I turned the first few pages. . . . I did not put the book down until I had read that last, characteristic prayer of the man who, more than any other, had ensured the survival and prosperity of the emigrants:

Let the Lord have the praise, Who is the High Preserver of man.

I have since read the journal, one of the great works of the English language, again and again, and it still holds for me that first fascination. By any standards the voyage of *Mayflower* was a most remarkable exploit. Any voyage of exploration in the seventeenth century was likely to produce its rounds of hardships and perils, but few can have revealed the wisdom and courage which marked the Pilgrim Fathers' endeavors.

The Beginning

The distinguished American historian, S. E. Morison, has written of their voyage and settlement:*

> The Pilgrims knew nothing of the coast they had reached, except what John Smith had written in his *Description of New England*. Supplies on the *Mayflower* were gravely depleted after her ten weeks' voyage; and there was no opportunity to produce food for another nine months. Stephen Hopkins had perhaps been in Virginia; but the others for the most part were simple folk, farmers and artisans who were unused to handling firearms, ignorant alike of fishing and fur-trading, unfitted by training and temperament to cope with pioneer life on the edge of this savage continent. No group of Englishmen, Frenchmen, or Dutchmen arrived on our shores in the colonial era at so unfavorable a season or so ill equipped; few were so isolated from possible succor. Yet none came through so well. . . .
>
> They were few in number and poor in the goods of this world. They evolved no institutions of any value in American development. They were not great shipbuilders, successful fishermen or trappers, or notable farmers. They were not of gentle or noble blood. Yet those simple folk were exalted to the stature of statesmen and prophets in their limited sphere, because they firmly believed, and so greatly dared, and firmly endured.

The story of the Pilgrim Fathers, told by Governor Bradford, had excited my interest, but one paragraph in his journal, one prayer caught my imagination:

> May not and ought not the children of these fathers rightly say: *"Our fathers were Englishmen which came over this great ocean, and were ready to perish in this wilderness . . ."*

"Our fathers were Englishmen . . . " It was the obvious link between the two countries, the point where friendship could be renewed again and the age-old bonds strengthened. Quite suddenly I knew what I wanted to do and what I *would* do. In the fashionable postwar mood of doubt and disillusionment, my plan would recall a struggle and an achievement which held a message for both peoples.

* *The Pilgrim Fathers, Their Significance in History,* by Samuel Eliot Morison, Concord, New Hampshire, 1937.

The footsteps of the Pilgrim Fathers were not to be trodden in by human feet again, but it would be an honorable and a challenging task to point out whence they came and where they led.

I would rebuild *Mayflower* — and she would sail to America.

❉   ❉   ❉

How was one to set about rebuilding *Mayflower?* And when she had been constructed and had sailed to America — and of that I was certain, if hopefully so — what was to become of her, and what, if anything, was to be the permanent outcome of her voyage? These were all questions that would have to be answered sooner or later, but one could not be attempted until another was at least dealt with in part. I would never be in a position, financial or otherwise, to undertake the task myself, but would require a large measure of private or public backing: on the other hand, I could not expect people to interest themselves in my project unless I had some convincing and concrete answers to the leading questions I knew would be posed.

Somewhere, however, a start must be made, and that could only be at the center of the whole scheme, at the one common denominator of all the ideas that were passing through my mind — *Mayflower* herself.

But how big was she? What did she really look like? There was little to go on, but in such leisure as came my way in the next year or so I sought for clues.

Bradford's journal told me that she was of "burden about 9. score," and that her master's name was Jones. Presumably her burden was reckoned in tons, since the Pilgrims found her cramped for their number, and since one Christopher Jones, master of a ship called *Mayflower,* had loaded the vessel with a cargo of 161 tons, mainly "redd wyne," according to an entry in the port records of London for January 1620.

I was fortunate enough to make contact with Dr. R. C. Anderson of Blackheath. President of the Society for Nautical Research, a trustee of the Nautical Maritime Museum at Greenwich, he was the man regarded as the leading authority on *Mayflower* and he cheerfully offered his help and advice at all times in the rebuilding of the ship.

He stressed that there were no actual records of the Pilgrims' *Mayflower* at all. She was probably just any old tramp that was available at not too high a price to take on the job, and her name was not mentioned until years after her now famous voyage. It was no help that there were about a dozen *Mayflowers* listed in English records for the year 1620. He was insistent that the only evidence pointing to the identity of the ship showed that she was old — for her main beam split in a blow during the crossing — had topsails, and she was, as I have mentioned previously, about 180 tons. He had looked up full details of a contemporary ship, thought to be of the *Mayflower* size and vintage, and this could be our guide.

So that although I could not be sure how like she was to *Mayflower*, I would be building without doubt a replica of the ship of the period, of *Mayflower's* approximate size and rig, as far as these are known.

The next, and most important, question was: Assuming that there was in Britain a yard capable of building *Mayflower* in the style and manner of the seventeenth century — how much would she cost? With some trepidation I sought for rough estimates, and finished up with a figure of around £100,000 ($280,000) for the whole job.

At least I now had some concrete material on which to base my plans, and as I built them up I found that my ideas on the end product of the *Mayflower's* voyage were beginning to take some definite shape, in the form of a permanent foundation for educational and even travel exchanges between the two peoples.

Over the next year or so I continued to discuss the project and note reactions to it. Some were in principle interested, some skeptical, some suspicious. Could a builder be found? Would not £100,000 be better spent in other ways? Could a crew be assembled? The future was to give the answers, but at the time the project seemed rather remote. However, I believed my idea to be a good one, and like good wine, it would not be harmed by keeping for a year or two.

By 1954 many of my incidental problems had been settled. Timber control had ended, postwar shortages of material had eased, and nearly a decade of peace had shown to everyone the vital and enduring importance of Anglo-American unity. The organization which would be needed to control the project had more or less formed its own executive body. I had by then gone into partnership in a firm of economic and industrial public relations, and my partner, John Lowe, who soon got word of my *Mayflower* hopes, welcomed the idea with an enthusiasm which never flagged from that day forth.

The time, in short, seemed ripe for an all-out, do-or-die push.

We first sought to bring the project to the attention of a representative circle of public men, so that if their reaction was favorable we might enjoy their advice and perhaps support. The outcome of our tentative soundings was, rather to our surprise, uniformly encouraging, and a further step forward was taken when at a dinner at the House of Commons, John introduced me to the guest of honor, the American Ambassador Mr. Winthrop Aldrich. There and then I mentioned the project to him, and at his invitation, went to the embassy a day or two later with the full details of the plans as they then stood. A descendant of the Pilgrim Fathers himself, he was most enthusiastic about the scheme, and offered to make inquiries for a possible berth for *Mayflower* in America.

The general climate thus seemed set fair. I was to learn, however, that from interest, and even enthusiasm, to raising about £100,000 is a long way, which is covered by an unpredictable switchback of hope and disappointment. Even with the assurances of actual support which I had received, there was to be more toil and struggle than I foresaw.

Nevertheless, I soon had two major encouragements. At a Burma Reunion in the Albert Hall I managed to speak to Lord Mountbatten, on whose staff I had served in Southeast Asia in the latter part of the war. I told him about *Mayflower* and he in turn introduced me to the Duke of Edinburgh: they both expressed interest, though at the same time their interest seemed touched with incredulity that anyone should discuss such a project seriously. But I was happy that they should know.

By a second piece of good fortune I spoke to a young man, Dominic Elwes, the son of the well-known painter. He took me to a house in Hill Street, in the heart of Mayfair. As we ascended the staircase I was given a running commentary on the previous owners, the Duke and Duchess of Devonshire; the huge mural which nearly covered one wall, which was a Rex Whistler; and the man we were going to see, Felix Fenston, a connoisseur of the arts, a yachtsman, a big-game hunter, a classical pianist, "a jolly good chap," and one of the important names in the story of the second *Mayflower*.

That evening will remain in my memory forever.

In the entrance to the room on the first floor was a militant stuffed tiger. Felix Fenston stood up behind a desk at the far end of the room to greet us, a small, bearded man with powerful shoulders in his early forties. He struck me at once as a younger version of Ernest Hemingway.

At Fenston's invitation I proceeded to tell him of my idea and the difficulties I had met. He listened without interrupting and then said: "How much?" This was a new approach for me and for a moment I was caught off balance.

"How much?" he repeated.

"A hundred thousand to do the job," I said.

He stood up and came round to the front of his desk and I noticed that he walked with a slight limp. "If this project is going to be a success," he said, "it has got to have the support of a lot of people. Your difficulty is in making a start. I like the idea and that is where I am prepared to help you make a start. So when I say how much I mean how much to get it under way?"

I told him that £3000 was my estimate for meeting initial costs. "That would be sufficient to set up an organization which could go out and get the money."

He thought for a moment, a few seconds. It seemed longer.

Then he said: "Well, I like the idea. I will think about it and let you know." He smiled and accompanied me to the door.

While awaiting word from him I either wrote or spoke to public men and organizations of my acquaintance who I thought would be interested in helping the project.

The list of Honorary Advisers grew steadily while the list of Patrons, now headed by the Lord Mayor of London, grew until it included over a score of leading public men, either from their general interest in Anglo-American relations or from some more particular connection with the Pilgrim Fathers.

A few days later Felix Fenston asked me to call and once again I walked past the stuffed tiger guarding his door. I found him playing Bach's Two-part Inventions. He spoke while he played: "You know, Warwick, I see a lot of people, all of them with different propositions. In the time it takes them to walk from the door to that desk I think I can tell whether they are genuine or not." He stopped playing and rested his hands on the top of the piano. "You will find a check for five hundred pounds on that table. It's not much, but it is a start. I am going away tomorrow, to Nassau. As soon as I get back I'll see you again to hear how you are getting along."

If any tiger — apart from the well-known specimen of Riga — ever did smile, Felix Fenston's did to me that evening. I smiled back. The stairs of the house were the firm planks of *Mayflower's* decks, Hill Street led its narrow way to the Plymouth quayside, and the muted roar of Piccadilly's traffic echoed the long Atlantic rollers as they flung themselves in from the west. Overhead I thought I heard already the slap of the wind in the filling sails.

There was thus a cheering measure of interest and encouragement for what was known as the Mayflower Project, and Felix Fenston and my other friends had placed the proverbial penny on the drum in the late summer of 1954. During the following month I began almost immediately to make detailed plans which would lead up to a public announcement of our intentions. In the first place the project had to be given a legal entity, and after some discussions with legal and financial advisers a draft was drawn up for a new Mayflower Company.

In the Memorandum and Articles of Association I tried to express our aims and objects as simply as possible. They were as follows:

(A) To raise any sum required, by public or private subscription, in order to build, equip, and maintain a replica of the *Mayflower*.

(B) To sail the ship across the Atlantic and to present her to the people of the United States of America.

(C) To promote, support, and encourage Anglo-American relations in any form whatsoever, and to remind English-speaking peoples of their common heritage.

Nothing herein shall be construed as giving the right to the Company to carry on any of its primary objects for the purpose of profit.

The administrative plan we had in mind was that the day-to-day working of the project would be done by this company, which would be responsible for raising the necessary finance and entering into all liabilities. At the same time we realized that in order to ensure the success of the undertaking, it was necessary to have the support of public men and, if possible, the co-operation of the major organizations normally active in this Anglo-American field.

There was no lack of support from individuals who were willing to lend their names to the cause, but I found that the two best-known Anglo-American organizations, although they expressed approval in principle of the project, were unable formally to associate themselves with it. An example of this was the letter I received from an official of the English-Speaking Union: "As I told you, the English-Speaking Union has in hand a large number of projects for increasing Commonwealth-American understanding for which it has to seek the support of its members and well-wishers, and under these circumstances would find it very difficult to lend its name to a project of this kind."

Sir Campbell Stuart, the chairman of the Pilgrims, which

counted among its members the Prime Minister, the Archbishop of Canterbury, and many other distinguished men, regretted that the Pilgrims was not able to become a co-operating organization since such a project, with its associated fund raising, lay outside its normal functions.

However, many leading personalities in public life adhered to the project. The Lord Mayor of London, the Duke of Argyll, Sir Patrick Hannon, Sir Alfred Bossom, Sir Harold Webbe, Sir William Rootes (the chairman of the Dollar Exports Council and a Pilgrim himself), Lord Milner (a Privy Councillor and a former speaker of the House of Commons), Alderman Norman Prichard (chairman of the London County Council), as well as my old friend Sir Francis de Guingand were among those who all agreed to become patrons. But before I could call a meeting of the patrons there were a number of important questions to which I had to have the answers. First of all: Who was to be the builder?

My inquiries over the years had shown me that the number of firms in England capable of building *Mayflower* was limited. The demand for wooden ships had been falling away and consequently even firms who had the facilities to do the job doubted that they could find craftsmen to carry out the work. These men were a dying race. But despite these difficulties there were at least three yards capable of building *Mayflower* if they could get the men, and each of them had a nucleus of shipwrights to do the job.

I was confident, when I announced our plans, not only that a builder would be forthcoming, but also that he would find the craftsmen, too. As matters turned out, this confidence was justified.

We were not unduly worried about getting the necessary finance. Perhaps we should have been, but we had already received sufficient assurances of financial support to feel reasonably confident that we could get under way, and that once building had begun there would not be any great difficulty in this direction.

The most depressing matter concerned the berthing of *May-*

flower in the United States. Mr. Aldrich's inquiries had un-
earthed no organization which would be able both to berth her
— which was easy and for which there was never a lack of
volunteers — and afford to maintain her in the years to come —
which was the stumbling block.

This threatened to be a serious setback. After all, building
replicas of famous ships and delivering them in the United States
was by no means a new idea. My inquiries on this subject produced some depressing information. At least two hulks of
"Columbus's vessels" had been seen rotting on the foreshore in
Chicago a few years previously (they had been sailed across
from Spain for a world's fair in Chicago in 1893), and a replica
of Hudson's *Half-Moon* had decayed to pieces up the Hudson
River. She had taken part in some celebrations and then had been
forgotten and neglected. Then there was the case of a replica
of Leif Ericson's longboat, which was sailed across from Sande-
fjord in Norway to the United States. This was also for Chicago,
and although she did well on her Atlantic voyage she, too, was in
due course forgotten.

Nearer home there was another reminder of the difficulties of
berthing: the famous *Cutty Sark* constituted a considerable
financial headache until the powerful intervention of the Duke of
Edinburgh and Lord Mountbatten.

Disturbing as these reports were, I decided not to allow them
to prevent our going ahead with the plans, but at the same time
I realized that we would be open to serious criticisms indeed, if
£100,000 was spent to rebuild *Mayflower* and sail her to America,
only for her to lie forgotten in some yard when all the excitement
was over. But here the answer to the problem was to come from
an unexpected quarter, and to be one of many examples of what
I should like to think was a benevolent Providence taking a hand
in our affairs.

II

Plimoth Plantation

Some six months after the first soundings, when plans were proceeding at a careful pace, two events occurred which both helped and embarrassed us. They helped, because they eventually provided the solution to two major problems: the permanent berthing of the ship, and the public announcement of our plans. A colleague who had been busying himself with historical research one day returned from a visit to the Maritime Museum with a copy of the American magazine *The American Neptune*. In it I was astounded to find an article by a Mr. W. A. Baker which was illustrated with detailed drawings of *Mayflower*. These were based on Dr. Anderson's work, but with an important difference. Mr. Baker was a naval architect, and his drawings represented the translation of Dr. Anderson's research into full-scale plans from which a shipyard could work. There was an acknowledgment in *Neptune* that these plans had been drawn up for an organization in the United States called Plimoth Plantation, of Plymouth, Massachusetts. I at once rang up the American Embassy and asked if they could give me any background on this organization, but they were unable to do so.

There were two questions in my mind: For what reason had Baker drawn up the plans, and what was the purpose of Plimoth Plantation? I decided I could best get my information at firsthand through the transatlantic telephone, and although I had no address, the American operator eventually connected me to Mr. Arthur Pyle, the secretary of the plantation. My first question to Arthur Pyle was: "Are you building a replica of the *Mayflower?*"

[14]

"No," he said, "we are not; but we have done a lot of research on the subject."

I told him of the Mayflower Project and then asked: "Would you be interested in berthing *Mayflower* if we built her?"

There was a pause on the line while he considered this proposition, and I thought I could hear the sound of the Atlantic Ocean intruding. Then: "Why, yes. But I think the best thing to do is for you to send someone over here, so that it can be discussed with our Board of Governors."

This was a most reasonable suggestion and I told him that I would try to send someone over within a few days.

"Let me know whom you are sending and when we can expect him," he said, "because I am sure that our president, Mr. Hornblower, would like to make him welcome."

I gasped, suddenly suspicious that I was on the receiving end of an elaborate practical joke, and asked Arthur Pyle to repeat the name to make sure that I had heard aright.

I heard Arthur chuckle. "Yes: Mr. Hornblower," he repeated. "Harry Hornblower," and spelled the name out for me.

I reported this conversation to John Lowe and asked him if he would be prepared to go within the next few days to the United States to see the plantation, and he agreed to do so. There was some consternation at the American Embassy when he went there to get a visa and gave as the reason for the visit "the rebuilding of *Mayflower*."

While the visa was being obtained and we were getting the necessary Bank of England authority for dollar expenditure, I had a telephone call from Fleet Street which disturbed me. Someone to whom the project had been mentioned had been overheard discussing it, and the information, in garbled form, had found its way to "Ephraim Hardcastle," the pseudonym for the society gossip columnist on the *Sunday Express*. Clearly, a premature and inaccurate disclosure of our plans in the national press might be damaging to the project. I took a taxi to Fleet Street and saw the journalist in charge of the column, and asked if he would hold the story until plans had advanced far enough for me to make an announcement. I promised that in view of the situation he would be given an exclusive report, but although he undertook to use my story in preference to the version overheard, like any good newspaperman, whose job it is to get news and print it before his colleagues, he could not agree to my proposal. I decided therefore that my only course was to make John's flight to America the occasion for an official announcement. This meant that I was once and for all completely committed, but there was no other course to adopt. I saw Stanley Mason, the news editor of Reuters, and gave him a statement.

Perhaps it erred on the side of caution and was cast in too formal terms. Anyway, the news was noted in most of the leading newspapers, and on the following Monday I was pleased to see this comment by Cassandra in the *Daily Mirror*:

> So the *Mayflower* will sail again. A replica of the Pilgrim Fathers' ship, meticulously exact in detail, is to be built in Britain at a cost of £100,000. It will then be sailed from Plymouth to the United States and presented to the American people as a gift from the British people.
> An excellent idea.
> A few years ago the Danes had a similar inspiration, and brought a Viking ship across the North Sea to visit us. It was great fun and the goodwill between ourselves and Denmark was helped enormously by the cruise.
> When people start building decorative boats for each other instead of H-bombs, well it makes a nice change.

My story had also been sent by the news agencies to the United States, and I wondered what the reaction was going to be. Would they dismiss it as a stunt? Would they suggest that it would be better if Britain paid them some of the dollars they owed instead of sending the ship? Or would it awaken no interest at all, except in a small section of the New England coast where the Pilgrims had made their home in America? Neither John nor I could give the answers to these questions. We had to wait and see, and he would be the first to know.

I decided it would be good for his morale if he bought a new bowler hat for the journey, and as I saw him board the plane at London Airport, complete with new bowler and dressed in his customary pin-striped trousers and black jacket, I thought that he looked a most impressive ambassador, all six feet five inches of him. I waited at the airport until the aircraft had lofted into the gray skies and reflected that a great deal depended on the success of his mission to America.

John's train was met at Route 128 by a slim young man in his early thirties, Henry Hornblower II, president of Plimoth Plantation, Inc. After an exchange of courtesies, when I am sure Henry regarded John, wearing his brand-new bowler, and with his formal turn of speech and manner, as an erudite undertaker, there was dinner in a country pub at Windsor. There John changed into a dinner jacket of Victorian cut. Many months later, when I too met Henry, he recalled for me the astonishment he and his fellow countrymen had felt when they saw the dinner jacket. Nevertheless, they managed to give their visitor the impression that it was an everyday occurrence.

First of all, over dinner, John was introduced to the governors of Plimoth Plantation. The plantation consisted of a group of private citizens, headed by Henry Hornblower, a Boston investment banker, keen archaeologist and a trustee of the Pilgrim Society. They were rebuilding the original Pilgrim settlement in Plymouth, Massachusetts, and in fact had already built two houses and the fort-meetinghouse, as well as having carried out a great deal of archaeological and historical research.

There was Bill Brewster, who looked like a young Cary Grant. He was a twelfth-generation direct descendant of the Pilgrims' first religious leader in America, the Ruling Elder William Brewster, and had seventeen other lines of descent to members of the *Mayflower* complement. John was impressed to find that the plantation, although a small body and right at the center of the Pilgrim tradition, had avoided the narrow exclusivism which characterizes some descendants of the Pilgrims. None of the remaining governors was a direct descendant of the Pilgrim company, but had joined the board from a profound respect and enthusiasm for the tradition which it represented.

The treasurer of the organization, Mr. Walter H. Neave, was another banker, and a robust Republican of the type found further south than New England. Another governor, Mr. George P. Olsson, was of Swedish origin. It was, however, yet another governor, Judge Amedeo Sgarzi, who was in some ways the most remarkable personality of the group, and indeed of all the people met in Plymouth. Italian by descent, he had come to enjoy a standing and influence, not only in the plantation, but in the municipal life of the town, which would never be equaled in any English community. Apart from being invoked and universally accepted as arbitrator in any contentious matter, he appeared, from subsequent conversations with civic leaders, to be entrusted with decisions and whole ranges of policy matters which gave him the authority of a New England Solomon.

Later in the evening came a visit to the First House, a replica of the typical buildings which the Pilgrim Fathers must have erected in the first year or two after their landing. Illuminated by a single street lamp, this tiny structure, hardly the size of a garage, was more impressive in its first impact than any building John had yet seen in America. It was a strange thought, he reflected, that this wooden cabin, albeit in replica, was in some sense the birthplace of the nation whose vast skyscrapers were among the modern wonders of the world.

On Sunday he attended a service at the First Church, which is in direct descent from the Pilgrims' religious meeting place. After church came lunch, with the traditional turkey and cranberry sauce, and in the evening he was shown the plans of *Mayflower* drawn up by W. A. Baker. Among earlier intentions of the plantation had been the building of a waterline replica of *Mayflower*. We were subsequently to learn, although I naturally did not know it at the time, that this had been mooted as much as seven years earlier, and Mr. Baker, a naval architect by profession, but also an internationally renowned authority on the history of shipbuilding, particularly of the seventeenth century, had prepared a complete set of working drawings, based on Dr. Anderson's research, but the difficulties of rebuilding had proved insuperable.

John realized that if we could have the use of Baker's plans the project would be advanced by at least six months, the time we had estimated it would take to have similar plans drawn up from the information made available to us in England by Dr. Anderson.

He therefore told the governors that he wished to reach agreement with the plantation on two main points:

(1) The berthing of *Mayflower*.

(2) The use of Baker's plans.

The discussion lasted into the small hours and was subsequently continued at the Neaves' house. On Monday morning Heads of Agreement were drawn up in Bill Brewster's Boston office, and were approved by the attorney for the plantation, Mr. Lothrop Withington. These formed the basis of all future cooperation between our two organizations.

They formed an important part of the basis on which our own work was to be built, and conditioned the future of *Mayflower's* journeys to and in the United States. For these reasons I give at some length the considerations underlying the Heads of Agreement and the main points which they covered.

First of all, it was important that the sailing of the second *Mayflower* should be a gesture to the whole American people and not, as it could in other circumstances have become, a re-emphasis of a particular episode, however vital, or a commemoration of a particular place, however hallowed in American history. It was therefore stipulated that the ship should, after reaching Plymouth, visit other parts of the United States, returning there for the permanent berthing and maintenance which the plantation undertook to provide.

The governors of the plantation further undertook to make available not only Mr. Baker's plans but also the considerable volume of research material which it had amassed on the Pilgrim period. As a guarantee of accuracy and workmanship, they requested that Mr. Baker be appointed design agent to the project, which we naturally welcomed, and were to welcome still more in the years to follow.

Demarcation of responsibility was obviously of the first importance, since both organizations would have their own obligations to consider and both had much to contribute.

The building, Atlantic journey and coastwise or inland journeys of *Mayflower,* prior to handing over to Plimoth Plantation, were to be with the English organization, though the plantation agreed to help with arrangements in the United States. This left the question of meeting regulations of the Ministry of Transport with the project.

The plantation accepted the responsibility of berthing, exhibiting and maintaining the ship after her handing over, thus overcoming the problem of finding a suitable and adequate organization to look after the most vital side of the undertaking.

The job of public relations affecting the undertaking was left to the British organization, though the plantation also undertook to make available facilities in this respect.

The document then outlined the expected sources of revenue and likely classes of expenditure, and defined the apportionment of each between the plantation and the project.

The general principles governing the division of income and expenditure as these concerned the building, operation and berthing of the ship were fairly clear, and merely required definition. It was reasonably to be expected, however, that whatever happened in the interim, there would be some surplus of revenue when the ship had finally been brought into her berth.

John therefore proposed the establishment of a trust fund for the receipt and management of such surpluses. Its object would be the furtherance of study and education in Anglo-American relations, with especial reference to the Pilgrim period. Since both bodies would be concerned, the plantation by its current responsibilities and the project by its contribution of the vessel, it was agreed that both should be represented in the management of the trust. It was agreed further that the general object of the trust should be to provide academic and cultural exchange and scholarship facilities to study in the United Kingdom and to further research, publications and reconstructions.

The plantation could hardly have realized it at the time, but their undertaking to berth the ship was eventually to grow into an enterprise costing a million dollars.

The document was completed by an outline of the liaison arrangements which would govern the corporation of the two bodies. For our part the meeting and the subsequent agreement could not have been more felicitous.

Before John left America he was received by Christian A. Herter, Governor of the Commonwealth of Massachusetts. He applauded the project and described it as "a striking and imaginative contribution to the fostering of Anglo-American relations."

When I went to meet John at London Airport, he had in his luggage a five-foot waterline scale model of the hull of *Mayflower* which had been made to Baker's specifications. The agreement secured, together with the plans, meant that within a few days our major problem, that of berthing, had been solved, and we were also in a position to approach a builder to start work with full-scale plans and detailed specifications. Never in the course of the project were obstacles to be so smoothly and completely overcome.

Now I had to find a builder and turn promises of financial help into hard cash so that he could start work. The latter was to be far more difficult than the first.

III

Keel Laying

Pᴵʀᴀᴄʏ and *Mayflower* did not seem to go together, despite the fact that the seventeenth century and piracy are synonymous, but when we took out our first insurance on the ship, Lloyds gave us a policy which contained the old wording protecting us against "fyer, enemyes, pirrattes, rovers, theeves, jettezons, letters of marte and countermarte, arests, restraints and deteynments of Kings and Princes." However, there was an attempt at piracy before we had reached the stage of taking out insurance, and the news of it came from an unexpected quarter.

The telephone message from the American Embassy gave no storm warning. The message simply said that Mr. Robert Ames, special assistant to his Excellency the Ambassador, would like to see me at Grosvenor Square as soon as possible. In the taxi, on the way there, I pondered the possible reasons for this summons. Perhaps the embassy wants to know how we are getting along, I thought. After all, they have had no information except for newspaper reports since I saw Mr. Aldrich. In the event, it transpired this was only part of the cause.

Ames was a Bostonian, polished, urbane, with a quiet manner. He came straight to the point.

"Mr. Charlton, when are you going to lay the keel?"

I told him I had not decided on a date, but we had found a builder.

"How long before work starts?"

"About two or three months."

"Could you get started sooner?" he persisted.

[22]

"Well, I suppose . . ." I hesitated, and he asked me another question.

"How about the financial side?"

"That is well in hand. Now that I have found a builder I plan to get together for an inaugural meeting all the people who have promised us support, so that those who have promised may turn their promises into fact and those who have indicated their interest may be persuaded to take similar action.

"The position is that although we have a quotation for the ship of sixty thousand pounds, we do not wish to make a contract with the builder until after our inaugural meeting."

"How much money can you call upon *now*?" asked Mr. Ames.

"Between three and four thousand."

"Then my advice, Mr. Charlton, is that the sooner you lay that keel the better."

I was puzzled by the sense of urgency he conveyed. I could not see that a few weeks would make any difference to the project. Indeed, with the summer holidays and the Parliamentary recess taking people out of London, and with a number of my own business affairs to look into, it was a highly inconvenient moment to set a major effort in train.

He could see I was puzzled and continued: "Tell me, does the name of Wallace mean anything to you?"

I shook my head. "No, I don't think so."

"A few days ago," said Mr. Ames, "a Mrs. Wallace called to see the Ambassador. His Excellency was engaged and I saw her myself. Mrs. Wallace had a complaint to make, a serious one. She and her husband had been approached by a young man who stated that he was the organizer of the Mayflower Project. This was in late March, just after the first reports had appeared in the press. This young man persuaded the Wallaces to part with a thousand pounds."

"Could you give me his name?" I asked.

Mr. Ames did so, and at once it rang a bell. I recalled reading about him in a newspaper and on one occasion he had been pointed out to me at a West End restaurant. He was known to the police as an extremely clever confidence man, and a few weeks before, the French Sûreté had announced that they wished to interview him in connection with a robbery at a villa in the South of France. I told Mr. Ames what I knew. He nodded. "You will forgive me for asking this question, Mr. Charlton, but I am sure you will understand that I have to do so, just for the record. Has this man at any time had any connection with the project?"

"None at all," I assured him.

"I was confident that would be your reply, but you understand I had to put the question. I do not think that there is any way to guard against this sort of thing happening, but the fact that it has could be most harmful to your project. Naturally the Wallaces feel they have been tricked out of their money. I do not know whether it will get into the newspapers, but if it does, although you are the innocent bystander, the consequent publicity would inevitably be harmful."

I nodded assent.

"So you see now why I suggest to you that you should try to lay the keel as quickly as possible," he continued.

I realized that if the news of the fraud on the Wallaces made headlines before I started building, many of my supporters would be frightened away. Even if the story broke after building began, it would be harmful, but having begun, there would be a fighting chance of riding the storm.

I thanked Mr. Ames for the information he had given. The only way to stop piracy of this or any other sort was to take a hint from Mr. Ames and start building. The keel must be laid within a matter of days. I reckoned that I could call upon just over £3000. But how much would the builder need to start work and what guarantees would he require for future payments? Again, the same benevolent Providence was to come to our aid.

While John had been in America, the *Illustrated London News* had published a double-page drawing of *Mayflower*, together with a long caption which gave our plans for the rebuilding. One of the results of this had been a letter signed by Stuart Upham, a shipbuilder of Brixham in Devon. He wanted to build *May-flower*.

His firm, J. W. & A. Upham Ltd., had been building wooden ships for nearly two hundred years. Their records show the first vessels built by them were the little fruiters of round about 150 tons. These craft were built for £9 a ton.

After the trade of these craft declined, the firm started on probably one of their best-known types of vessel — the Brixham trawler — of which many were supplied to the great fishing ports around these islands. There is no doubt that for the fishing industry, these little, sea-kindly vessels with their snug ketch rig were unsurpassed for laying about in the fishing grounds, and whenever Stuart Upham spoke about them he did so with a sadness at their passing and said: "When I was a boy the harbor was dark with their sails and now, to the best of my knowledge, there is not one Brixham trawler working under sail today."

During the war years the firm armed and equipped ships and ran Admiralty trials and builders' trials from their dry dock; they armed and equipped and dry-docked over eleven hundred vessels, excluding the building of thirty-five wooden motor mine-sweepers and M.T.B.s, all of which were over a hundred feet long.

With this vast background of experience of heavy wooden ship-building accumulated over the years, they were, I felt confident, capable of carrying out the *Mayflower* reconstruction.

I cabled Upham to say that I would be flying down to Exeter and would be grateful if he would meet me there. I have often wondered what he thought of the tousled-haired man who stepped out of the little plane that day and drove with him to the yard. He did not speak much until I was in his offices and then he said suddenly, as though he were breaking through a dam which held back his excitement: "You know, we *can* do it! This is the place to build her."

He took me for a tour of the yard, saying very little, but when he did he spoke about wooden ships with such affection that the feeling was communicated. I do not think I have ever been so impressed with a first meeting as I was with Stuart Upham.

I had found our man. He patently possessed two important qualities: great enthusiasm for the project in hand and the integrity of the true craftsman.

I asked him if he thought it would be difficult to obtain the necessary timber for building, as John had been told in the United States that they estimated that this alone would take nearly two years. "I think I know where to get it," he said. "No, that won't be the problem. It's the men, but we have got a nucleus of them. They are old ones, but they are the ones with the craft and they will teach the others."

After my visit to the embassy and the disquieting news I had received there we decided to take Upham into our confidence and see how far he would go along with us. "I know that in the normal way," I said to him, "contracts with shipbuilders stipulate so much down and guarantee regular time payments. We are not in a position to do that, but if you have confidence in the project and will accept a first payment in good faith, we could get started."

His reaction was surprisingly free of complications. "I am prepared to make a start," he said. "We're only a small firm with limited resources, but such as they are, they're at your disposal. Lay the keel, start building, and my belief is that the little ship will start talking for herself."

He held out his hand. I shook it, and our first contract with Stuart Upham, shipbuilder and gentleman, was made. On the Fourth of July, American Independence Day, 1955, work on *Mayflower* began.

A few days later we sealed the contract with the company's check for £1000, and I also sent out invitations to all the people who had expressed interest in the project, inviting them to a meeting on July 27 at Felix Fenston's house in Hill Street.

Felix had been away in Nassau and we had been out of touch during John's visit to America. He was pleasantly surprised when I told him of the advanced plans for building and of the arrangement for the permanent berthing of the ship in the United States.

Keel Laying

I did not tell him the story I had heard from Mr. Ames at the embassy, but simply stressed that the time had arrived for action.

Sir Patrick Hannon presided, acting as joint host with Felix Fenston for the inaugural meeting of our supporters. I told them what had gone before and announced that the keel was to be laid on the following day. I think some of them were puzzled at the haste with which they were called to Hill Street and the keel laying was announced: the earlier pages of this chapter are my reasons — and my formal apology.

Applications for places in the crew had already begun to arrive at the office from men and women stirred by the romance of the venture. One came from a Commander Kenelm Winslow, a collateral descendant of Edward Winslow, who sailed on the first *Mayflower* and who emerged as the Pilgrims' most eminent diplomatist. Edward was three times governor of the New Plymouth Settlement, a member of North America's first "Parliament," and one of Cromwell's right-hand men in Commonwealth affairs. Kenelm Winslow wrote on behalf of his own son John, who was in the Royal Navy and an expert yachtsman and swimmer. We invited Commander Winslow to officiate at the formal keel laying of the ship and thus provide a link with the Pilgrims. As the months went by, I became more aware of the deeper significance of the voyage of the Pilgrim Fathers' vessel, which had sailed as a defiance of autocracy and exclusivism, and had in some sense over the centuries achieved her goal to a degree beyond the Fathers' imagining. Her successor, in fact, must be made to typify the fulfillment of the toleration and universality for which, in their way, the Pilgrim Fathers had risked their all. Nevertheless, in was their heroism which had begun the battle, and a due observance of their feat was our proper duty. If we could find a descendant's family which had continued to epitomize the link between England and America over the intervening centuries it would form a living connection between the two vessels.

I was, moreover, influenced by other considerations. Edward Winslow, the Pilgrim leader, had embodied in his way the connection between enlightened scholarship and printing characteristic of the European Renaissance, of which the first *Mayflower's* journey was one of the last expressions. Kenelm Winslow was himself closely connected with printing and the Fleet Street where Winslow had dwelt and been married. Kenelm's son John was by his own qualities a very proper and indeed obvious choice for inclusion in the crew.

The story of the family's descent over the centuries is worth telling as an example of the link between the English and American peoples symbolized by *Mayflower*.

No British family was more intimately identified with the birth of the American nation, or has remained more closely allied to it since. Ten generations linked Commander Winslow's son John, the modern Winslow boy, with the seventeenth-century Pilgrims, John and his bride Mary Chilton, the first of the *Mayflower* women to set foot in America.

John Winslow I, Kenelm's ancestor, was one of five sons of a Droitwich merchant who all emigrated to America as Pilgrims, though not in the same ship. Two of them, Edward and Gilbert, were among the first batch of Pilgrim Fathers in the *Mayflower* in 1620, together with John's bride-to-be, Mary Chilton.

When *Mayflower*, after a two-and-a-half-month voyage, limped into New Plymouth she had a collapsed main beam. That she survived the voyage is probably due to the ingenuity of Edward Winslow, a printer, who had taken his press along with him, for when the main beam collapsed he jacked it up with his press, a support which kept the ship intact for the rest of the trip.

John met Mary Chilton, the *Mayflower* heroine, when he arrived at New Plymouth in 1621.

He sailed in *Fortune*, which proved prophetic for him. For it was John who founded the Winslows' prosperous Boston shipping business that flourished for one hundred and fifty years.

Next in the family tree was Edward, one of eleven children born to John and Mary. Edward, a captain in his father's ships, was born in 1634 and died in 1682.

His second wife was Elizabeth Hutchinson, granddaughter of Ann Hutchinson, one of the most interesting and controversial women in New England. For daring to challenge the religious opinions of the Puritan settlement, Ann Hutchinson was condemned as a heretic and banished with her children to Rhode Island. There she and all but one of her children were slain by the Indians.

Sole survivor of that family massacre was the father of Elizabeth Hutchinson, who became Edward Winslow's second wife. Edward and Elizabeth had five children. One of them, another Edward, was born in 1669 and died in 1753.

In 1709, four generations after the *Mayflower* pilgrimage, Isaac Winslow was born in Boston. He inherited the prosperous family shipping business and married twice. During the period of growing revolt against "interference" from Britain, Isaac Winslow was a prominent Loyalist and Addresser to Governor-General Gage. Although a Loyalist, he married Lucy, daughter of the famous Revolutionary General Waldo. She died in 1765 and at her funeral he proposed to Jemima Debuke, who married him and bore his two sons, Thomas and James. They were happy and prosperous, but in the Revolutionary War of 1775 the family had to flee from Boston with the retiring British troops.

Two years later Isaac died a penniless exile in New York, and within ten days baby James was also dead. Jemima and her five-year-old son Thomas sought refuge with friends in London, where the widow died in 1790. Reared by his widowed mother in England, Thomas became a captain in the Army. While he was stationed in Bermuda he married Mary Forbes, daughter of a Scottish settler, and they had thirteen children.

Wealth returned to this branch of the Winslow family in the shape of two fortunes inherited by Thomas on his return to England. But the retired soldier speculated on the Exchange and lost everything. So another penniless Winslow widow crossed the Atlantic to start life afresh — this time from London to New York.

But not Thomas Forbes Winslow, the eldest son. He was a midshipman with the Royal Navy in Bermuda when his father died. T. F. Winslow left the Navy to try his luck in England.

There he married Elizabeth Matthewson, daughter of a Calcutta jute merchant. They had eleven children. He took a degree in philosophy at Glasgow University, became a Presbyterian preacher and, through his wife, inherited yet another fortune for the Winslows.

The next two Winslow generations spent most of their lives in lunatic asylums — not as inmates but as residents.

Henry Forbes Winslow, T.F.'s youngest child, born in 1834, became an M.D. specializing in lunacy. He married Mary Grant, a Scot who had been reared in Canada. For years the family lived in two lunatic asylums which the doctor conducted at Hammersmith and Hayes Park.

After a hectic early life in the asylums, Dr. Winslow's son Ernest Henry evidently sought refuge in orthodoxy. He married an English wife, settled down with five children as the company secretary to a Manchester dye firm and died in 1942.

It was his third son, Douglas Kenelm, who laid the keel of the new *Mayflower*, and their midshipman son, John, whom we chose to sail with us.

In the shipyard the British flag and the Stars and Stripes hung over what Stuart called "the stick." This was the keel, a naked chunk of wood, with true edges stretching fifty-eight feet on the straight and curved upward at the end. It was not all one piece but joined by a keel scarf, and had been hewn from a one-hundred-twenty-year-old oak.

The Vicar of Brixham, the Reverend Yeomans, conducted a short service, and then Commander Winslow formally tapped the two pieces of timber into place. There was a splutter of flash bulbs, a whirl of newsreel cameras, and the job had been done.

Standing next to me during the ceremony were Bill Baker and his wife Ruth. They had flown over for the ceremony, and afterwards Bill Baker said: "Warwick, I feel sure you have the right man to build her." I was to learn that Bill was a man of few words and that for him this was a lengthy speech.

Keel Laying

Before I left the yard to return to London, I asked Stuart how he thought the ship would sail, for to me, in the excitement, she was already halfway to completion. He replied with a smile which lit his light-blue eyes: "Like a pig!"

On my way back to London I reflected that one very important hurdle had been taken, anyway; one that would discourage the pirates, who could have been a nuisance, and silence some of the skeptics, though they didn't matter so much. As John said: "The only pity is that Ken Winslow had his hands the wrong way round on the hammer."

A few days later I went into hospital to have attention for my leg, which I had broken some months previously in an accident and which was not healing as well as it might. John came to see me one evening, looking downcast. "I have some bad news," he said. "Sir Patrick Hannon has withdrawn his patronage."

"Did he tell you why?"

"He gave a reason," said John. "He said he was getting on in years, and that is true, for he is over eighty, and that he had too many other commitments."

"Do you think that is the real reason?"

"I honestly don't know," John admitted, "but I do know his going is a great loss."

So did I, and I have always wondered just how far the story of the international crook who used *Mayflower* to steal £1000 had spread, and made people, even those who knew us well, apprehensive of being involved in disputes and acrimony.

I must have looked very depressed when John gave me the news about Sir Patrick, for before he left he said: "Don't worry, it won't break the project. Anyway, here is something to buck you up," and he gave me a cutting from an American newspaper. "Go on," he said, "read it, and remember there are many more like it in the office."

Here is what the Michigan *News Advocate* had to say about the rebuilding of the *Mayflower:*

There is something heart-warming in this gesture by the peoples of England. It can hardly draw the two nations closer together than the present alliance, dictated in part by the exigencies of current international politics, in part by common friendship and understanding, between them. Rather, it is a tangible reaffirmation of that friendship. It is a gesture, not at the official, governmental level, but from people to people. It is a personal salute, deeply appreciated.

It is a reminder that time can heal wounds, that bitter enemies can become friendly allies. The entire world is in need of such a reminder today.

Reading this dispersed my depression, and I soon returned to my normal condition of optimism. All we needed now, I reflected, was the best part of £100,000, so the sooner I was out of hospital and getting the money, the better for the project. I rang for a nurse and told her I felt well enough to leave.

She went for the sister.

IV
Getting the Money

THE American humorist Steig is not very far away from the truth in the cartoon where he portrays an executive slumped over his desk with a knife in his back, and standing behind him "a business friend" carrying a dispatch case. The caption reads: "Sorry, Charlie, business is business!" When we decided that one of the best sources for obtaining finance for *Mayflower* was the business world, we either had to show them that association with *Mayflower* was good business, or make them forget that business was business.

Early on I came to appreciate the words of Albert Schweitzer:

> To obtain the necessary funds for my undertaking I undertook a round of begging visits among my acquaintances, and experienced in full measure the difficulty of winning their support for a work which had not yet justified its existence by showing something achieved, but was for the present only an intention. Most of my friends and acquaintances helped me over this embarrassment by saying that they would help my adventurous plan, because I was its author. But I must confess to having also experienced that the tone of my reception became markedly different when it came out that I was there, not as a visitor but as a beggar.

During the two years in which we were engaged in raising approximately £100,000 for the project, I became something of a chameleon. I would change my approach by a sort of mental radar to suit my victim. There was only one morality, to keep the supply of cash flowing to pay the craftsmen working on the project.

Prelude to a Voyage

When Stuart gave a rough first estimate of £60,000 for building, it was soon apparent that it was very "rough." Timber alone cost nearly £30,000, but even this figure does not include some ideally shaped pieces that Stuart required and which were not for sale. They mysteriously disappeared from a copse near a house where a timber-concession officer lived. One morning the timber officer was disturbed by what he must have thought was the sound of giant woodpeckers at work. When he looked out of his window he could see only a number of ordinary human beings, so I suppose he went back to bed and counted *Mayflowers* instead of sheep. It was fortunate at times that the people of the West Country were with us, for in the morning not only had the suitably shaped pieces of oak vanished, and, it was rumored, reappeared in Upham's shipyard, but the copse itself had disappeared.

The ropes, which took months of research and over a year to make, we knew would cost nearly £7000. When you add to this the scores of smaller items necessary to fit out and equip even a tiny ship like *Mayflower*, it is not surprising that material charges alone should account for nearly £45,000.

In addition to this there was the cost of labor and a reasonable profit for Stuart Upham's firm. In view of the fact that no one had built a ship like *Mayflower* for over three hundred years, it was very difficult to say how long the ship would be a-building.

In addition to the monies raised, we were given considerable quantities of materials. Some we accepted with thanks, and for some we charged. I will go into this latter and perhaps surprising practice later.

Throughout the project I kept going a steady flow of news through all the popular media of the press, radio, television, magazines, and this resulted in what is known as "impulse giving." A number of firms read about the project and it captured their imagination sufficiently for them to make very generous contributions to our cause.

The first news stories had hardly appeared before a representative of the Marconi International Marine Communication Company, for example, called to see me and told me his company would be delighted to supply the radio equipment which they had read we would have to carry to comply with Board of Trade regulations. This would have cost us nearly £2000, and we were delighted to accept it.

When Websters of Arbroath, the famous sailmakers, offered to supply the canvas without charge, this again was accepted with grateful thanks.

The many gifts to the project which can be described as "impulse giving," and the patience, time and craftsmanship which were often spent upon them, make it difficult to put any precise value upon them. An example of this was the gift, very early on, of navigational instruments by Kelvin & Hughes. They not only offered us replicas of seventeenth-century navigational instruments, but also volunteered to equip us completely with up-to-date navigational equipment, all of which they were prepared to donate.

No precise information exists about the navigational equipment carried by the first *Mayflower* when she set sail in 1620, but the instruments which Kelvin & Hughes made were as exact as it was possible to get them. No materials which could be not obtained in the seventeenth century were used.

The instruments made were a cross staff, a traverse board, two compasses, a binnacle and a candle lantern.

The cross staff, the forerunner of the modern sextant, was copied from an exquisite model in ivory held by the National Maritime Museum, and was made of pear wood. The wood was commonly used around the seventeenth century for mathematical instruments, since it is close-grained, free from knots and very suitable for engraving, which in this case was done by Mr. F. Grey of Hornchurch.

A traverse board was simply a recording board on which the distance in nautical miles (and their fractions) and the mean compass course were recorded every half hour. The board was made from oak, pegs being placed in a row of holes to record the distance. More pegs on a length of twine come from the center of the board to the cardinal points to record the ship's course.

Two compass bowls were turned in deal by patternmaker Mr. Harry Copping of Romford. The dimensions and shape are exactly the same as compass bowls of the *Mayflower* period.

The compass card may have been made by "Daniel Foster near Wapping Old Stairs" a little after the *Mayflower* sailed, but its copy is exact in every detail. Magnets, made from pivot steel, which was believed to have been available in the seventeenth century and to have been used by watchmakers for a long time, were arranged in diamond fashion around the pivot. This was turned from brass and pressed through the center of the card. It rests on a pointed stem forced into the wooden base of the bowl.

The card was protected by a circle of glass resting in a bed of putty round a recess at the top of the bowl. Access to the card was obtained by removing the bottom of the compass bowl. The bowl, swung in gimbals, was kept in a deal box.

Compass and lantern were housed in a binnacle, a square box of unpainted deal. No information exists on how the compass was illuminated at the time, so a candle lantern was built up from materials available in the seventeenth century — principally copper sheeting — and based on shapes which were known to exist then.

The people of Brixham, where I had had long discussions with Councillor Bewley, then chairman of the Urban District Council, gave us our ship's bell, which had been cast in 1638. Since the passing of the trawler fleets Brixham had been a poor town, dependent mainly upon a fickle summer-holiday trade. There are nine thousand inhabitants in Brixham and the bell cost them the equivalent of about five cents a head, man, woman and child.

Some of the gifts we received touched the heart, particularly those from children, nearly all of whom fell in love with the idea of *Mayflower*. The school children of Boston in Lincolnshire set about making a table for the captain's cabin. Some of them must have a future in the antique trade, for they evolved an aging process so perfect that it eventually had the appearance of a seventeenth-century table.

But despite gifts from firms, towns or individuals, a great deal of ready cash had to be found. The estimate of cost with which I started out was around £100,000, a figure which has been borne out by subsequent events to within 1 or 2 per cent. This, then, was to be the real expenditure. The period covered was limited by the need to avoid any delays in a project so widely noticed. Two years seemed a generally accepted figure for the time the job would take. This, then, meant finding an average flow of £1000 a week. As an exercise in raising capital for a new venture at a time of credit squeeze and general upheaval, it was big enough to be a worthwhile challenge, but I was reasonably confident that it could be done.

There were two ways of raising this money. One was a public appeal. We felt very strongly and, as it proves, with some justification, that such an appeal would expose the project to some very real dangers. The first of these was the possibility that the appeal would fall short, a not unknown peril in recent instances.

It was also repugnant to us that Anglo-American relations should be thought of as requiring a passing of the hat. Not indeed that we particularly quailed before the task. It was simply that we felt that it would be lacking in dignity. I don't mean the stuffed-shirt sort of dignity, but the dignity of people who want to make their own way without charity.

Finally, much as we appreciated the steady confidence of the patrons who had accepted the invitation to come into the project, we did not wish to reward their kindness by press-ganging them into an endless round of money raising. The project should go ahead alone. This meant exactly what it says: going out and getting the cash to keep the craftsmen at work.

I was to discover that Felix Fenston, who had given me the wherewithal to go ahead and get the project under way, was the one person on whom I would be able to call whenever the occasion demanded. I have to add one rider to this: first, he had to be found. He is a man who travels a great deal. On one occasion

I saw him on Friday and rang him on Monday to hear that he had gone off to Africa on safari!

Although Felix was by far the largest personal subscriber of the project, he was not the only one. All our personal and business acquaintances were approached, and usually enlisted to participate in some way or other. An example was at a luncheon I attended given by the Saints and Sinners. One of the speakers was inaudible, and this baffled Sir Louis Sterling, who had been born on the East Side of New York, made a million, and come to make his home in England, where he was knighted for his services to Anglo-American relations. Sir Louis, whom I had not met before, asked me what the unheard oration was all about. Instead of telling him I spoke about *Mayflower*.

"Why haven't you asked me for something?" he said. "I am famous as the man who can't say No." I did ask him — and his claim to fame was not diminished.

In case this gives the impression that the task of separating people from their money is an easy one when it concerns a project as glamorous as *Mayflower,* I must recall that like the wolf on the street corner who approached every pretty girl that passed, I also got a lot of "No's."

But it was not our intention that individual subscriptions should provide the main bulk of the necessary resources. It was clear that in this age of oppressive taxation and egalitarian leveling, industry was the best source of income. Even this was no easy solution. In England, industry is less used to supporting this sort of thing than in America. There were those who told us that industry would take a skeptical view of so romantic an undertaking, and that in these staid times they wanted to see a good return for their money, even if they were attracted by the venture itself.

This was nothing new, for the merchants of London who financed the Pilgrim Fathers to the extent of about £7000 had loaned and not given the money, and had charged 70 per cent interest. The merchants' terms were so exacting that the Pilgrims had not only to sell their butter but to pawn their future to leave England and it was many years before they were able to clear their debts. The twentieth-century merchants were fortunately less exacting. I evolved a scheme for them in which we would sell the space in the vessel's hold while she was building. Down at Plymouth, near the Barbican, where the Pilgrims left England, there is a firm called S. J. Lethbridge Ltd., which has been making furniture for well over a century.

I had some drawings prepared of a Treasure Chest in seventeenth-century style, 4' 6" x 2' 6" x 2', pleasing in design, robust enough for long handling and yet easy to assemble. I visited Mr. Roger Lethbridge, the present head of the old Plymouth firm, conferred on the designs and asked if he would manufacture the chests. This was agreed, at the bare cost of labor and materials. I offered them to British industry for £460 each, which was at that particular time the cost of a week's building less materials.

Industry was told:

> These "Treasure Chests" and their contents will represent the twentieth-century trading links between the United States and Great Britain.
>
> They will be on exhibition before sailing from this country and on arrival in America. Their contents will be selected to represent the highest standards of British manufacture and craftsmanship.

This scheme proved attractive to industry and eventually over £30,000 was raised as a result of it. Some of the finest examples of British craftsmanship and merchandise were shipped on *Mayflower*. When one considers that people began to buy these chests a few weeks after building began in the summer of 1955 although she was not sailing until the spring of 1957, then I think it can be agreed that merchants have changed for the better during the last three centuries.

The chest scheme was not our only source of revenue from industry. A number of firms, other than those mentioned earlier, all offered either materials or equipment. It was obvious that many of these firms would be able to obtain great promotional value from their gifts, and it was in these cases that we suggested that they "buy" the gift from us. It sometimes took a little explanation before they saw this point, but we were able to convince most of them.

Within a few months of commencement of work, Stuart Upham was forced to complain that he was being plagued with sightseers to the yard. They all showed such interest that he did not like to turn them away, but at the same time there was a real danger that if their numbers continued to grow they would interfere with work on the ship.

It was clearly time to turn this potential difficulty to advantage. I went down to see Stuart and told him of my plan, to which he agreed, and it was immediately put into effect. An exhibition would be staged at the yard and the public charged for admission.

It was, in the first stages of the plan, rather a big decision to add the responsibility of an exhibition to the task of building the new *Mayflower*. No one knew for certain how many people would come, and there was hardly such a thing as a precedent to guide us. (That, however, was true of the project as a whole.) Sketches of the layout were prepared, however, and the job of converting the boat shed into an exhibition hall was begun. Extending such things as approach stairways, parking grounds and paths meant extra outlay, and a staff of some ten "Pilgrim Maids," in the costume of 1620, were engaged as attendants, which added considerably to the administrative work of the project.

After it was all in order I cabled Harry Hornblower and asked him to send plans of the Pilgrim House erected for the plantation, and had one set up in the shipyard. It had taken the plantation several months to build, and Hornblower was quite surprised, visiting the shipyard only a fortnight later, to see the English version, complete.

At Easter 1956 the exhibition was opened. There was plenty for the public to see. A collection of models of ships which the Upham family had made over a period of two hundred years, a photographic display which gave the background and purpose of the project, seventeenth-century shipwrights' tools, examples of equipment which we would use on the voyage, a display of Pilgrim costumes, and "Mayflower Books" which we invited the public to sign if they wished to associate themselves with our goodwill mission to America.

My decision to have an exhibition was justified, and the revenue from admissions contributed £18,000 directly towards building. It also provided a means whereby a quarter of a million people associated themselves in a particularly spontaneous and genuine way with *Mayflower's* work of education in Anglo-American history and common heritage.

The Customs and Excise rose to the occasion. They decided that in view of the educational appeal of the project, and the number of school children who attended the exhibition, no entertainments duty was payable, a gesture which encouraged us no less than it helped the building of the ship. This represented an important ruling from at least one authority. The educational aims, on which both the Mayflower Project and Plimoth Plantation set such store, were thus acknowledged officially for the first time.

The arrangement with Stuart Upham was that we would pay for all the materials directly, and would pay him the cost of his labor plus an agreed sum for overheads and a fair profit.

Stuart understood the difficulty of committing the project to specific dates for payment, the more so as we were not able to overcome this as shipowners would have done when building a normal commercial vessel, by obtaining accommodation at the banks. Throughout the period of building, Britain was in the midst of a credit squeeze. Anyway, I was not in a very good position to obtain loans for the project as I had already used what security we could furnish in order to get the project and the building under way, and all else was anticipation. This latter, even in such a unique case, the banks were loath to accept as a substitute for security.

The result was that we had to pay our way as best we could. This would have been far riskier had it not been for the attitude of Stuart Upham, who said in effect: "I trust that you will pay me as and when you can, and so long as I can afford to do so I will not worry you." If his firm had large financial resources this would have been a fine gesture: considering that the yard operated on a slim budget and was itself suffering from the credit squeeze, it was nothing short of magnificent.

Not everyone agreed that support from industry on the scale we planned was in keeping with the project. The purist said: "If you ask industry to help you, then the project will become tainted with commercialism." I replied to this by pointing out that all mankind lives in the last resort by industry and commerce, particularly in Britain. It would be a sorry reflection on the great firms of Britain to doubt that they would use their association with the project in a dignified manner: and though not strictly relevant, it was an undisputed fact that the sailing of the first *Mayflower* was in essence a commercial venture.

We were not disappointed: there was no "sensational" use by industry of the project as a vehicle for advertisement. Without exception the various companies associated with *Mayflower* by their gifts or support announced that association with a quietness and dignity appropriate to the broader and deeper aims of the Mayflower Project and the Plimoth Plantation.

Unfortunately, and to our deep regret, this did not convince the purists, one of whom was Admiral of the Fleet Lord Fraser of North Cape. He took the view that the only proper way to finance the project was a public appeal, and that anything dealing with industry would inevitably lead to charges of commercialism.

He was one of the most enthusiastic supporters of *Mayflower*, and as he was one time First Sea Lord and a most distinguished sailor of the Second World War, his views carried special weight.

In December 1955 I had decided it was time the project had its own journal, and so set about publishing the first issue of the *Mayflower Mail*. This newspaper, which was self-supporting, gave all the news of our activities. In the first issue Lord Fraser expressed his views:

Getting the Money

To a seafaring man, this undertaking is the more striking because it is a maritime venture, and the ocean, as in all our history, will be one of the principal actors. It is, therefore, not surprising that public attention in this country has already been captured by the Project, and that it has attracted interest and support in growing measure.

I wish to recall, however, some of the deeper significances of the Pilgrim Fathers' voyage. They have been variously acclaimed as the founders of American democracy, as the champions of liberty and as near martyrs (almost half of them did die in the first terrible winter of 1621) in the cause of religious toleration.

In different degrees they were all these things, yet these were not their unique glory. Between their system of self-government and the democracy of today a long road remained to tread. In politics their few surviving writings show them to be anxious to remain loyal subjects of the English monarchy, and less than solicitous about the niceties of political rights for others who came from outside their own circle. In religious outlook, they were tolerant in a degree which is visible only in comparison with the general pattern of their age.

Only the most careful diplomacy kept the English authorities in a state of neutrality instead of active persecution. The Pilgrims were shamelessly exploited and swindled by some of their backers and emissaries, and it was finally as much as they could secure to be left alone. Yet despite their tribulations they became one of the most successful and well-ordered colonies of the age. What sustained them was a living faith in God, and though He subjected them to grievous trials, they were time and again saved by what can only be called a miracle.

When *Mayflower* cracked a main beam in a storm, they had of all things a printing press on board which they used to jack up the damaged timber. They landed in a district which the Indians had left untenanted after an epidemic. They were met by an English-speaking Indian, who had earlier been captured, taken to Europe, escaped and returned to America, and whose woodcraft repeatedly saved their lives. In the most perilous straits of all, when food was exhausted and all aid from England cut, a pirate captain on a chance visit traded them vital commodities, albeit at an extortionate price. Through all these vicissitudes the Pilgrims remained undaunted, shrewd yet visionary, humble but exalted.

The re-enactment of the *Mayflower's* journey is thus a memorial to more than a physical connection. It recalls one of the most heroic achievements in modern history, and embodies virtues of which humanity ever stands in need.

This public and movingly written expression of support from a great sailor greatly advanced our cause. It was therefore all the more distressing for me when at a meeting in the House of Lords in January 1956, having confirmed my views to Lord Fraser on the dangers implicit in a public appeal and having reaffirmed my intention to finance the venture in the manner indicated here, I received a broadside from him. "If there is to be no public appeal, Charlton, I don't think my presence as a patron is any longer required. I wish you all the luck in the world, mind you. It is a wonderful idea, but if you are not going to have a public appeal, I don't see that I can be of any help."

Everyone shared my distress at his decision and I personally could understand that a man of such high principles, who had spent all his life since boyhood in the relative seclusion of the services, would find it difficult to understand that the support of industry did not necessarily lend itself to commercialism. But he was right in one thing he said before retiring from the scene: other people would share his view. They did, and from time to time we were criticized upon this point. This criticism was fortunately not widespread, but it was none the less irksome.

There was one potential source of income from which a fleet of *Mayflowers* could have been built, but this we firmly chose to eschew. Hardly a day went by without an American offering a donation, and they were most insistent, particularly at the shipyard.

I remember on one occasion early in the morning going down to the yard and seeing an American woman on her own passing through the ticket barrier. Our attendants had instructions that no Americans were to be charged, and they became expert at recognizing Americans, often before they spoke. There is an American look, difficult to define but easy enough to recognize.

I followed our visitor down through the exhibition to the ship, where she stood stock-still, looking up at the scaffolding. Her shoulders were shaking and for a moment I thought she was laughing. Then I saw that she was crying, and the tears were of pride, not sorrow. Later, she pressed us to accept a donation. I had to refuse her, as I refused so many others.

Although it is fair to say that getting money for the project was difficult, it must be remembered that the project had imposed limitations by the very methods it had chosen to use. Nevertheless, I believe that we were justified in the course we adopted. A great deal of spontaneous support came our way and although industry represented a major source of income, over a quarter of a million of my fellow countrymen, either through the exhibition or through personal and unsolicited subscriptions, associated themselves with the project. No public appeal could have produced much greater numerical support.

Certainly I have no doubt at all that the Pilgrim Fathers would have seen my point, and in gratitude I can only recall a few more words from Dr. Schweitzer:

> Still the kindness which I experienced on these rounds out-weighed a hundredfold the humiliations which I had to put up with.

V

Building

Much has been written in the press of the second *Mayflower's* being an exact copy of the first. This, I am afraid, is just not true. How, when and where she was built, what she was like and what was her fate are, and will remain, a mystery. Much has been written in this book of Bill Baker's plans, to which Stuart Upham built our own *Mayflower;* so a summarization, in Bill's own words, of the results of the five years of fascinating research which led to the working drawing from which a seventeenth-century vessel, of the same size as Christopher Jones's *Mayflower,* was built, will be found in the Appendix. Although the data arrived at is mainly a matter for the discussion of the experts, the story is one of applied detection and analysis of the most exciting sort.

I don't know whether I have met anyone keener on the preservation of the old arts and crafts of shipbuilding than Stuart Upham. He treated the reconstruction of *Mayflower* with the inspirational approach of a great artist creating his masterpiece. From the beginning the work filled him with pleasure, because it enabled him to discover the way our forefathers went to work. But his enthusiasm was tinged with sadness, for no one knew better that the building of *Mayflower* was probably the last occasion on which a ship of this size would be constructed without the aid of modern materials and methods.

His old-established firm was able to draw on its long-accumulated lore in building, but familiarity with the honest craft of wooden shipbuilding was not in itself enough. The construction of the new *Mayflower* involved considerable research with a view to the revival of tools and techniques long since discarded by shipbuilders.

Some of the tools could have been used on the first *Mayflower* — their very names have an old sound: the adz, the first tool of the shipwright's tool chest; the ax, for the rough trimming of logs; the gimlets, for boring holes before brace and bit were invented; gauges, for scribing; augers, for long boring to ensure water-tightness; timber girt measurer and wood rasps, for shaping of the wooden tackle blocks; clipper mauls, for driving bolts.

I was determined that in every detail the new *Mayflower* should not only look like her predecessor, but be fashioned after the same manner, and Stuart Upham was delighted to carry this through.

The treenails — wooden pegs used to fasten the planking to the frames — he made from old Devon cider casks. The treenails had to be dry and seasoned, as unseasoned timber would shrink, weaken the fastenings, and cause our ship to leak. The cider casks, which were one hundred and thirty years old, were ideal for the purpose. The treenails made from them (twenty inches long) were driven home by the most experienced shipwrights, who could be relied upon to strike true and well; otherwise they would break off.

One problem which the builders of the original *Mayflower* would not have had to face was that in the old days they almost certainly worked to the size of the available timber. But Stuart had to work to Bill Baker's specifications and timber had to be found to meet them. And that meant getting the biggest oak growing in Britain.

Stuart saw from Baker's plans that *Mayflower* was one of the most shapely and therefore the most complex vessels ever laid down on the firm's mold-loft floor. With so much shape the timber had to be specially selected, and searching for it entailed an immense amount of work, for trees reaching the bulk needed are near the maximum size to which British oak grows and by that time the timber is usually getting too old. An abundance of crooked timber was needed for the first stages to make the complex curves of the ribs and timbers. In *Mayflower* they were particularly difficult to match.

When he was worried about possible holdups over timber, the word spread in the West Country and folk told him where it could be found. Some of the trees weighed up to ten tons, with an age of anything up to two hundred years, and it would be almost truthful to say that it was one tree to one piece, which had to be worked truly and accurately.

When all the curves were assembled and the vessel was finally framed, the outer skin of 2½-inch-thick planking was added. This was cut from straight timber, which was needed in considerable lengths. Individual planks were clamped to the ribs, those at the bows being bent to shape and put on while steaming hot after treatment in the steam kiln.

The oak tree used for the main stem was one of the biggest to be found in Britain, 6 feet in circumference and consisting of 116 cubic feet of solid Devon oak. Trimmed to size it was reduced to about 55 cubic feet. Another enormous log was needed for the keel, measuring 14 x 12 inches and 58 feet long.

I was naturally impatient for the ship to be launched, and when I saw the sort of tools Stuart was using I asked him if he might not get the same results with modern equipment.

His reply, albeit accompanied by a grin, was a check to my impetuosity: "Warwick, the tools which we used for the construction of these heavy wooden ships have not varied much in three hundred years. The main difference is in the sawing of the timber, which used to be done by the pitsaw, adz and ax. I am also using electric drills, but they have to be used carefully as they tend to wander at the soft grain. Believe me, except for sawing and drilling, modern machinery cannot be used if you want me to build *Mayflower*."

When work began I told Stuart that I hoped he would have the ship finished in a year. His only comment was: "We'll do our best, but we won't cut corners."

I used to go down to the yard at least once a month to see how work was getting on, and the operation seemed painfully slow.

Building

The keel remained lonely and insignificant in the yard while Stuart was busy laying the lines of the ship on his mold-loft floor. When the first ribs were in place it looked for all the world like the skeleton of a giant whale washed up by the sea. I could have jumped for joy. This seemed enormous progress, and then months went past while the planking and decking were meticulously put in place.

There were times when I wondered if she would ever be ready for launching, but whatever doubts I had, they were allayed by Stuart. He used to take me round the yard and explain why and how everything was being done, and I began to realize that no good could come of hurrying craftsmen who knew what they were about and worked at the unhurried pace which belongs especially to the West Country. Woe betide the ignorant foreigner from London who tries to change the way of their world!

All the materials were bought in England, except for the timber for the masts and spars, which was of Oregon pine from Canada. Transporting these logs alone was a big job. The largest of them, for the mainmast, was 80 feet long and 24 inches square. After crossing the Atlantic they were moved from ship to rail at Manchester, by rail to Torquay in Devon and floated across Tor Bay to Stuart's yard, as they were too cumbersome to take through the twisting, narrow streets.

The 24-inch-square log for the mainmast had to be shaped by hand with adzes to its specified diameter of 21 inches in the widest part, and cut to length, which was 67 feet. The main-topmast was 33 feet 9 inches long and 9 inches in diameter.

The foremast had to be 57 feet 9 inches tall and 17 inches in diameter and the fore-topmast 29 feet tall and 7½ inches in diameter; it was surmounted with trestletrees and crosstrees and by the characteristic crow's-nest, looking like a large shallow bowl, 9 feet in outside diameter. Specifications for the mizzenmast (that is, the aftermast) were 41 feet 8 inches tall and 10½ inches in diameter, and there was a large bowsprit, tilted sharply upwards from a box in the bows, measuring 57 feet 9 inches, with a largest diameter of 13½ inches.

While Stuart was busy building the hull and superstructure and shaping the three masts, a number of specialist firms all over Britain were engaged manufacturing materials as near as possible to those that were in use in *Mayflower*. Among these were two old-established Scots firms who were making the ropes which were to be our "engines" and the sailcloth for our "wings."

I placed an order with the Gourock Ropework Company soon after the keel laying and it was fortunate that I did, for the job took over a year.

The company originated in Gourock in 1736, but in 1797 it took over the Port Glasgow Tent and Duck Company and transferred to Port Glasgow, the home port at that time of a number of full-rigged ships. Records show that the firm had a flourishing export trade in 1745, much of it conducted by sailing ships between Scotland and the ports on the developing eastern seaboard of America. At one time the company itself had three full-rigged ships sailing to Baltic ports with cargoes of Scottish wool and salted herrings and returning with Russian hemp for the rigging of sailing ships.

The firm's own ancient handwritten records provided some guidance on early practice and techniques of making ropes able to stand up to the strain and stress which a seventeenth-century rig imposes. Some ropemaking techniques unused in normal production for nearly one hundred and fifty years were revived and put to the test, and veteran retired members of the staff were consulted, including master ropelayer Jimmy Starrett, who returned from retirement after sixty-three years' service to give expert advice.

All the ropes are of lightly tarred squadron Italian hemp, a high-grade true or soft hemp, and specifications called for 4¼ tons for standing and running rigging, 3¾ tons for working ropes, ground tackle ropes, towing and deck tackle ropes, plus essential spares.

The plans called for nearly three hundred and fifty separate ropes in the rigging proper, including ratlines and robands, and in addition such things as flag halyards and deck tackle ropes, bringing the total to over four hundred.

Building

The principal working ropes were four 90-fathom lengths of hauling line 5 inches in circumference; the main tow, a 120-fathom length of 9-strand cable rope 12 inches in circumference; the drogue rope, 120 fathoms of 4-inch-circumference rope, and its trip line, a 120-fathom length of 2-inch-circumference rope.

For the rigging proper, we needed twenty-eight different sizes of rope in over twenty different lays and constructions. The shrouds had to be of 4-strand ropes, wormed, with a central heart, varying in size from 6¼-inch circumference for the lower main shrouds, to the mizzen shrouds 2⅞ inches in circumference.

The largest rope in the ship was the 10-inch-circumference mainstay, of 9-strand cable construction. As with all the shrouds, this secured and hove taut by deadeyes and lanyard. All the stays are hove out on the stretch until a permanent stretch of 8½ to 10 per cent is obtained, a very difficult operation as too much stretch might have damaged the rope, while too little would involve risk of damage to the mast.

Shrouds were also stretched, but in this case the operation, also difficult, was continued until the heart in each shroud was broken, ensuring that the standing rigging ropes were "dead."

The main and forecourse tacks are of 9-strand cable construction and are tapered throughout their length. They were made on ropewalks in pairs. Their manufacture is very intricate and laborious work, but tapering is essential for a seventeenth-century rig because an ordinary rope of the size of the small end would do one job and one the size of the larger another, but neither would do both.

An unusual feature of the work was that there was not a single splice in the rigging, although the art of splicing was known when the original *Mayflower* was built. Instead of splices, throat, round, crown and other seizings were used.

In this manner cordage as near as possible to the original was produced, with this difference: three centuries had taught how to eliminate weaknesses inherent in seventeenth-century ropemaking, so our ropes would be more reliable and uniform.

Bill Baker specified that for historical accuracy flax was to be used as the fiber for making the sailcloth. Francis Webster & Sons Ltd. of Alma Works, Arbroath, a firm founded in 1795, offered to give us flax canvas for two suits of sails, and I accepted this gift.

The name "Webster" means weaver, and the firm is a family concern, four Websters having succeeded each other at the head of it. During the nineteenth century Websters were known all over the world as suppliers of flax sailcloth. Today much of the output is devoted to the manufacture of marine, industrial and transport covers and tarpaulins, but some sailcloth is still made.

There was no need for these Scottish weavers to search their archives to discover how to make the sailcloth for the second *Mayflower*. The knowledge had been handed down to them by succeeding generations and improved upon as new methods and an up-to-date plant dispensed with the old hard tasks.

In the great days of sail, many a square-rigged ship rounded Cape Horn under Websters' canvas and the mills supplied Finland's well-known Erikson fleet until it was broken up during the war. The surviving ships of the fleet, *Pamir* and *Passat,* which were sold to Germany, are still in service wearing Websters' canvas.

In the old days Scotland grew its own supplies of flax, but production has now died out, although it was revived by the British Government as a necessity during both World Wars when European supplies were cut off. Today the raw material comes mainly from Holland and Belgium, and some from Soviet Russia.

Before reaching the mills it is "retted" by steeping in tanks or rivers or by being laid out in the dew, to induce fermentation and to dissolve the natural gums. It is also "scutched," which means breaking the core and cleaning the fiber. The strong resemblance that flax bears to human hair is heightened after it has been combed free of waste by the hackling machine. The flax is then drawn into a continuous sliver 250 yards in length, and six of these slivers are combined into one by a doubling machine. This process is repeated three times on drawing frames, giving a strand made up of 1296 slivers and looking like a fine, strong string, which is run onto bobbins ready for the spinning frame.

After spinning, which increases its strength and reduces the bulk still further, the flax yarn is reeled into hanks for processing at the bleachfields. It is then wound onto spools ready for the warp beam, a large roller on which threads from the canvas warp are mounted. To feed the weaver's shuttle which makes the weft of the canvas, yarn is wound onto small bobbins, known as cops. The flax yarn is now ready for the weaving department, where the clacking looms turn the yarn into the finest canvas, "as durable and almost as impenetrable as chain mail," say the makers.

About 2500 yards of this canvas, in rolls two feet wide and in three different weights, were supplied to make the two suits of sails for the ship and sent to Brixham's only remaining master sailmaker, Mr. Harold T. Bridge, who has spent fifty of his sixty-two years as a sailmaker.

When he began to learn the trade as a boy in 1908, Brixham was a leading British fishing port. There were eight master sailmakers, each with his own sail loft, and the talk of the journeymen in the lofts was "all about sails and sailing."

In those days, Mr. Bridge recalled, they used to see as many as half a dozen tall square-riggers anchored for shelter from a westerly gale in Tor Bay and the old sailmakers would reminisce about the work that was done for such ships in the golden days of sail.

Mr. Bridge learned his trade from these men, some of them seventy or eighty years old, whose jobs in their youth had included making sails for full-rigged ships. As a boy Mr. Bridge himself made sails for Brixham's trawlers. The fleet was large at that time, but was mostly sunk during the First World War; the fishing grounds were littered with the wrecks and Brixham has never recovered its importance as a fishing center.

As a young man Mr. Bridge went to sea as sailmaker in the square-rigged, three-masted, single-t'gallant *William Mitchell*, of 1884 tons, and in her made the trip from London to Australia.

Later he was for nine years sailmaker aboard *Westward,* a two-masted, privately owned schooner.

Eventually he gave up seafaring to establish his own sail loft in Brixham and he had lived to become the last master sailmaker in this traditional seafaring port, where in the old days almost everybody knew how to race a trawler.

Although much of Mr. Bridge's work was in cotton sails, ranging in weight from 2¼ to 35 ounces per square yard, made in 36-inch rolls, it was not unusual for him to be working in flax canvas. "Although in America they used their native cotton, British wind-jammers always had flax canvas sails," he told me. "I worked in flax canvas on the *William Mitchell* and today we often use it for hard-weather cruising sails for yachts. I think it's definitely better for square-riggers; it's harder wearing than cotton and less liable to mildew, unless the cotton is proofed, and cotton gets hard to handle when wet. Still, flax has its difficulties and the racing man, even in small boats, wants a high standard of sail and prefers cotton. Some of them are using terylene now, but so far I haven't worked in that."

I used to visit him in his sail loft, in an ancient building hidden behind the fire station in Bolton Street. A modest notice bore his name and through a sliding door I would pass in and pick my way through rolls of sailcloth and sails awaiting repair. The floor was covered with old canvas on which small boat sails were marked out in chalk before being cut to size, and on one wall hung a picture of a square-rigger, the *Archibald Russell.* He worked seated on a plain hard bench, helped by his young assistant, Louis, who was learning the trade. Here they began in August 1956 to make the first suit of sails for the *Mayflower.* Although the loft contained a sewing machine, the only concession to modernity, all the canvas for *Mayflower's* first suit of sails was stitched by Mr. Bridge's strong hands in flax twine. Along the head, leeches and foot of each sail he stitched stout boltrope, a 3-strand rope of special "sails' lay," and into it he worked — and it is hard work — the bowline cringles, martinet cringles and clew cringles, all made from the same boltrope and covered with hard-wearing leather as protection against chafe.

This work began soon after the keel was laid, with interruptions for routine work, and by the end of a year Mr. Bridge was well ahead and only waiting until the *Mayflower* could have its first suit of sails bent on before going ahead with the completion of the second suit.

We had set September 22, 1956, as the target date for launching, almost fourteen months after keel laying. Early in August I went down to Brixham on one of my routine visits to the yard. There were rumors in the town that we would not make the launching date, and these had filtered through to the press.

I told Stuart that I had had an urgent request from Henry Hornblower to fly to America to meet the governors of Plimoth Plantation, to discuss the plans and see the land where *Mayflower* was to be berthed in perpetuity. "They also want to be sure," I told Stuart, "that we are going to launch her on the day we have promised."

I might just as well have given Time a push as try to hurry Stuart Upham from the pace of the craftsman. He frowned slightly. "Well, Warwick," he said, "she's got to be fastened and dubbed down, and then the seams have to be calked and paid up with pitch, all before she's watertight — and we can't launch her till then." The blue eyes lit up with the familiar smile. "Still, we'll do it."

I booked my flight to America.

VI

Captain and Crew

Wʜᴏ wanted to sail on *Mayflower?* Everyone, or so it seemed from the cables, phone calls and letters that came to me from over three thousand people who tried to bluster, bounce, badger, buy, charm, and wheedle their way on board. But some of them just asked, and asked, and asked again, hoping to wear me down. And the trouble was that I found it difficult to turn any of them away. We all have in us the desire to please and I find it more difficult than most people to say "No," so I acted the coward even when it was obvious that a flat refusal would, in the long run, have been the kinder course.

I initiated a filing system for all applicants and sent or gave an evasive reply which left them on the hook of hope. I used to thank them for their interest, apologize for not being able to give them a definite answer and end: "The choice of the crew must be with the captain. When he is chosen your application will be put before him and then we will be able to give you a definite reply." Pat Jeans, my secretary, did not tell me in so many words that she considered some of my replies close to being downright dishonest, but she indicated much. "Wouldn't it be better," she used to suggest, "if we were a little more definite to those who haven't a chance?"

"How can we?" I replied. "That wouldn't be fair. After all, everyone has a chance. It *does* depend on the captain."

"Even this old man of eighty-two who thinks the long sea voyage would cure his arthritis?"

"Everyone," I insisted, "everyone has a chance until the captain chooses his crew." She didn't believe me and I didn't believe myself, and I came to long for the day when we had a captain, a down-to-earth sea dog of a man who had no desire to please anyone but himself.

I suppose men *are* more polite than women: at least, they accept an excuse in silence, but women are not so easily put off. When they wanted to sail on *Mayflower* and received my pie-in-the-sky letter they usually came back with mutations of this question: "Are you taking women?"

"Well, are you, Mr. Charlton?" Miss Jeans would ask.

"Everyone has a chance . . ." I began.

"Until the captain chooses his crew?" asked Miss Jeans, with mock innocence.

"That's right," I said, but I knew it was not good enough. It would be fairer, much fairer, I reasoned, to tell them there was some doubt as to whether we would take women at all. I still used the captain gambit but added the doubt for good measure, taking a stumbling step towards honesty, and soon found pleasure in this; pleasure flavored, I think, with a certain cruelty. I would stress the hardships and discomforts of the voyage, but the women who volunteered to sail on *Mayflower* were, in the main, serious about the project. Some of them were deeply stirred by the adventure and romance of our venture, and talk of hardship usually produced the inevitable reply: "Women went before, why not now?" How I longed for a captain to give the answer. I could not forget that out of the one hundred and two passengers on the first *Mayflower*, twenty-nine were women and two of them became mothers either during the voyage or shortly after landfall. Mistress Hopkins gave birth to a son on the high seas, named Oceanus, and Mistress White had a child on board soon after the ship arrived in Cape Cod harbor — Peregrine, the first Englishman born in New England.

Not a great deal is known about the Pilgrim women individually, but we know they endured persecution and hardship enough before they set sail. During the sixty-seven days' voyage they must have sometimes despaired for the safety of the ship as *Mayflower* was tossed about by the Atlantic storms. The Pilgrims searched the shores of New England in November, and in that first winter nearly half of those who sailed on *Mayflower* — many of them women — died through sickness or privation. Those who remained shared the hazards of primitive life in a hostile territory: the men building their stockades and shelters, the women weaving into the coarse fabric of the new life the love, devotion and patience which made their earth-floor homes the foundations of America.

Knowing this background it was not easy to give women a reason why they could not sail on the twentieth-century *Mayflower*, when hardships and hazards would be limited to the voyage. The modern woman was quite prepared to undergo the same physical hardships of the voyage as her forebears. I even met a mother of three children who wished to go. She wrote: "Please will you consider an application for a mother of three sturdy boys, 9, 11 and 14 years, to sail on *Mayflower?* We are all used to roughing it and I have travelled thousands of miles in cargo boats before the war."

I was intrigued and asked Mrs. Marie Lloyd to call and see me. She arrived with her entire family, confirming that the application was a serious one.

"And why do you want to go?" I asked, striking a bet with myself that the answer would be "To emigrate." But she replied: "My husband feels it would be a wonderful experience for the children, as they have never had more than two days' holiday since they were born, and we could never afford a holiday ourselves."

How she made me wish the captain was by my side, banging the table with mirth, stifling an oath, and then saying: "Shiver m'timbers, Mrs. Lloyd, I'll take you and your husband and those three boys there — we'll make shipmates of them and have a holiday into the bargain."

But there was one would-be member of the crew who made me wish for the presence of the captain for a different reason, our most persistent applicant, a peer of the realm who claimed descent from both Henry VIII and Robin Hood.

He arrived at my office one morning and asked the usual question: "Any room for crew?" I gave him the stock reply, but far from discouraging him this information was a spur to his ambition. "I must sail on her," he said. "And if you haven't a master, then what about me? I've had some sailing experience and I can get some more while *Mayflower* is being built. I've thought about nothing else since I heard you were rebuilding her."

I asked him to make a formal application in writing, hoping that this would keep him busy. Nothing of the sort. Every day for three months he turned up at the office asking for news. Sometimes he would walk up and down the corridor, wearing a duffel coat, looking for all the world as though he were pacing the decks of a ship. Then one day he said: "I don't mind waiting for your decision so long as I can be near the ship, so I think the best thing to do is for me to go down to Brixham and see if I can give your builder some help. I've spent hours at the National Maritime Museum, and I think I have learned a lot that would help."

I tried to be firm and told him that our builder was working on the result of five years' research and two hundred years' experience; that he was not short of information but of shipwrights. He smiled. "All right, then, I'll work in the yard."

As soon as he was out of the office I phoned Stuart Upham and reported the latter part of the conversation. "If he does turn up," said Stuart, "I think I can deal with him."

The noble lord duly arrived, and Stuart emphasized that the shortage was skilled shipwrights and not laborers: the peer promptly insisted he did not mind how he was classified so long as he could work on the ship.

Stuart played what he thought was his trump card. "Then you will have to be a member of the union before I can consider you," he said, and returned triumphant to his work.

The next thing that happened was that the general secretary of the Ship Constructors' and Shipwrights' Association, Mr. Sydney Ombler, received an application at the head office of the union at Newcastle for union membership. I asked Mr. Ombler what chance there was for the union's agreeing to the request.

"I think there are some difficulties in the way," he said. "Union members at Brixham must be satisfied that he has served an apprenticeship and worked for a number of years in the trade. He certainly knows something about sailing, but that's another matter."

Meanwhile, the descendant of Robin Hood and Henry VIII told me glumly: "I don't think I am going to get that union card. It's a bad show, considering I took my seat in the House of Lords as a Labour peer." He was right about the union card.

I did not see him again, and the last time I heard of him he had signed on as a deckhand at the nominal wage of one shilling a month on a cargo ship bound for Konakri, a tiny port in French Equatorial Africa. His reason? "I am getting experience to make sure I am selected for the crew of *Mayflower*."

At last, one Saturday morning, six months after the keel was laid, I was going through the mail when I came across the one application for crew I wanted. It was signed "Alan Villiers."

I had read his books about the sea. From his boyhood days in Melbourne he was determined not only to go to sea in sailing ships, but also to command one. Despite the discouragement of his father he achieved his ambition.

He recalls in his autobiography, *The Set of the Sails*: [*]

> My father said that it only seemed adventurous [life at sea] because I was building up my ideas of it from my own imaginings, fed on books, and the sight of ships in a safe port. The sea, he pointed out, was no safe port. But the cool loveliness of the silver-grey wind ships lying in the bay, and the song of the wind in their high riggings, stirred me deeply, and I vowed I would sail in such ships as soon as I could. My parents' pleadings that I should devote myself to school and win a scholarship there which would take me on to Melbourne University were largely wasted on me. The essential thing, said my father, was to become qualified in a profession. There was no way for the unqualified save Dead End Road, and the sea for me would be

[*] Charles Scribner's Sons.

a dead-end calling. I knew that he was talking sense, but my ambition to go to sea in sailing ships grew rather than lessened.

When he was fifteen he shipped as a cadet in the Tasman Sea bark *Rothesay Bay*, an ancient Scot in the New Zealand timber trade. The next quarter of a century he wandered over the globe, voyaging whenever he could find a suitable vessel. At the age of seventeen, stranded and penniless at Bordeaux, he boarded *Lawhill* for Australia, and when she collided with a buoy and he was pitched off the yard, he had a miraculous escape, striking the rigging all the way in his fall to the deck.

He joined a whaling expedition to the Antarctic in the ship *Grace Harwar*, in which one man was killed, the second mate went mad and jumped overboard, food ran short, and the ship's company nearly starved. He was in the famous Cape Horn grain racer *Herzogin Cecilie* and later became part owner of the record-breaking *Parma*.

There seemed to be no type of sailing ship in which he had not gained experience, even putting in a spell with deep-sea dhows, and then before the last war he had set out on his greatest adventure, in his own vessel, a Danish training ship which he renamed *Joseph Conrad* and sailed round the world.

During the war he commanded a squadron of landing craft during the Allied invasions of Sicily, Italy and Normandy, and was awarded the D.S.C. In addition to being a man of action he was also a trustee of the National Maritime Museum and a member of the council of the Society for Nautical Research. Above all, he had a passion and love for the sea and sailing ships.

The morning I received his letter I replied inviting him to the office.

Although he wore civilian dress and a thick overcoat, he seemed to bring the sea into the office with him. "Commander Villiers," I said, once he had time to sit down, "will you captain *Mayflower*?"

He gave me a slow, secretive smile, one Drake might have given before he left for Cadiz.

"I could do it," he said at once, paused, and continued quickly, the questions spilling out as though he feared they would be blown away by the wind or overcome by the sound of the waves.

"Is there any auxiliary? No? When will she be ready to sail — a year? Have you chosen the crew? No? Well, I have some good lads who sailed with me. There are problems, that's for sure, but they got there before and we'll get there again.

"Human memory is a poor thing at the best of times, but it amazes me how it has distorted the picture of the square-rigged ship. They magnify the dangers, extol the difficulties, elaborate the problems. Yet the deep-sea sailing ship was used by all the great discoverers and explorers.

"It was the little sailing ship which opened up the world, found the new continents, established the trade routes — not powered vessels. They came in later. The sailing ship was the backbone of the commerce of the world almost up to the end of the nineteenth century. She carried passengers, armies, freights. She sailed regular passenger schedules across the North Atlantic, to Australia, round the Capes. She did the world's work and she did it well. In the process, she became no fragile, balky, hard-to-handle little beauty of a ship — though, by Heaven, she had the beauty all right. She was a powerful and a reliable machine, and one of the finest products of human brains.

"She reached the highest development in a great five-masted full-rigged ship, built of steel, with a five-thousand-ton hull capable of going through the water at seventeen knots and more. She could carry eight thousand tons of cargo and a crew of forty-six. That was *Preussen,* and she had no engine power.

"*Mayflower* will be no *Preussen,* of course. The point is that the sailing tradition they had in ships like the *Preussen* and others isn't dead yet. The art and science of handling square-rigged ships are still there. Are these your plans of *Mayflower?* Good.

"How is she to be rigged?"

"With rope, like the original," I said, while the Commander drew breath.

"Um — we're used to wire. Her rigging is complicated beyond

necessity: we're used to utility style. What about the steering?"

"A whipstaff."

"We're used to a wheel."

"They weren't invented when *Mayflower* sailed."

"We'll make do. How about accommodation?"

"As it was . . ."

"Poor, and no headroom down below. We're used to full head-room and decent living quarters." He studied Baker's plans for a moment.

"Well, Mr. Charlton, the short answer is that, galleon or no galleon, *Mayflower* is essentially a handy bark," he said. "She will be square-rigged on fore and main and fore-and-aft on the mizzen — and she'll sail and handle as good little barks do. The best and handiest sailing ship I was ever in was a bark of around seven hundred tons, which is well over twice the *Mayflower* size, and she had a lot more sails than the Pilgrim ship, and a lot less crew too. The old-style ships had short, snug rigs, and a very work-easy sail plan. There was none of that fighting with iron-hard canvas in a gale aloft, as we had to do in the Cape Horners. Those tops'ls in *Mayflower* brail into the tops, and the two big course-yards come down on deck, with their sails.

"In our big sailing ships," he recalled, "all the square sails had to be handled aloft, and the deuce of a job it could be at times. We'll miss that particular headache anyway, and I doubt not the ship will be handy. The hull will slip along very nicely in anything of a sailing breeze at all; it's just that towering after-castle that worries me. It shouldn't be too bad: after all, it's a style of construction that survived at sea for a good many hundred years. Maybe they helped the old ships to lie-to, without any canvas set, and apparently the *Mayflower* did ride out a blow or two on her first crossing. She probably also made a lot of leeway."

Leeway or not, he did not doubt that she would sail quite well. What bothered him a little was not the voyage. No, it was the awkward sails, like the lateen mizzen, which suggested difficul-ties, and the fact that all the rigging was of cordage.

"Hempen shrouds were long gone from seagoing ships when I first sailed," he said.

"There must have been a lot of 'give' in them. I can remember really old salts talking of pretty little wooden ships which they spoke of as being 'alive' because they were built of wood — which, according to them, was a much more shipshape material than metal could ever be — and because their cordage rigging 'lived' with the ship, and accepted all the movements of the hull in a natural manner."

I told him our cordage would be of best hemp, laid up especially in Scotland by Gourock Ropeworks, and he brightened visibly. All the stout hempen shrouds were being stretched properly: every lanyard, every ratline, every tack and sheet and brace and halyard was good stuff, to be relied upon. The sails would be of best Scots canvas.

"They will stand all right," he said, and came back to the rigging plan. "She bristles with awkward leads and complications, like that steeved-up bowsprit, braces led to stays, and so forth. It will be difficult to accept all this, when we know how the whole rigging could be improved so easily. Yet we shall accept her as she is. That is the job. It is some time since anyone had the chance to find out what sailing such a ship was like, and I certainly wouldn't miss the chance to try her out and see."

Next we discussed the possible route the ship would take and he emphasized that this would depend upon the time of year she sailed. No one could be sure of the precise route Captain Jones had taken on the first voyage. It was sufficient for him if he sailed, got an offing, beat across and arrived more or less where he was bound. It seemed from Bradford and Mourt that Captain Jones had not taken the southern route, but had made as direct a passage as he could. The Gulf Stream, the Hope cycle of the westerly winds, the difficulty of beating out of the English Channel for a start, all these were against Captain Jones.

"They will be against us, too," said Alan, "and make no mistake about it, getting across the North Atlantic to the westward can be difficult. Even the famous clippers used to take six weeks to beat from Liverpool to Boston or New York, on the average."

I knew that coming towards Europe was much easier, because of the prevailing westerly winds and the east-setting Gulf Stream. But Alan Villiers confirmed that there were good ways to make westing. We know a great deal more of the ocean winds and currents now than Captain Jones did, and it would be plain common sense to make use of the knowledge.

Yet, he felt, the voyage would be no picnic. "She is a very small ship and the Atlantic is still a wide and stormy ocean. But I think we ought to get along all right."

It was a great relief that the entire selection of the crew would be in his hands. "Some experts have been telling us that they did not think we were going to find a crew who would be able to handle the ship," I said. "Their point is that it is over three hundred years since anyone sailed such a ship across the Atlantic."

He laughed. "The sailing-ship spirit isn't dead yet. Why, I know where I can put my hand on a mate, second mate, third mate, bos'n, and four A.B.s, all of whom have been around Cape Horn in sailing ships. There's Godfrey Wicksteed, who would be a good mate, for instance. He has an extra master's license, and he's a qualified master in deep-water sail. He and I were together years ago in *Bellands,* a big lime-juice four-masted bark. Since then he has sailed in Scandinavian ships, among others. He knows his stuff. There's Adrian Small, who would be second mate: he took his mate's license in sail a few months back, and before that he served his time in big 'P' Cape Horners since the end of the war. Ike Marsh would make a good bos'n, and he has been at sea all his life. His last square-rigged ship was John Huston's whale ship *Pequod.* The A.B.s are all chaps who served in the Erikson square-riggers.

"I could man the ship entirely with young certificated officers from the merchant navy if I wanted. Many of them have sailing experience from the Outward Bound Sea School at Aberdovey. That's tough, too, and they learn fast there. I can get several from *Conrad.* I shall want a steward, though. He's an important man in a sailing ship on a long voyage. He has to know how to make salt horse palatable, and how to bake sea bread and good sea pies. We don't have refrigeration, and food is important.

"As for good boys, we could fill the ship with them. I wish we were able to take thirty of them."

I had one final question. The women.

"Well," he said, "I take it *Mayflower* will have no conveniences, and there will be no privacy. No, I rule women out. And it's no use quoting the original. If you tried to copy things completely according to history it would soon be just a stupid stunt. For one thing, you would have to throw one of the Mrs. Bradfords over the side." This was a reference to Mrs. Dorothy Bradford, the first wife of William, who drowned off Cape Cod.

"You are quite sure about that?" I said. "There are to be no women?"

With a possibly wistful reflection on conditions in 1620, he said: "In those days, women were chattels. They're not now. They talk back and you can't handle them. No! No women." Then he added, with a twinkle in his eyes: "Unless I take my wife. I know she would like to go."

When he left the office I called in Miss Jeans. "In future," I said, "will you please refer all applicants for crew to the master of *Mayflower*, Commander Alan Villiers."

I felt sorry about "no women," but no one could argue with a man like that — not even a woman.

VII

Visit to America

With Alan Villiers busy selecting his crew and Stuart Upham working confidently towards the date of *Mayflower's* launching, I set off in a lighthearted mood on my trip to discuss berthing plans with Plimoth Plantation.

Over lunch at Boston's Union Club, Henry Hornblower came straight to the point: "I suppose," he said, "you're wondering how and where we are going to berth the ship?"

I had always been confident the plantation would do her justice, but I was not prepared for the ambitious development Harry outlined to me then, and later, when he drove me to the Eel River site, at Plymouth, which was the scene of a massacre in King Philip's War, the only time the Plymouth settlement was ever attacked by Indians.* There I met the other governors: Herbert F. Boynton, George C. P. Olsson, Judge Amedeo Sgarzi, and William S. Brewster.

"Bill Brewster goes right back to the original Pilgrims," Harry said. "The rest of us caught later boats. He and his wife will represent us at the launching."

The governors were beginning a national campaign to raise enough funds to build a million-dollar replica of the first Pilgrim village at Plymouth as it looked in 1627. They planned to have it completed by the spring of 1958.

They showed me over the hundred-acre tract which was to

* "King Philip" was Metacomet, chief sachem of the Wampanoag Indians. His brother (Wamsutta) and he were called Alexander and Philip by the English.

become the permanent resting place of *Mayflower* as part of a historic exhibit of the beginning of their nation. They were going to build a complete village, including houses, a trading post, a grist mill, a museum and an Indian village, on a site only two miles south of Plymouth Rock, the place where the Pilgrims first stepped ashore.

"The project started as the result of a twenty-thousand-dollar contribution in 1945 to purchase land on which to build a village and prepare plans," Harry recalled. "We bought some land, but the state put a bypass through it. That slowed the whole program. We built one typical Pilgrim house near the Rock to test the reaction," he went on, "and in the first year it was visited by three hundred thousand persons. After two years of operating the house we accumulated enough money from the sale of postcards and from the settlement of the land-damage case with the state to reproduce a fort-meetinghouse. Later we built a 1627-type house.

"Then when John Lowe came over and said you were going to build a *Mayflower* and present it to Plimoth Plantation as a gift from the British people, we began to scout round wondering where to put the ship, because we are just squatters on state property near the Rock."

But a provident windfall, if touched by tragedy, came their way when Henry's grandmother died in October 1955. It was discovered that she had left the hundred-acre estate along the Eel River to the plantation. The land closely resembles the topography of the place where the Pilgrims first settled and is a perfect setting. *Mayflower* could wish for no better home.

"We have raised a hundred thousand of the estimated million dollars we'll need," Harry said. "Money is coming in from divers sources — individual people, corporations and patriotic societies. We'd like to see the place built by the people rather than one large donor and it seems they all want to lend a helping hand."

Before I left New England for New York, I had a date to keep in Provincetown, Cape Cod, where I had received an invitation from Mr. Horace Hallett, president of the Provincetown local bank. This appointment gave some cause for alarm to the governors of the plantation. The people of Provincetown were agitating for *Mayflower* to make their town and not Plymouth her first port of call. My friends at Plymouth argued that if the ship called first at Provincetown it would have an adverse effect on their campaign to re-create the Pilgrim settlement and berth the ship. This was not unreasonable, but the people of Provincetown argued that if we ignored their claims we would not be faithful to history, and Harry Kemp, the famous poet of the sand dunes, cabled the Queen demanding royal intervention. Local historians based their prior claim to the ship upon four points:

(1) *Mayflower* stayed at Provincetown for five weeks before going on to Plymouth.

(2) The Mayflower Compact, forerunner of the Declaration of Independence and the Constitution's Bill of Rights, was signed in *Mayflower's* cabin while the vessel was anchored in Provincetown harbor.

(3) The Pilgrim women went ashore at Provincetown to establish the Monday washday tradition.

(4) Provincetown harbor was the base of operations for Captain Myles Standish's explorations that led to the first encounter with the Indians at Eastham and the discovery of the Indian store of corn on Corn Hill in Truro.

The plantation sent David Patten and George Olsson along to watch that I did not concede too much to their rivals.

My host, Mr. Hallett, introduced me to members of his committee, and after fattening me at lunch, put the point-blank slaughterer's question: "Will you give us an assurance, Mr. Charlton, that *Mayflower* will call here?"

"I will give you an assurance," I said, noting anxious glances from George Olsson and David Patten, "that Provincetown will be appropriately included in our arrival ceremonies." I did not feel this double talk was good enough, but did not want to commit myself any further until I had spoken to Alan Villiers.

Prelude to a Voyage

I saw that Mr. Hallett was not satisfied with my reply and was returning to the attack, so thinking to divert attention, I said I did not want to leave Provincetown without meeting Harry Kemp. I thought they looked surprised at my request, but with characteristic American courtesy where a guest is concerned, they sent out a search party, which located the poet working in the back room of a store building.

He proved to be a turkey-necked old man, hard of hearing, with a good supply of words. He was considerably less restrained than Mr. Hallett in his discussion of the problem.

"A hidden gang of powerful people are trying to do a silly and grievous thing here," he told me. "It wasn't anticlimactical when the first *Mayflower* dropped anchor here before going to Plymouth, and it won't be today.

"This is the last great adventure of my life. I'm seventy-four now, and I'll walk to Washington to see what can be accomplished by that sort of a protest if I have to. But I've got all sorts of fantastic and dangerous plans. Some of the fishermen here are with me on this and we'll go out and intercept that ship and bring her in here ourselves if we have to. I'd even be in favor of using live shot to shoot the rigging down if we have to, but I suppose that would be regarded as piracy."

I got in a word quickly to confirm that shooting our rigging down would be regarded as piracy, or at least as a very unfriendly action.

"I love to do outrageous things," he said. "I start each day reading from a replica of Shakespeare's First Folio. It sets me on fire. I am also a fanatic on the subject of *Mayflower* and the Pilgrims. They were innocents who came to the codfish grounds with hooks too big. They didn't believe that the end justified the means. I am starting a national program to have Provincetown recognized as the place where the greatest thing in history took place. And now some of these Plymouth people think they are going to be able to jam up historical truth. I'm warning them now that we'll do any desperate thing in the world to thwart them."

[70]

At which point I could only remark that I hoped the people of Plymouth would pay heed to his words.

❋   ❋   ❋

One evening I spent in Plymouth on that first visit to America will remain with me always; it was my first meal in an American home, dinner with Harry's mother and father. Their house was embraced by the lush green of the New England countryside, the grounds were thick with tall trees and bushes, but there was an ordered casualness about the gardens, and a permanence, and I had a sense of Old England in the New.

It emerged that evening that Ralph Hornblower was an ardent supporter of the plantation and of the Mayflower Project, but he preferred to remain in the background. It was he who had started the plantation off with an anonymous donation and I hope he will forgive me for breaking this confidence here.

From Plymouth, David Patten took me to New York. George Stewart, who had arranged the insurance for *Mayflower,* has offices in New York and had promised to introduce me to a group of his friends who might help me arrange *Mayflower's* reception and exhibition in the city.

There was Fred Glass, a tall Southerner whose gentle manner and voice could be misleading until one knew that he ran the Empire State Building with the ease and efficiency of the born administrator.

There was George Sanders, a stout, fresh-faced, middle-aged man, a former Commissioner of Trade for New York, and now president of the city's oldest tourist corporation, the Hudson River Day Line, which operates ships from Pier 81, adjacent to where the *Queens* tie up.

There was Paul Bird, a business associate of George Stewart's, a Bostonian who traveled the world regularly once a year and had the tolerant good humor that comes from meeting and mixing with people of all races and discovering how much alike we all are. The C.B.E. noted after his name was a mark of his repute.

I started off by explaining to them that we wanted to bring *Mayflower* to New York, and to exhibit her during the summer months, so that millions of people might see her before she was handed over to the plantation for permanent berthing.

George Sanders spoke first. "You can put her at Pier 81," he said. "But that is not enough, just to tie up a seventeenth-century ship." He turned to the others. "It isn't the presence of *Mayflower* that matters so much. She and her voyage are the physical representation of the ideas of these people. To promote, maintain and run an exhibition worthy of those ideas is going to cost a lot of money — but I think it's worth doing, because the ideas are worthy."

With that short speech he virtually carried the meeting. On the following day I was given their formal promise to set up an organization for *Mayflower* in New York, which would work in co-operation with the New York Convention and Visitors Bureau and prepare for the arrival and exhibition of the ship. The basis of this agreement was thus reached in two days and I had only one telephone call to make before leaving with my mission accomplished, but I could not make it until I had the number.

Before I left for America, we had had several discussions as to whom we should invite to launch *Mayflower*. We wanted it to be someone who was of the people as the Pilgrims were, and at the same time someone who had contributed in a practical and signal way to Anglo-American friendship. I was talking this over with my friend Edmund Jessup, the rector of Babworth with Ranby, near Retford, where the Pilgrim ideals first took root, when he remembered the story of a young American airman, a nonswimmer, who had risked his life to rescue some thirty British men and women during the East Coast floods of 1954. He had been decorated by the Queen for his heroism, and the Rector thought that the airman, whose name, we found after making inquiries, was Reis Leming, would be a choice in keeping with the project. But when I had spoken to the American Third Army

Air Force, I was told that he had been demobilized and was back in America.

Charles Strickland, the architect to the plantation, offered to trace Leming for me. He was true to his word and came through with a telephone number in Toppenish, a small town in the state of Washington. I put through a call and after introducing myself, said: "Mr. Leming, have you heard that we are rebuilding *Mayflower* in England?"

"Yes," he confirmed, "I have."

"Well, we want you to come and launch her."

There was a gasp. "Do you mean that?" he exclaimed.

"A round-trip air ticket and expenses paid — how about it?"

"Are you serious?"

"Yes, Mr. Leming."

"When is this?"

"Ten days' time — the twenty-second of September."

"Well, O.K. — er," he hesitated, and then said hopefully: "Don't suppose I could bring Mary Ann? She's my wife. We were married in England."

"Yes, of course," I said. "We'd like you both to be our guests."

The voice at the other end of the line said simply: "Gee!"

VIII

Launching

No one has ever set out upon a great enterprise without meeting with a few Jeremiahs, critics and fainthearts, and as the time for launching the ship approached, I took some pleasure in the knowledge that this event would forever silence a good section of them, the criers of doom who said *Mayflower* would never get as far as the water. I had not seen her for nearly three months, and now in a sense I was looking at her with a fresh eye. At first glance she appeared disappointingly small: a swollen lifeboat crowned with a curved wooden stockade. As I stood on deck with Stuart Upham he said: "How does it feel?"

"To stand on the deck for the first time?"

"Yes."

I took a long time to reply. "She *is* small."

Stuart smiled, and took me by the arm and led the way below. Here all was dim, and smelled of tar and oak. It might have been the Ark. He broke the silence. "People forget," he said, "that it all began from a damned acorn."

I went back to the office in the shipyard with renewed confidence, and checked over the arrangements for the following morning. We were expecting three thousand visitors, nearly a third of whom were coming from other parts of the country and from the United States. The event was being mirrored for the world by newspapers, radio, newsreel, television and still cameramen. While the shipwrights were putting the finishing touches for the launching, placing the blocks upon which they had carved their initials, I walked up the road to the hotel where we had installed Reis and Mary Ann. They had flown six thousand miles from their home town for the ceremony and arrived at London Airport only three days before. Felix had invited them to stay with him while they were in London, and his butler, Mr. Hynd, looked after them, took any messages, and reminded them of their many appointments. There was a press conference when they got off the plane, a welcome from General Wilson, commander of the Third Air Force, a trip to Scotland to see the ropes being made — such a packed schedule that I had little time to go over the details of the main purpose of Reis's visit. But from their contact with the press a few moments after touchdown and the speech Reis made forty minutes later at a crowded Saints and Sinners luncheon, both he and Mary Ann confirmed by the dignity of their bearing and the sincerity of their utterances that they typified the youth and future of America.

Mayflower was to be launched according to the seventeenth-century procedure, recalling the still earlier religious ceremony of christening a ship, and in this the central role was played by a man. Bill Baker had drawn my attention to a description of a typical launching written by Phoneas Pett, one of the greatest of English master shipwrights. The vessel was the *Prince Royal*, and the launching date September 24, 1610.

> The noble Prince himself [James I], accompanied with the Lord Admiral and the great Lords, were on the poop, where the standing great gilt cup was ready filled with wine to name the ship so soon as she had been afloat, according to ancient custom and ceremony performed at such times, by drinking part of the wine, giving the ship her name and heaving the standing cup overboard.

By 1664 the practice of presenting the cup to the master shipwright had become fairly common. Builders supplied the goblet and after it was thrown overboard some "hardy swimmer" recovered it and usually tried to sell it back to the builder.

"In this case," I told Reis, "we are presenting the cup to you and Mary Ann."

"But what if the swimmer doesn't recover the cup?" said Reis.

"Yes. How about that?" joined in Mary Ann. "We want a memento to take back to Toppenish."

"You've no need to worry," I said. "Our 'hardy swimmer' is Beric Watson, who is a good skin diver, and with our customary prudence we have a duplicate cup."

"We want the real thing," Mary Ann said firmly.

"Or a reasonable facsimile thereof," I said, airing a legal phrase I had picked up in New York.

"The real thing, that's what we want," insisted Reis.

"Don't worry about that," I said. But they did. They both did. And I did.

I could not sleep that night, but stayed in the hotel at Torquay, nine miles away from the yard, drinking coffee and talking to Felix in the lounge. It was past four when he suggested that although there was little prospect of sleep, at least it was worth going to our bedrooms for a lie-down. I dozed off into a half sleep, never going far below the surface of oblivion, when I was roused by the sound of a storm. Outside as I looked, the dark morning rain streamed, cascading over Devon, and thundering like Niagara.

When we arrived at the yard most of the crowd were already in place, standing under the shelter of the drumming iron roof of the yard. We pushed our way through to a platform by the bows of *Mayflower,* over which there was no shelter. Reis and his wife were in their position next to General Wilson and Felix joined them. I glanced round and saw John, who had been shepherding our visiting patrons, smiling through the rivulets of rain running down his face. Umbrellas bobbed and rocked and poured water every now and then onto the hats and over the collars around them.

In the outer harbor on the storm-glass sea, pleasure launches pitched and rolled under a tent of umbrellas. The fishing wharves were crowded, and behind every window of the higgledy-piggledy houses fronting the crooked alleys and stone stairways of the steep Brixham hills people were watching. The band of the Somerset Light Infantry waited with their instruments poised.

Mr. Yeomans, Vicar of Brixham, followed by his choir, walked to his place at the bow of the ship, the Service of Dedication began, and all our voices were raised in defiance of the storm in the hymn "O God of Jacob, by Whose hand Thy people still are fed. . . ."

Then we said a prayer of Sir Francis Drake, asking the blessing of God on our venture and grace to finish the work:

> *O Lord God, when Thou givest to Thy servants to endeavor any great matter, grant us also to know that it is not the beginning but the continuing of the same unto the end, until it be thoroughly finished, which yieldeth the true Glory, through him who for the finishing of Thy work laid down his life, our Redeemer Jesus Christ.*

The choir sang an American merchant seaman's version of the Twenty-third Psalm, and there followed a prayer from the inauguration speech of Abraham Lincoln.

> *Grant, O merciful God, that with malice toward none; with charity for all; with firmness in the right, as Thou givest us to see the right, we may strive on to finish the work we are in.*

Overhead, lightning forked and there was a long burst of thunder.

Then there was quiet. And as the rain began to ease we sang the closing hymn, written in the house at the end of the road above the shipyard by the Reverend Francis Lyte, a former Vicar of Brixham, "Abide with Me." The words floated across the harbor and were echoed by the crowd in the streets.

Mr. Yeomans pronounced the blessing, and in the silence that followed Felix stepped forward.

"I'll cut it short," he whispered in my ear. "The sooner we get the ship away the better." He stood in front of the microphone, some sheets of rain-drenched papers in his hand.

"All free men know that their future hangs on the continued friendship of America and this country," he said, "and that is why we are here today — to see *Mayflower*, the symbol of our common heritage and enduring community of interests, go down to the sea again."

He read extracts from messages of goodwill, including one from Christian A. Herter, Governor of the Commonwealth of Massachusetts: "I am stirred by the spirit of goodwill that prompted your people to give so generously to a craft that will soon sail far away. God speed your valiant ship to our shores."

General Wilson came forward to introduce Reis Leming, and before so doing told the assembly: "All Americans, regardless of race, color or creed, have inherited the tradition of courage and fortitude which belongs parficularly to the Pilgrim Fathers and which you seek to commemorate here." I was reminded as he spoke that one of the messages of goodwill had come from Mr. Hulen Jack, President of the Borough of Manhattan, and the highest Negro officeholder in the United States.

Reis, tall, fair-haired, the George Medal pinned to his rain-soaked overcoat, walked up to the microphone on the stand in front of the choir, looked around, caught the eye of Mary Ann, and said in a silence broken only by the sound of the gulls wheeling on high and the waves lapping against the shore: "This is one of the greatest things that has happened to me. You British don't forget."

Stuart Upham handed him the christening chalice and together they passed it round the shipwrights, each man taking a sip of wine until the chalice returned to Reis. Then he and Stuart went up the ladders onto the ship and walked to the bows, where Reis drained the cup. According to the old custom, he cast it into the sea, with the words "I name thee — *Mayflower*."

When Reis threw the chalice into the sea I turned to John and signaled that I was going down to stand with the shipwrights. He joined me. Beric Watson, in bathing trunks and goggles, came running up to the bows, the christening chalice in his hand. "Look," I shouted to Reis, "he's got it!"

"Are you sure it's the right one?" Reis shouted back and I nodded, but later I had to produce the two cups before he and

[78]

Mary Ann were convinced they were not being fobbed off with the "reasonable facsimile thereof."

Now came the real business of the launching of the ship, when the shipwrights came into their own. Ten of them lining each side of the ship held their long-handled maul hammers at the ready and waited for the foreman shipwright to make his calls.

"Are you ready?" he shouted. And then began to chant: "One blow, two blow, three blow," and twenty hammers rang a sharp explosive tattoo, driving the wedges that would by tiny fractions inch the full weight of *Mayflower* onto the cradle of the slipway.

> One blow, two blow, three blow,
> Strike her hard, strike her hard.
> Inch a blow, up she go,
> One blow, two blow, three blow!

George Phillips chanted, and as he chanted I heard Stuart's voice: "Hit, m'hearties!"

The foreman's calls were slow, rhythmic and clear, and I felt as though my heart was beating with the blows of the hammers. Then came the moment when all of us, three thousand people, were united in an almost unbearable silence. The pulsating chant and chock of the hammers were finished. The final word of command came from Stuart. He gave the order for two men to strike away the dogshores under the forefoot. One advanced and with a gentle blow knocked out a single wooden block. Then with no check, the *Mayflower* swept down the greased slipway, gathering speed, and launched herself for the first time on water.

She scattered the little boats as she ran on across the harbor, dragging the anchor flung over her bows, and then she turned and faced broadside on as though to take her bow. The whole crowd gave three crying cheers, and I found myself shouting and cheering with them, and John leaping up and down at my side, shouting in my ear: "It went all right! It went all right!" and wringing my hand at the same time.

I found it difficult to answer, my throat dry and my eyes wet with tears forgotten since childhood. Nor was I alone. I ran to Bill Baker and his wife Ruth, and they could not speak as we clasped hands. Then in the excitement of congratulations, with the band of the Somerset Light Infantry playing the "Battle Hymn of the Republic," I saw Bill Brewster, smiling, nodding his handsome head in silent approval, thinking perhaps of his ancestors who had sailed in just such a ship over three centuries ago to the New World.

I sought out Alan Villiers, who had stayed in the background during the ceremonies. "Tell me, Alan," I said, "what did you think of it? Are you happy?"

He tilted his head on one side and said in his rasping voice: "Warwick, I am sure Drake would have been delighted with the way little *Mayflower* took the water. He would have felt at home at the launching ceremonies, too, with the blazing and the golden goblet and the old shipwrights' chantey.

"She slipped down the waves like a bird, and I was delighted with the way the hull slipped through the water."

He paused and spoke slowly, picking his words carefully, "Sure there was somewhat less of her there than I would like to see, and I had hoped that at least she would be a finished hull, with the aftercastle and that long, characteristic beak. You know the hull as launched was planned only to the 'tween decks and the ribs stood gaunt and naked above that; but now she is in the water Stuart and his craftsmen will make rapid progress. Whenever you get impatient you must remember that building the replica has bristled with problems, all of which have had to be overcome the hard way. The ancient craft of fashioning fine ships from English oak — done as it used to be — had to be remastered in Upham's yard. Now it is done and progress will be rapid."

There, too, was Stuart, standing apart from the crowd, and staring happily out at his ship.

"Well," I said, knowing his dislike for superlatives, "do you think it went all right?"

At first he did not answer, and I thought that he had not heard my question.

Then, with his eyes still fixed on *Mayflower*, and in his soft West Country burr, he said: "It was a *proper* launching."

[80]

IX
Final Arrangements

ALMOST immediately after the launching the project began to run into heavy weather and there was no calm until the ship set sail from Plymouth six months later.

The first storm warning came in October with the Suez crisis. My first thoughts were that war in the Middle East might lead to a world war, and if that happened the project would be wrecked.

These events were far beyond our control and I was resigned to the fact that if my worst fears were realized we'd have to get some guns for *Mayflower* and join the Royal Navy. In fact, the crisis gave added importance to the purpose of the project, but that was not easy to see at the time.

When it became apparent that the Americans did not approve of the Anglo-French action in Suez, there was a howl of indignation among government supporters and an outburst of anti-Americanism.

The *Daily Mirror* cartoonist Vicky summed up the situation with a cartoon of the British Foreign Secretary returning to England from America in *Mayflower*, battered by storms and being greeted by members of the government carrying anti-American slogans. The caption read: "Return of a Pilgrim." This breach in Anglo-American relations did some material damage to us. A number of the firms who had promised financial support suddenly discovered reasons for withdrawing, and this happened when we needed every penny to meet mounting building costs. Although none of the firms concerned suggested their change of heart had come about as a result of a change in Anglo-American relations, I decided the only policy was to sit tight, say nothing, keep working and wait for calmer waters.

I rang Harry Hornblower to assure him we would not allow international events to interfere with progress on the ship. I also told him not to accept reports of violent British criticism of the American Government as representing the mass of public opinion in Britain. He seemed almost embarrassed at his end of the line. "We are naturally very worried," he said, "but please don't think there is bad feeling for England here."

I had previously arranged for Alan Villiers to fly to America to speak for the plantation, to help them launch their major fund-raising campaign to achieve their target of one million dollars for the berthing site, and I saw no reason to change these plans. On the contrary, it seemed to me we might usefully steal some of Nasser's headlines. So Alan flew to America as planned, and during the week he was there, never a day went by without stories of the Mayflower Project, the plantation's plans, and our basic aims of Anglo-American friendship being given prominence through the press, radio and television. He returned tired but triumphant, with the front page of one American paper, the Boston *Globe,* giving him more space than the Suez crisis.

Meanwhile, progress at the yard was slower than we had anticipated. Stuart had estimated the previous summer that the ship would be ready for trials on or about December 31, 1956. With this date in mind I had approached the Port of London Authority and negotiated St. Katharine's dock, near the Tower of London, as a berth for the ship for her London exhibition, which was to be the major fund-raising exercise before we set sail. I consulted architects and drew up detailed plans for the exhibition, including a reconstruction of seventeenth-century London adjacent to the berthing place; advertising space in the national press was provisionally booked and all our supporters were circularized with these plans.

Stuart Upham is an optimist and his optimism had, in the past, moved him to surmount many obstacles. I know he was loath to disappoint us, but towards the end of November bad weather, combined with the shortage of skilled hands, forced him to admit that the ship would not be finished for at least another four months. This was a great disappointment, but the slow pace of building gave me cause for alarm on another count. On the other side of the Atlantic, Ronald A. Forth, an Englishman who had lived in Massachusetts for thirty years, was the chairman of the National Reception Committee organized to welcome *Mayflower*. He had gathered together an impressive committee to ensure the second *Mayflower* would not be greeted with the still, stony silence of an unconquered continent which greeted our forerunners in 1620. Since the launching, his reception committee had been meeting, getting into the spirit of the occasion by meeting in the Myles Standish Room of the Plymouth Memorial Hall.

He wrote and told me of these plans, which included ten days of celebration to start the moment the ship showed sail over the horizon, with nightly performances of the Pilgrim Operetta, a number of parades, and an official welcoming ceremony set for noon on Saturday, *May 25*. Yes — they had even set a date! When I had spoken to Mr. Forth during my visit to America he had naturally asked me for a date of arrival. How do you give such a date when your motive power is the wind? After talking it over with Alan Villiers and Upham, however, I felt it fairly safe to say we hoped to make a landfall about May 25, 1957, and not later than the first week in June.

He told me that with a firm date he might get President Eisenhower to welcome us, and also Sir Harold Caccia, the British Ambassador to Washington.

The energetic Mr. Forth went before the Massachusetts State House committees to ask for seventy thousand dollars in state funds for the celebrations and to seek an act to permit Plymouth to vote up to twenty-five thousand dollars for the event. At the same time the Government of Massachusetts voted nearly three hundred thousand dollars for the dredging of Plymouth Bay channel to be completed for our arrival. This sum, authorized by the state, also enabled them to construct a cement walk round the Pilgrim First House, adjacent to Plymouth Rock, and a fence for the safety of the crowds.

Mr. Forth was also budgeting for a temporary stage and grandstand on the roadway next to Plymouth Rock, to accommodate nearly four thousand people.

I had not anticipated a welcome on such a large and costly scale, particularly after Suez. I felt, however, that the Anglo-American quarrel gave added purpose to the project, and the reception of the ship in the New World might help to warm the coldness and bitter words that blew over the Atlantic. I wrote to Forth:

> We realize, if only from our own experience, how important it is that you should have as much notice as possible of our date of arrival. However, we would point out that setting the precise moment of landfall for a seventeenth-century sailing ship without auxiliaries, after a three-thousand-mile journey, can only be done within certain brackets, and to go further than this would merely run the risk of unconsciously misleading your organization. We are advised that as far as can be foreseen the week of May 25 is the safest to posit for the time of arrival.

I had hedged my bet a little but not so as to upset the plans for our reception.

Paul Bird, the Bostonian president of the group I had met in New York, informed me of equally elaborate plans for our reception there. Pier 81 was to be transformed into an exhibition with a seventeenth-century Anglo-American theme. They were collaborating closely with the New York Convention and Visitors Bureau and *Mayflower* had been adopted as the central theme for the annual New York Summer Festival. They had made administrative preparations to receive some three million visitors during the ship's five months' stay in New York before she was formally handed over to the plantation. This would mean that she would be seen by people from all over the United States who pour into New York at that time of year.

There was evidence of the widespread interest in the project in the States in the increasing volume of requests that arrived from Americans who wished to sail on *Mayflower* either as passengers or crew. I felt that the inclusion of an American in the crew would make for increased interest in the project. Some months before, the National Association of Boys' Clubs had suggested to me that we should take one of their members as a cabin boy. I had agreed to this and they had run a national competition which had ended in the selection of Graham Nunn, a sixteen-year-old boy from Corby, at a ceremony presided over by H.R.H. the Duke of Gloucester. I invited the Boys' Clubs of America to run a similar competition and this they had agreed to do.

Every year the Boys' Clubs held a national competition to select their Junior Citizen of the Year, and this year they added a prize of a passage on *Mayflower*. The final selection was Joseph Meany of Waltham, Massachusetts, by a committee headed by former President Hoover.

I had resigned myself to the fact that delays in building would mean an alteration in our program before leaving England. We had always intended that the ship should go to London and then, after the exhibition, make as many ports of call as possible before she left Plymouth. The civic authorities of Weymouth, Boston, Dartmouth and Southampton were among those who wished to give us a ceremonial send-off.

We were going to have to disappoint most if not all of them if we were to have a chance of reaching America on schedule, and eventually I had to announce that we would not be calling. This news brought a storm of protest from Southampton and the two Southampton Members of Parliament who were on our Board of Patrons resigned. I behaved in a somewhat cowardly fashion when it came to giving this news to the city, and asked Alan if he would do it for me. He did so in his usual forthright manner.

The main worry, however, was not support from civic authorities but whether or not the ship would even be completed on time to set sail early in April, the date I had promised our American friends. Alan Villiers told me he would need about forty days for the crossing, taking the northern route, which had the advantage of being more direct and therefore faster. It would involve greater risk, but I felt that in view of our commitments on the other side of the Atlantic the risk was warranted.

When we discussed this Alan said: "The original *Mayflower* didn't have to worry over a problem that's just about our worst, I reckon: the risk of collision. She sailed a North Atlantic that didn't know any liner lanes. She was just about alone. That has advantages when the navigation lights aren't too good. We'll carry the best of sidelights and a strong white sternlight, but that's all we're allowed.

"And there's no doubt that there is some deterioration in the lookout kept at sea today, aboard some ships. Fellows get the idea — very naturally — that all ships show white masthead lights, and a sea where there aren't any such lights — to them — can't have any ships in it. Well, we don't carry masthead lights, because we're not allowed to. The normal red and green sidelights and one white sternlight are all that are allowed to pure sailing ships. So I will do the best I can to keep away from steamships of all kinds."

With all the irritating delays I had a surge of hope soon after the New Year. A nearby shipyard had laid off some skilled shipwrights and we were able to increase our labor force. I also formed what Americans call a "crash" program committee to help speed up completion. Alan was the chairman of this committee, which received daily reports from our on-the-spot surveyor Norman Vine. Towards the end of February it became apparent that unless something serious interrupted the pace of building, the ship would be out of her dry dock by the beginning of April. Most of the shipwrights' work was completed, the three lower masts were in and there was excellent progress on the rigging. It really began to look as though nothing short of continually bad weather would impede progress. Then in March I heard the faint warnings of *Mayflower's* running into trouble. Some nine months previously the Confederation of Shipbuilding and Engineering Unions, representing forty unions engaged in the

shipbuilding industry, had approached the employers' organization to ask for a 10 per cent increase in the basic rates of pay. The
union leaders pointed to rising profits, full order books on the
one side and the increased cost of living on the other. But the
employers refused to discuss the matter. They felt that increased
wage claims were rapidly spiraling to inflation and that Britain
was in danger of pricing herself out of the world markets. The
union leaders thought the employers selfish and arrogant.

During the ensuing months the attitude of both the unions and
the employers had hardened, until in March the unions issued
an ultimatum to the employers that either they agree to a 10 per
cent increase in the basic wage of skilled men or they would call
a national shipyard strike to start at noon on Saturday, March 16.
The government tried to act the role of peacemaker, but neither
the unions nor the employers would give way.

I asked Stuart if he thought the threat of a national strike of
shipyard workers would affect *Mayflower*. For once he was not
optimistic. "Yes, Warwick, it will mean the closure of our yard.
There is no way in which we can carry on.

"How much the work on *Mayflower* will be affected will depend on how long it is before a settlement is reached. It is all
very disappointing for us, but it is something over which we have
no control."

He added hopefully: "I am keeping my fingers crossed. Perhaps there will not be a strike, or if it does happen, perhaps it will
not last long."

I took a train to the yard and went round talking to the men,
telling them of the plan for *Mayflower's* reception in America.
I did not mention the strike. The ship towered high above her
dock. Craftsmen who might on Saturday be told by their unions
to down tools were busy putting finishing touches to the superstructure.

This was on Tuesday and the following day I heard that the
strike notices had been served at the yard and decided that something could be done and that I would do it.

Apart from my natural desire to see *Mayflower* finished, I felt that strike action on this symbol of Anglo-American unity would do more damage to Britain's reputation in America than all the rest of the strike put together.

I made inquiries to discover who was the most hardheaded of the strike leaders and I was told my man was Mr. Ted Hill, the chief of the Boilermakers' Union. I telephoned him and put my case. "Mr. Hill, I suggest it would be good public relations for the British labor movement and a gesture of fraternal goodwill to the American labor movement, if your confederation exempts *Mayflower* from the strike." I found Mr. Hill more willing to listen to reason than I had been led to suppose.

"I am inclined to agree with you, Mr. Charlton," he said, "but you will have to get on to the secretary of the confederation, Gavin Martin, and tell him that it is all right with me. He has the final say."

I took this advice and spoke to Mr. Gavin Martin, who agreed with Mr. Hill, but said that the final say was not with him but with Mr. Sydney Ombler, the general secretary of the Ship Constructors' and Shipwrights' Association. I spoke to Mr. Ombler. My luck held. He had worked on wooden ships himself and had followed the progress of *Mayflower*. "I think if Ted Hill and Gavin Martin have agreed, then you have my support," he said. "We will exempt *Mayflower* from the strike action." And then he added: "Let me know when you get her finished and I will try to come down and see her off."

I telephoned the yard at Mr. Ombler's suggestion and spoke to the branch secretary of the union there, Mr. John Lamswood. "Would the men like to go on working?" I asked.

"They would like to well enough," he replied, "but what can we do?"

I told him my news. "Mr. Ombler wants you to telephone him straightaway and he will confirm to you verbally what I have told you and follow it up by a letter. This letter will state that no other work is to be done in the yard excepting that on *Mayflower*."

My plain record of what transpired cannot convey the dramatic effect that this news had when it reached the press. On the following Saturday at noon every shipyard in England was silent except for the one at Brixham where the men were working on *Mayflower.* I released my news to the press with the following comment:

> The decision by the Confederation of Shipbuilding and Engineering Unions to withdraw strike notices at the *Mayflower* yard is a magnificent gesture on the part of the men working on the ship and the union leaders. When *Mayflower* sails she will not only represent the finest of British craftsmanship, but also carry a message of goodwill from the shipyard workers of this country to the shipyard workers in the United States of America.

Over the week end the news of this friendly act by the union reached the United States, and on Monday a message arrived from the president of the International Seafarers' Union in New York thanking the British union leaders for what they had done. But the fight was still not won.

John Lamswood called me from Brixham and read a letter he had received from the district secretary of his union:

> I have to inform you that following our meeting with you this morning, we held a meeting with the shop stewards when a report on the position relative to Messrs. Upham's was submitted to them.
>
> From reports which we have now received from the various yards throughout the whole of the South West area including Falmouth, it is very apparent that there is considerable resentment over the fact that work is continuing on the Mayflower Project and 100 per cent of the employees of Messrs. Upham's have now been engaged on this work.
>
> After very careful consideration it was Unanimously Agreed that I should be requested to write to you and appeal for the full support of your fellow workers in our present struggle.
>
> While it is appreciated that permission has apparently been granted by the Executive for work to continue on the *Mayflower,* at the same time it has not been indicated that the employees concerned could not come out on strike if they so desired, and we therefore hope you and they will appreciate the present position and cease work forthwith.

[89]

Prelude to a Voyage

The letter meant that despite the national ruling, the men working on *Mayflower* were being asked to join the strike. A meeting was being called locally which was to be attended by all shop stewards in the West Region and a vote was to be taken over the confederation's decision. Mr. Lamswood warned me: "I am attending the meeting, Mr. Charlton, and I will do my best, but I think it will go against us. The trouble is that although I have received official confirmation from the national executive to continue working, the South Devon branch has not."

I decided to call on the union leaders who were meeting at their national headquarters at Transport House: the main purpose of the meeting was to broaden the strike until it would affect 2,500,000 men, and possibly call a national strike.

The corridors of Transport House were crowded with press men waiting to hear what was going on behind the doors of the conference hall. I walked past them and let myself in. Two stewards came up to me. "You cannot come in here," they said, rather belatedly I thought, as I closed the conference hall doors behind me.

"I have an urgent matter for the executive," I replied. "One that requires immediate action if their members are not to be victimized."

They called for Mr. Ombler and I told him that there was discontent among the South Devon shipyard strikers because work was being allowed to continue on *Mayflower*.

"They are calling your men blacklegs," I said. "There is talk of the yard being picketed. Has the decision definitely been confirmed by your executive?" He assured me that it had.

"Will you please confirm this or get the executive to confirm this without delay?" I asked. Mr. Ombler was kindness itself and he agreed to do so. Our battle was won.

When I got back to the office I was in a jubilant mood and at once telephoned the yard to tell Lamswood what had happened. But scarcely had one problem been disposed of than another hove into view. Doubts began to be expressed about the ability of *Mayflower* to cross the Atlantic safely.

Transatlantic News Features

From left to right: Warwick Charlton, founder of *Mayflower II*, Stuart Upham, the ship's builder, and William A. Baker, naval architect and designer of *Mayflower II*, discuss early plans

Mayflower Studio

Felix Fenston and John Lowe

Commander Alan Villiers, master of the *Mayflower*, Stuart Upham, and the ship's first mate, Godfrey Wicksteed, examine silver model of the ship

Henry Hornblower II, president of Plimoth Plantation, Inc., on ship with Upham during her building at Brixham, Devon

Wide World Photos

The mold loft where the shapes and sizes of the timbers for *Mayflower II* were worked out full scale on the floor

Mayflower Mail

Stuart Upham (*right*) examining a crooked oak from which to cut specially shaped pieces for the new *Mayflower*

Early building stages

Mayflower's anchor waiting for its wooden stock to be fitted

Men at work on the crow's-nest, at top of mainmast of Oregon pine, 67 feet in height

International News Photos

Mayflower Mail

Calking seams prior to launching

Mayflower M...

"She appeared disappointingly small: a swollen lifeboat crowned with a curved wooden stockade"

The ship's bell, given to *Mayflower* by the people of Brixham, was cast by Miles Grave in 1638

Nicholas Horne

"It was a *proper* launching," said Stuart

The "hardy swimmer" presents the goblet to Reis Leming (*second from right*). On Reis's left stands General Wilson, U.S.A.F., and choir boys

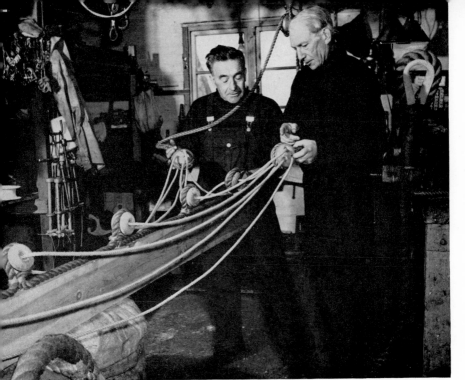

Mayflower Mail

Rigging for the ship . . .

Sport and General

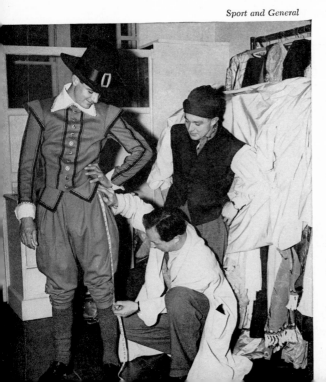

. . . and for her crew. David Cauvin of Cape Town, South Africa, is fitted for his Pilgrim costume as John Winslow watches

The little ship takes shape in the
final stages of building

Mayflower Treasure Chests are brought aboard

Mayflower II under full sail for first sea trials in Tor Bay, Devon

The Lord Mayor of Plymouth (*left*) smiles as Commander Villiers
toasts the venture's success in ancient loving cup

Warwick Charlton and Commander Villiers (*second and third from
left*) in rowing pinnace on day of sailing, April 20

Under way with all sails set

Eating in the Great Cabin . . .

. . . and in the tiller flat

Laundry day for Dick Brennan

Scrubbing the decks

Ike Marsh tarring the lines

The galley. Dick Brennan and Wally Godfrey, the ship's cook (*right*)

Gordon Tenney from Black Star, reprinted by courtesy of Life magazine

The crew of *Mayflower II*

1) MAITLAND EDEY
2) GRAHAM NUNN
3) WALLY GODFREY
4) GODFREY WICKSTEED
5) ADRIAN SMALL
6) ALAN VILLIERS
7) JAN JUNKER
8) STUART UPHAM
9) PETER PADFIELD
10) JOE MEANY
11) JIMMY HORROCKS
12) WARWICK CHARLTON
13) JOHN WINSLOW
14) DICK BRENNAN
15) JUMBO GODDARD
16) JOE LACEY

17) FRED EDWARDS
18) BERIC WATSON
19) ANDREW ANDERSON-BELL
   (SCOTTIE)
20) IKE MARSH
21) DAVID CAUVIN
22) JACK SCARR
23) JOE POWELL
24) CHARLES CHURCH
   (CANADA)
25) HARRY SOWERBY
26) EDGAR MUGRIDGE
27) DR. JOHN STEVENS
28) MICHAEL FORD
29) DAVID THORPE
30) ANDY LINDSAY

Prelude to a Voyage

Stanley Bonnett, the shipping expert of the *Daily Mail,* voiced all these forebodings. He wrote:

Will the 183 ton *Mayflower II* survive the Atlantic rollers which rock the 81,000 ton *Queen Mary?* While sailors debate I will be bold.

To me she has an even chance of making a scheduled landfall at the Plymouth, Massachusetts, end of her ocean pilgrimage. No more. I believe more in Commander Alan Villiers, her master, than in the *Mayflower* herself. For no matter how little sail she may have left to catch the wind or how much sea may have slipped into her oaken belly, I believe he will keep *Mayflower* headed for the New World.

I put this on record too: I do not envy his job. I have yet to talk with a square-rigger specialist who does. The *Mayflower* is a replica of a 17th century ship — a breed which were not famous for comfort or ability to get home. Exactly what the *Mayflower I* looked like no one knows. Mr. William Baker, the American naval architect who designed *Mayflower II,* has been as authentic as the records have allowed him. But whether his *Mayflower* is as seaworthy as that of his model's unknown designer remains to be seen.

Mayflower II was launched in a thunderstorm and appeared in danger of capsizing due to lack of ballast.

She canted over as heavy chests were put aboard, and one 81-year-old retired sea captain, who sailed four-masters, said: "I would not sail that ship outside the breakwater."

The only thing really sweet about her 1620 predecessor was the wine in the bilges which seeped there from days in the Bordeaux wine trade.

Her biggest danger is that she may be caught aback — get the wind on the wrong side of her sails. Expert opinion on much of *Mayflower's* design is divided. Many think her tall sides are too high.

Others say that if the sea casts *Mayflower* over on her side her "tender" shape will encourage to keep her going over. . . .

All that hempen rigging is criticized too. Hemp stretches. If *Mayflower's* sails have to be adjusted because of it, the job could be really tough.

With sea trials not beginning until next week, the crew will have little time to get to know their ship.

The views were shared in part or whole by others. One of our Olympic yachtsmen regarded the whole scheme as dangerous, and Dr. Bennett, a Member of Parliament, experienced in sailing everything from a Shamrock to a Firefly, said that he felt the designer had been faced with a difficult task. This arose not from any lack of talent, but from artistic license in contemporary seventeenth-century drawings, which did not sufficiently demonstrate the enormous beam and ballast necessary to counteract the great poop and forecastle. Alan replied to these doubters.

"Why all this pessimism about the *Mayflower*? My crew have the greatest confidence in the ship, and so have I. We get a little tired of armchair critics who say she cannot sail, or is not safe, or something of the kind.

"I will pay attention to critics who have experience — square-rigged sailing-ship experience, I mean. In this business, no other kind of seamanship counts.

"Our little ship is stoutly built and well rigged. True, she looks odd to modern eyes, used to wall-sided steel sea-wallers. But we do not forget that our ancestors sailed ships like this for centuries, and they were not fools.

"Already some features of the rigging, which bothered us at first because of their apparent inefficiency, have proved to be perfectly workable. The method of steering with a whipstaff, for example, works very well, though we are using ordinary wheel steering for the voyage. The spritsail is a handy piece of canvas, placed just where it most assists the ship's maneuvering, and the lateen mizzen is a useful balancing sail.

"The *Mayflower* is essentially just a small and handy little bark — and she will sail as such. Drake and Hawkins could walk aboard her and take over."

The views of private individuals as to the safety of the ship, whether or not they were based on contemporary sailing experience, did not unduly disturb me as I had sufficient confidence in Bill Baker's design, Stuart's construction and Alan's seamanship not to listen to pessimists.

But there was one voice which claimed our attention: it came from the Ministry of Transport Marine Safety Section. I thought at first that their inquiry as to whether or not we were to be escorted was based on interest and not concern. But after a number of discussions with them I realized that they had to be satisfied on several points, all of them to do with our safety.

Mr. W. P. Shovelton, the chief of the ministry's marine-safety branch, explained his department's attitude: "Now that you have made it quite clear that there is to be no escort we are concerned, in view of our general responsibility for the safety of life at sea and in view of the general interest aroused by your voyage, to assure ourselves for the safety of your venture. We want to know the course you are going to follow, the nature and number of your crew, what trials you are going to carry out, the proposed life-saving and fire appliances and whether radio is to be carried. Most important of all we wish to be assured of the stability of the ship."

The regulations governing marine safety have obviously progressed in the three centuries since the Pilgrims sailed, but there was nothing to be gained by cocking a snook at the ministry on these grounds; they were genuinely trying to help and whatever our personal feelings about rules and regulations we had to consider the lives of everyone who would sail with us. I therefore arranged that as soon as Alan returned from America we would have a meeting with the Ministry of Transport, at which Stuart would also be present, and at any rate make the position clear even if we could not allay their misgivings.

I think the three of us were a little taken aback when we entered the ministry conference room to see ten officials waiting for us. I had the feeling that the project was on trial, and this assessment was not far from the mark.

I thought I had met one of the officials before and told him so. He introduced himself. "My name is William Penn," he said. Then I remembered that we had met last in Calcutta eleven years ago when he had told me he was a descendant of William Penn. "I hope you are not going to be too exacting," I said.

"We are here to help you," said Mr. Penn.

"In view of your ancestry," I said, "I don't think you could do otherwise." At this there was some laughter and the ice was broken, and we settled down to answer their questions.

Final Arrangements

First of all they wanted to know what course we were taking. "I did hope that time would permit me to take the southerly course," Alan said. "Unfortunately, due to the arrangements which have been made in the United States and the fact that the ship will not be ready before the middle of April, I will have to take the quicker route. I have checked over something like five thousand such voyages across the Atlantic during the last hundred years and hope to achieve the voyage in something like thirty-seven to forty days. However, I have no intention of sacrificing trials or the precautions of good seamanship during the voyage merely to arrive on time.

"In view of the scale of the reception, which includes a pageant of Anglo-American history to which the President and British Ambassador have been invited, we are most anxious to avoid any delay which could not be accounted for by bad weather on the voyage."

He added that he would be receiving the regular ice reports by radio, and again emphasized that he would not sail until he was satisfied that he could safely do so and he intended to take no chances en route. If he was late for the reception committee, that would be "just too bad."

We told them there would be a crew of twenty-one, of which nine possessed master's certificates and were thus all competent seamen. The first three mates were masters of sail. I told them that Marconi Transarctic Wireless Radio and Radio Telephone equipment would be installed and a qualified certified operator would be carried on board.

The discussion switched to rigging and stability and Stuart explained that the rigging was essentially simple in character. All the standing rigging had been amply tested and stretched. Since then tests over the previous two weeks had shown that no further stretch had taken place. The ship would be out of dry dock in a few days and would be ready to undergo her inclining experiment.

Our discussion covered bilge pumping arrangements, steering gear, ventilation to crew space and our compliance with collision regulations; they agreed that the use of standard navigation lights would be satisfactory, as would our hand-operated foghorn, fire appliances and life-saving equipment.

They told us that in view of the nature of our voyage and the absence of a lifeboat we should require 200 per cent life-raft accommodation, a minimum of three rafts. We agreed to this and they for their part promised that if there was any difficulty in obtaining rafts they would help us. With regard to other life-saving appliances, we would have six lifebuoys, one line-throwing appliance and twelve parachute distress rockets.

They appeared to be satisfied on all these points.

I was just beginning to congratulate myself that we had been able to give the satisfactory answers to all their questions when one of the ministry men said that he would be responsible for the inclining equipment when the ship was out of dry dock. "The curves developed by the department are not in agreement with the estimates sent to us by your consulting naval architect," he said. "Our curves show a result about half as good as Mr. Baker's."

I explained that I had no technical knowledge and would be grateful if they would tell me why the difference between their figures and Bill Baker's gave them so much concern, and they explained that according to Bill's figures the ship was in grave danger of capsizing even if she ran into only moderately rough weather.

I cabled Bill to fly to England for the inclining tests at a date we agreed to be the first week in April. On April 1, Stuart confirmed the ship was ready to leave the dry dock. Thousands of people lined the cliffs to watch her go, and in the yard press and cameramen and hundreds of onlookers lined the dry dock.

For more than an hour the crowds had stood round the quayside and the ship waiting for high tide to enable the dock gates to be opened. Because of an easterly wind, high tide, which was due at 7:18, was cut by two feet, and for more than an hour Alan, Stuart and I waited aboard until the tide was high enough for the ship to take the water.

Final Arrangements

At five past seven the last of the blocks holding the ship was knocked out. Water in the dry dock seemed to be insufficient to lift her, and her keel rested on the bottom. We had only eighty tons of ballast. As the tug *Penley* began pulling on the stern, *Mayflower* listed dangerously and heeled about fifteen degrees to starboard. There were many white faces on board hidden in the evening gloom. I caught hold of the rigging, while Stuart jumped ashore to the dockside so that he could see what was happening. Many of the crowd, including women and children, ran from the narrow concrete pathway by the dock to higher ground.

For a few minutes it was touch and go whether *Mayflower* would get out of the dock. She moved several feet forward and heeled to port.

Bill Baker muttered between compressed lips: "Insufficient ballast."

The crew on board worked feverishly as *Mayflower* righted herself and got into the open harbor. As the tug began turning her, she continued listing one way and then the other.

While she was only about ten yards outside the dock, Stuart was making hurried arrangements to take another ten tons of ballast aboard when she was at anchor. I think all of us felt at one time she was in danger of heeling over altogether. The continued swaying of the ship kept us praying and the crowd watching until she reached her mooring point.

Stuart soon recovered his composure; the trouble was indeed insufficient ballast, although it had been necessary to bring her out of the dock that way. We needed at least another eighty tons of railway lines.

One of the paradoxes of the newspaper business is that had *Mayflower* entered the water without any trouble there would have been very little comment, but pictures of her listing were printed everywhere and were pointed out as confirmation of their views by all those who had expressed doubts as to her seaworthiness. But Alan, Bill and Stuart were all confident that there was nothing amiss which could not be righted by more ballast.

Half the crew were already in Brixham and I had sent the rest letters asking them to join the ship. Cargo, stores, victuals were arriving in the yard. We had only to pass the inclining test the following Friday and the ministry would be satisfied. I was not able to return to the yard to watch these tests, as I was busy in London seeing that the extra ballast was delivered in time, but on the following Saturday William Penn telephoned me. "We haven't worked out all the figures yet," he said, "but I thought I would let you know that we are satisfied with her stability."

For two years I had been working on the project, worrying about a score of details and never for a moment questioning that *Mayflower* would be seaworthy when she was completed, but I must admit that the obvious concern of the ministry, their questioning of Bill Baker's figures, and her performance when she left the dry dock had insinuated some doubts into my mind. These doubts were unspoken and only half admitted to myself, but the whisper of them could not be shut out of my mind, particularly at night when I tried to sleep.

I shuddered at the prospect of hearing from the ministry that somewhere along the line miscalculations had been made and that if *Mayflower* sailed at all it would be with an escort. I don't know what I would have done had this been the case, but during the four days in which I waited to hear the verdict on her stability the truth of Voltaire's comment, "There is something displeasing in the misfortunes of your friends," impressed itself upon me.

The past month had provided the greatest challenges for the project since we began, but the strain involved and the victories won seemed worth while when Henry Hornblower wrote to me from the plantation:

Alan is most enthusiastic about progress on your side, and confident that he can meet the Plymouth dateline for the reception on May 25. Needless to say, this information was a relief to the Town Reception Committee, which has been working night and day to shape things up.

We have completed and launched the Pilgrim shallop. It is truly beautiful. The Governor's wife, Mrs. Furcolo, had some difficulty breaking the bottle of champagne, but it was finally accomplished and the boat slid down the slipways complete with the Harvard crew with oars at attention. Bill Baker was aboard, and so became the first in history rowed by the Harvard crew. Alan can fill you in on other details. Crowd estimated at 3000 to 3500. Next day even more showed up — about 10,000.

Work at the site continues to progress satisfactorily. We are cleaning off brush and renovating buildings that will be kept. Within a month or so, we should have one of them finished as an office and reception center.

Charles Strickland's plans have been completed although we are still waiting on the engineers with regard to some final details on roads, paths, and other creature comforts demanded by the touring public.

The publicity on this side has been increasing in tempo. The news that the ship was to go to New York for the summer after its two weeks' stay in Plymouth triggered a lot of front-page comment from the Boston press. Much of the comment was critical, but at any rate everyone is talking about *Mayflower* as a result of it.

We continue to add members to our team and presently have about as strong a Board as any historical association in the country.

Please keep me posted on departure time, as I would like to be on hand to wave good-by to all of you when you start your journey westward. We shall all be on hand in May to greet you, and again on Thanksgiving Day when the ship comes back to Plymouth to be turned over to the plantation.

It was time now for me to become a sailor. I bought some kit, a duffel coat, thick woolen sweaters, sea boots, oilskins, long woolen underpants and thick woolen vests, and a storm cap which made me look like a refugee from Siberia. I had no knowledge of sailing or of the sea except what I had read.

Now, in *Mayflower*, I would learn what it was all about. Ten years of hopes and dreams, of criticism, encouragement and cynicism were behind me. From a wild idea on a tropic night, *Mayflower* had become a reality. Sturdy, stout and brave, the little ship had become more than her promise. It awed me to realize that she was probably nearer to me than my closest friends, that in ten years she, and all that she stood for, had snowballed to so great an extent that I should never know or be able to imagine the ultimate effect her voyage would have.

I closed the door of the Mayflower Project office in Coleman Street, handed the key to Miss Jeans, and went off to take the train for the *Mayflower.*

PART TWO
The Voyage

Being thus arrived in a good harbor, and brought safe to land . . .
Governor William Bradford, *Of Plymouth Plantation*

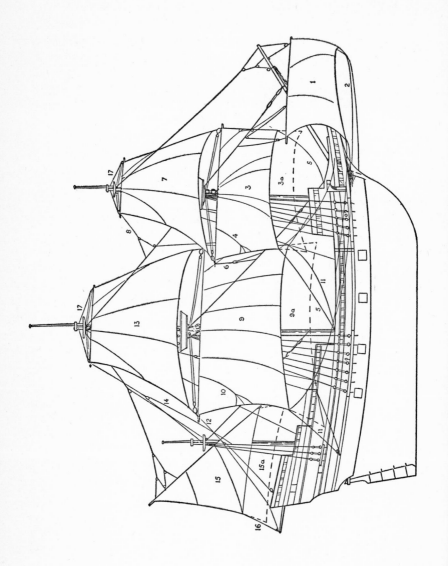

SIMPLIFIED SAIL, SHEET AND BRACE DIAGRAM

(Based on the original blueprints drawn up by
W. A. Baker for the building of Mayflower —
Copyright Plimoth Plantation, Inc.)

1	Spritsail		9a	Main bonnet
2	Spritsail sheets		10	Main martinets
3	Forecourse		11	Mainsheets
3a	Fore bonnet		12	Main brace
4	Fore martinets		13	Main-topsail
5	Foresheets		14	Main-topsail brace
6	Forebrace		15	Mizzen
7	Fore-topsail		15a	Mizzen bonnet
8	Fore-topsail brace		16	Mizzen sheet
9	Main course		17	Lifts

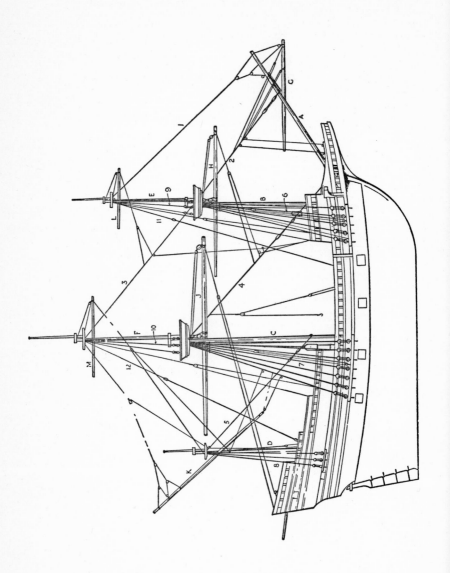

SIMPLIFIED STANDING RIGGING AND SPARS DIAGRAM

(Based on the original blueprints drawn up by W. A. Baker for the building of Mayflower — *Copyright Plimoth Plantation, Inc.)*

STANDING RIGGING

1	Fore-topmast stay	7	Main shrouds
2	Forestay	8	Mizzen shrouds
3	Main-topmast stay	9	Fore-topmast shrouds
4	Mainstay	10	Main-topmast shrouds
5	Mizzen stay	11	Fore-topmast backstay
6	Fore shrouds	12	Main-topmast backstay

SPARS

A	Bowsprit	G	Spritsail yard
B	Foremast	H	Foreyard
C	Mainmast	J	Main yard
D	Mizzenmast	K	Mizzen yard
E	Fore-topmast	L	Fore-topsail yard
F	Main-topmast	M	Main-topsail yard

I
Trial Run

I JOINED the ship at Dartmouth, where she had been towed from Brixham the previous day. I had not been able to board the ship at Brixham as I was still completing last-minute formalities without which the ship would not be allowed to sail, including the acceptance of formal delivery of the *Mayflower* from the builders and, finally, the registration of the ship herself.

In the ordinary way, we should have preferred at least a week of sea trials to test the ship and to give the crew a chance to get used to handling her before she set sail to cross the Atlantic. But there was no time for lengthy shakedowns. We were already late in starting and those in America were anxious to set close to specific dates for our arrival.

Alan Villiers was impatient to get away — as were all of us. He felt, as I did, that it would be unwise to wait any longer. So there was only time for the ship to set her sails in Tor Bay on one day's trial run before being towed to Dartmouth en route for Plymouth.

Dick Brennan, who had joined the ship ten days previously as a member of her crew, told me later that she looked a lovely sight with all sails set for her first run. From early in the morning people had gathered at Brixham at all vantage points. The public were there in tens of thousands and the press, television, radio, newsreel and still cameramen were there in scores.

Finally at 4:45 in the evening the tug *Penley* towed *Mayflower* out into the bay. As she glided forward in the evening sunshine on calm water, throngs of pleasure and sailing boats gave her a signal on their sirens and the Brixham Yacht Club a salute of cannon. Before *Mayflower* cast off her tow line, members of the crew swarmed up the rigging and unfurled her sails. The red ensign fluttered from her lateen yard and the flag of King James, flown by the original *Mayflower,* flew from her mainmast.

When the last of the six sails was unfurled in the mild southwesterly wind, the ship moved sedately across the bay along the coast towards Teignmouth. A flotilla of small boats followed in her wake and on her sides. Small aircraft dipped in salute as they flew overhead.

Below decks in the Great Cabin, Jim Horrocks, the ship's radio officer, sent his first message that *Mayflower II* had officially cleared the harbor. In the adjoining galley the cook, Walter Godfrey, was busy preparing the evening meal of minced scallops, spaghetti and sauté potatoes.

On the return run to Brixham, Bill Baker took over the wheel. "I am pleased with the way the ship has behaved," he said. His smile of satisfaction and the happiness shining from his eyes told their own story of the wonder and delight he felt that *Mayflower* had come to life.

As *Mayflower* approached Tor Bay, the tug *Penley* drew alongside and began towing the ship back into the shelter of the harbor. Sir Alan Moore, who, at seventy-five, is vice-president of the Society of Nautical Research, was on board and went aloft to help furl the mainsail as *Mayflower* returned to harbor. Fifty feet above decks he worked alongside the youngest member of the crew, Graham Nunn, sixteen, of Corby, Northants.

For more than two hours the ship had sailed along the coast line before returning to Brixham harbor shortly before 8 P.M. Stuart was exuberant with the ship's showing, but Alan put in a rider to our builder's enthusiasm; he said: "We still have one or two things to iron out and I hope this will be done before we get to Plymouth."

While the ship was en route from Brixham to Dartmouth, Michael Farr gave a farewell dinner for the captain and crew in the cellars of James Hawkes and Company on the Barbican at

Plymouth. Only a few of the crew were able to be present, but in many ways the dinner, which was attended by nearly three hundred guests, was evidence that *Mayflower* had captured not only public imagination but official notice, too. There was a message from the Prime Minister, one from the English-Speaking Union and another from the Outward Bound Trust, and many others from public men and national organizations on each side of the Atlantic.

When I went aboard *Mayflower* at Dartmouth, the ship was in darkness and I made my way below with the aid of a flashlight to inspect the 'tween decks where the twenty-two crewmen, who would run the ship and stand the watches, would sleep and eat during the voyage. I sat down on a bench in the tiller flat, which was situated directly beneath the Great Cabin. Wally Godfrey explained to me that the place got its name from the fact that the ship's tiller projected into it from a hole in the stern. Later during the voyage I found that the tiller swung back and forth constantly with a clicking, creaking noise just over the heads of those in the flat. All the dirt, greasy water, slops and stenches from the galley and fumes from the diesel generator seemed to collect there.

At the entrance to the tiller flat there was a small sign — 50/50 CLUB MEMBERS ONLY. This alluded to the 50/50 chance of arrival given the ship by Stanley Bonnet of the *Daily Mail*. Food for the tiller flat came down the companionway from the galley above. I reflected that whoever was carrying food would have a difficult time navigating the steps if a heavy sea was running.

The crew had their quarters in cubicles measuring 9 feet by 5 feet and equipped with double-decker iron bunks. These extended forward from the tiller flat along the 'tween decks, one on each side of the ship, with an open space along the middle, part of which was filled with cargo. The cubicles were partitioned off with hardboard.

I had a talk with Alan to decide in what capacity I should make the crossing and he asked me what I would like to do. I said I would like to join a watch. Accordingly he promised to assign me to the third mate's watch, but added a word of advice: "Warwick, you have been working very hard for the past two years; you also have a book to write. I suggest you try and take it easy. If you want to go on watch for the experience, then that is all right with me, but you only have to let Jan Junker know — he is the officer of your watch — and he will release you."

There was one complication during the tow from Dartmouth. One of the crew had inadvertently pulled the ripcord of one of our life rafts, which were stowed on deck. There was a sound of hissing, followed by a loud report as the raft exploded, unable to inflate properly because its outer canvas cover had not been unlaced. The Ministry of Transport official would not let us leave unless we had a replacement. I pointed out that we had four other rafts, that they would take care of forty-eight people and that there were only thirty-three of us on the ship. But he was adamant; five rafts or we did not go. Mr. Burnyeat, who was responsible for the victualing, came to the rescue and after a great number of telephone calls located one, which was delivered to us on the day of our departure.

John Lowe and I had a final conference. He handed to me a golden gorget (an ancient piece of armor) which was being sent by the Honorable Artillery Company of London to the Ancient and Honorable Artillery Company of Boston. He also gave me a Mayflower Medallion, commemorating the sailing, for Joseph Kasper, the president of the Associated Merchandising Corporation of America, who had arranged to show our cargo in fifteen of their stores. The crew had loaded the eighty chests, which had somehow, and it seemed to me quite miraculously, been stowed into the relatively small area of our holds. I could not help thinking at that moment of the back-breaking work that we faced to unload them in the same manner as they had been stowed. Then I remembered that I had made ararngements with Mr. John Sloan Smith, the president of Aero Mayflower Transit of America, who had agreed not only to help unload the chests but also to deliver all our cargo free of charge wherever it was consigned in the United States.

Early on Saturday morning Alan and I changed into our seventeenth-century costumes and were rowed ashore in a four-oar gig by members of the crew who wore their fawn tunics and short trousers. This was for the civic commemoration of our departure, which was held at the Mayflower Steps. Alan was in black with a wide-brimmed Puritan hat, large white collar, knee breeches, woolen stockings and buckle shoes. It was raining steadily as the oarsmen pulled us up to the Mayflower Steps, where a crowd of some ten thousand were waiting for us. The Lord Mayor was there in his finery, wearing his three-cornered hat, scarlet robes trimmed with fur and his chain of office. The town clerk was in his wig and gown. Mr. James T. Frazier, chairman of the Board of Selectmen of Plymouth, Massachusetts, Harry Hornblower, George Olsson and Arthur Pyle had all flown over for the ceremony. George Olsson presented Alan with a mounted chip of Plymouth Rock, upon which legend says the original Pilgrims stepped when first they landed in Massachusetts. This was to serve as a lodestone in the Great Cabin of the ship.

Alan spoke into the microphone, declaring: "I have the utmost optimism about the result of the voyage. I am glad to be in Plymouth — at last — to take the ship on her way to Plymouth, Massachusetts. The only regret is that there have been two weeks of nice easterly winds and we have not been able to take advantage of them. You can see how deep the ship lies in the water — laden with the goodwill of this country. I have read a lot of nonsense about her fifty-fifty chance of reaching America. Those who believe this should realize that it was little ships like *Mayflower II* which enabled famous seamen to open up the world — not giant liners."

The Lord Mayor replied: "It gives me great pleasure to see *Mayflower II* in Plymouth Sound. It has taken great energy and determination to guide the project to its present stage, and Mr. Warwick Charlton and those who supported him deserve praise. I am confident in Commander Villiers' ability and in the success of the voyage."

The Voyage

I responded briefly, saying that I was very proud to see *Mayflower* off Drake's Island, ready to sail to America as a symbol of our common heritage.

We invited the Lord Mayor and his party to come aboard and got back in the gig to return to the ship. I felt no sense of unreality about what I was doing. Here I was in seventeenth-century costume being rowed by seamen similarly decked towards a seventeenth-century ship. I had lived so long with the idea of *Mayflower* that the only incongruity seemed the motor vessels churning around us and the hundreds of cars on the shore. When I climbed up the ladder to board *Mayflower*, I felt a surge of triumph occasioned by the absolute certainty that our voyage was soon to begin.

I chided myself that my feelings probably had more in common with that of a privateer bound for the Main than of a Saint or Stranger boarding *Mayflower*.

II

The Voyage

First Day, April 20. I stood in the poop and counted the flotilla of small craft seeing us off from England, and including all of them, from our tug to rowboats, counted sixty-seven. In one launch I sighted my office staff, most of those who had worked with me to put the ship under sail. They stood up watching us go, sometimes waving, but most of the time standing motionless. Just before we cast our tow their motor gave out and I stood waving to them — Miss Jeans very upright, little Miss Beck beside her, and Mrs. Grimmett, her red hair distinguishable when distance made the faces of the others pink blurs. John, black jacket and pin-striped trousers, was in the tow ship, and when the moment came to cast adrift, it arrived so unexpectedly, at least to me, I barely had time to shout: "See you on the other side." There was the sound of the Captain's gravelly voice shouting orders, and movement in the ship as though she knew the moment had come, the purpose of her birth, to leave Plymouth, Drake's Island astern, cup the wind in her sails and make way as her predecessor had done across the waters of the implacable Atlantic. They braced the yards and let go her sails; they caught enough of the light air for her to sway gently and to move on her own. She was under way quickly, her course west-south-west. Stuart Upham joined me on the poop, his blue eyes dancing with pride. "The secret of this vessel is rhythm, everything giving in unison," he said, "from the ropes, transmitted to the spars and then to the hull, all working in unison to give her a hatful of wind." He braced himself as she swayed, looking up at the topmast: "She's a very lively ship — not a groan in her, tight as a fiddler's bitch."

I had been so preoccupied with last-moment administrative details which had to be completed in order for the ship to get away, that I had not had time to inspect my living quarters and I made my way to them now. I had the luxury of a cabin to myself, aft, under the quarter-deck, opposite the galley and near the Great Cabin. There was an iron bunk with half a dozen blankets, three of them pure wool, white with red, yellow and black stripes, a present from the firm who had made and exported them to North America since 1669. The Captain issued us some blue sheets and pillow slips which I thought an unnecessary luxury until later in the voyage. There were two lockers: one for my clothes and the other to store my cigarettes, soap, toothpaste, towels, shaving materials and some of my books. There were hooks to hang my seventeenth-century costume, and also for my yellow oilskins and duffel coat. There was an electric light, which we were warned to use sparingly, and a copper candle lantern as a standby. There was, of course, no porthole, and when the door was closed, I was in darkness. Stuart Upham was in the cabin nearly opposite, the same size as my own, but with two bunks. He shared with his friend Jumbo Goddard, a burly empire-builder of a man, who made his living prospecting for precious metals, in the past gold, now mostly for uranium. We messed, the Captain, the mates, Stuart, myself, Julian Lugren, who was making the film documentary of the voyage, in the Great Cabin. The Captain had chosen for his quarters the most uncomfortable place in the ship, the small charthouse high on the quarter-deck. "So I know what is going on," he explained with a wry smile. Not long after we cast our tow all hands assembled amidship and the Master addressed us from the quarter-deck. "Now, lads," he said, "the bull is behind us. We have to get down to the job of delivering this ship to America. We have to conserve water, a gallon per man per day for all purposes; the ship's radio is only for ship's business and for none of that damn press nonsense; there's no smoking on the quarter-deck, on lookout or at the wheel, and you must not whistle on deck! You approach the quarter-deck only by the lee ladder; and finally: the heads are in the beak!" This last referred to the sanitary arrangements, which were crude, open to the elements, but well serviced with water. You climbed onto the fo'c'sle and down into the beak, where a square of planks was cut away. There was a roll of toilet paper provided; the flush was the sea beneath. A sign read: WILL OFFICERS PLEASE ADJUST THEIR DRESS BEFORE LEAVING. One of the officers, the white-haired, ruddy first mate Godfrey Wicksteed, took this notice personally and always made anyone on the fo'c'sle check his dress. In the fo'c'sle there were two bunks, one for the bosun Ike Marsh, and the other for our chippy Edgar Mugridge. Ike is a leathery little man going on sixty. He wears a cloth cap, an ordinary gray single-breasted worsted suit, and well-worn shoes that were once brown. When the Captain gave the order to unfurl the sails, Ike was one of the first and fastest to clamber up the foremast ratlines. Edgar Mugridge, who had most of the fo'c'sle set apart as the carpenter's shop, worked on the building of the ship from the keel up. He is a Brixham man with the soft West Country burr, stubby, round and cheery, and, like his friend the bosun, scorns seagoing clothes and wears a cloth cap. I felt I should inspect 'tween decks now that we were under way, and the cargo hold to see how our sixty-five chests were stowed, but the excitement of the day, and those immediately preceding our departure, made me decide to turn in for my first night's sleep afloat on the *Mayflower*. The ship swayed gently underneath as I stretched out on my bunk, too tired to undress, and pulled a blanket over me. It seemed she was hardly moving at all, and when morning came, it transpired that we were still in sight of Plymouth, going towards Brixham.

Second Day, April 21. During the night the ship had to make way against a four-knot tide and with so little wind to help her could barely hold her own. We had the humiliation of an early morning visitor from the press — a representative of the London *Daily Mail* who had chartered a launch out from Falmouth. The Captain would not allow him aboard, but he climbed onto the port channels and posed for a photograph, promising to be over by air during the next two days to drop some newspapers for us. Later in the morning, a twin-engined aircraft circled over the ship, and the Captain could see his wife waving to him. She dropped a message, and Doc Stevens took out the pram, a light larch boat Stuart Upham built for his daughter Wendy, to pick it up. I was on the quarter-deck when the doctor delivered the message to the Captain, a few scribbled words wishing him well, but I could see they lifted his spirits.

Most appropriately, or so it seemed to me, the first person I saw at the wheel on this our first real day at sea was John Winslow, a collateral descendant of the Edward who sailed on the first *Mayflower*. John, a chubby young man full of high spirits, has taken unpaid leave from the Royal Navy to be with us. He has begun to grow a beard, but only down one half of his face, to win a wager struck with the other seamen that he will arrive in America with one half of his face clean-shaven, the other half bearded. If he does, he wins one hundred and fifty dollars, but I think Alan will enter into this matter before we make landfall. Our American friends might find it difficult to appreciate a half-bearded descendant of one of the Pilgrims; they might think he was taking his role too lightly.

At ten o'clock there was a muster in the waist. The Captain took Easter Sunday service, and read a chapter of Bradford's journal so that the ship's company would be well informed concerning the Pilgrims. He found Bradford too wordy and dry for reading from the quarter-deck, and skipped long passages to hold the crew's attention.

The ship was now nearer Brixham than Plymouth, and I think that everyone was praying the wind would freshen and take us out of sight of land. Later in the day, at the approach of dusk when it seemed our fate to be becalmed, a light wind filled our sails and soon we were moving sedately through the water at about three knots. There was no sound of creaking timbers, only the soft lap of the waves against her sides, and the Captain exclaimed to me: "Ah, now we're nipping along smartly." Our course was west-southwest. I was pleased that we were no longer becalmed and asked how long it would be before we were clear of the Channel. The Captain brought me up short: "We could be a few days in the Channel; we could be here for weeks. It has taken sailing ships four months to clear the jaws of the Channel."

Throughout the daylight hours we were an object of curiosity to other ships, most of them changing course to take a closer look at us, dipping their ensigns in salute. At night a little ship of our own tonnage warmed all our hearts; at 8:10 we were hailed by trawler BM10, the *Iago*, on her way home to Brixham. She turned on her deck lights and we heard a voice shouting: "Ahoy, *Mayflower!* Do you want a fry? Is Edgar Mugridge there?" Edgar called back: "Yes — here I am. Is Sam there?" And turning to me he said excitedly: "I'll be damned if my cousin Sam isn't out there!" The pram was lowered for the second time that day. Beric Watson took the oars and two buckets, the latter in answer to their call "Want a fry?" "Boy, this makes you feel good," said Edgar as Beric rowed out to the trawler. We had put two bottles of rum, one in each bucket, as a gift to the trawler men, and Beric returned with a boatload of fish: a seventeen-pound cod, plaice, put, red mullet, dover sole, lemon sole and John Dory. We shouted our thanks across the waters and gave "Three cheers for the local lads," and they replied with "Three cheers for the *Mayflower*" before they doused their deck lights, but we peered over the waters until the sound and shape of the trawler had merged with the night.

Third Day, April 22. All night the ship nodded along under a zephyr of wind, and we are quickly becoming accustomed to the confined world of wood, rope and canvas. The motion of the ship is more pitch than roll, up one side of the swell and down the other, almost a soothing motion, or at least it is to me, but a number of the crew, including Joe Meany, Dr. Stevens and David Thorpe, are seasick. I can quite understand Joe's feeling poorly, but I am surprised at Doc and David Thorpe, because they are both experienced yachtsmen, and Doc was in the Navy during the war, part of the time in submarines, but as he says: "It's calmer under water than on top." Joe does not complain, but stays most of the time 'tween decks, coming up the companionway hurriedly to seek the side and returning straightway to his bunk, silent and sad-eyed as though he is wondering whether this was the best year to be nominated Junior Citizen of America. Graham Nunn, our English cabin boy, is not troubled by the motion of the ship. He has just returned from a voyage to Australia as pantry boy aboard a passenger ship, but the sailors tell me that coming straight from sea has no bearing on seasickness; apparently it just depends on whether you are prone to seasickness or not. I tried to comfort Joe by telling him that Lord Nelson was sick every time he went to sea and what was good enough for Nelson should be good enough for everyone, but this did not make him any happier. Joe Powell, a friendly giant of a man who was a wartime commando and now earns his living as a film stunt man, appeared on deck today with two front teeth missing. He explained to me: "I lost a set when I was filming on *Moby Dick* with John Huston. I didn't want to take a chance with my new set, so I've stowed them for the voyage."

We had a muster of all hands in the afternoon when there was a slight sea, the lateen was set, and we were sailing easily under all plain sail on the starboard tack. We were greeted by the Danish steamer *Henning Maersk*, of Frederica. This especially pleased the third mate, Captain Jan Junker, a Dane who sailed with Alan on the *Conrad* and is now captain of the *Kaskelot*, a 250-ton fuel-powered motor ship with emergency sails, spankers and forestaysails, engaged in the Greenland trade supplying coal to Eskimos. I have volunteered to join his watch.

Alan decided, owing to the inexperience of the crew, to use the double watch system — four hours on and four hours off.

The watch is responsible for working the ship, manning the lookout — for'ard, on the fo'c'sle, or upon the foreyard. They also
take turns manning the helm and working the sails.

The watches are: First Dog, 4 to 6; Hour Dog, 6 to 8; Evening
Watch, 8 to 12; Middle, 12 to 4; Morning, 4 to 8; and the 8 to
12 and 12 to 4 watches. The reason for the two two-hour watches
between 4 and 8 P.M. is to break up the cycle of watches so that
the same men won't have the long night ones. The bells com-
mence at the beginning of each watch, one bell each half hour
and one bell a quarter from the hour before the end of each
watch to warn the relieving watch of the time. At twelve o'clock,
for example, they ring eight bells; at twelve-thirty, one bell; at
one, two bells; one-thirty, three bells; and so on until eight bells
are rung at four o'clock. They never go beyond eight bells,
except at midnight on New Year's Eve when the youngest member of the crew rings sixteen bells, eight for the old year and
eight for the new. However, I hope we shall have no need to be
reminded of this custom.

We logged 64½ miles for the day, the mileage being estimated
from noon till noon each succeeding day. Alan said: "We're
going fine and should soon be clear of the jaws of the English
Channel."

Felix, our kitten, is proving fiickle, sleeping in a different bunk
nightly. This evening I am honored by his presence.

Fourth Day, April 23. At last our little ship is well out into
the Atlantic, making five knots. Alan said to me: "The Lord
has been good to us." There are no longer any inquisitive ships
to turn off course to inspect us. We had only one visit today, a
Canberra jet MS-137 which gave us a display of aerobatics,
finally waggling its wings and speeding homewards. Now our
only companions are the occasional kittywake and herring gull.
We had two birthdays today: Ike Marsh, the bosun, was fifty-
eight and the cook gave him a cake with one candle and Alan
gave him a bottle of rum. He is surprisingly agile, not only for

his age but for any age. Today he went aloft while there was a quartering sea and the ship was lurching, pitching and rolling, carrying all sail. He has been at sea most of his life, but all the time in steamships until three years ago when Alan persuaded him to work on the *Pequod*. The other birthday was that of our cat Felix, who is quickly getting used to life at sea, using a coil of rope to rest on deck, and I noticed his legs adjusted themselves as easily to the motion of the ship as if they were mounted on gimbals.

Godfrey Wicksteed, the first mate, read me an extract from a letter of good wishes sent to him by ten-year-old Anita Harding of Upware School, Cambridge. She wrote: "We nearly all of us hope you don't have any accidents." Dick Brennan, who is settling down as second cook to Wally Godfrey, asked Wally, who had let it be known that nothing was to be wasted, what he should do with some cabbage stalks. Wally nearly told him.

This being probably the last day we shall be able to use the radio telephone, Alan tried to speak to his wife, but was told the number was unattainable; then he remembered that he had told the exchange he was not accepting any calls a few days before joining the ship, and had forgotten to cancel these instructions.

We have made 174 miles on passage; the seas seem to be building up and I have the feeling that Alan is not completely happy about the ship. He has too much to do now for me to trouble him, but in a day or so I shall ask him and see if I am right.

Fifth Day, April 24. I was called at eight bells and decided not to wash or shave: Joe Lacey, who sailed with the Master and Adrian Small, the second mate, on the whaling ship *Pequod*, said he wasn't going to wash until he got to Plymouth: "I don't bother with it; you only get sore from salt water." I was not prepared to go as far as Joe, but thought I might compromise and wash once a week. I am dressed in jeans, long woolen underwear, a thick blue roll-neck jersey, duffel coat and an astrakhan seaman's hat with flaps that pull down over the ears. No socks or boots during the day. I want to harden my feet and at the same time dispense with the necessity for sock washing. I have tried washing thick sea socks in sea water and Teepol, but it takes a long time to rinse them and even then they are sticky. Joe Lacey told me I'd never get rid of the stickiness unless I used fresh water, and we haven't enough of that. The saddle of the main-topsail slipped during the night and Joe went up the yard to try to get it back, but it was too heavy for him to move alone. There's a following sea and the ship is making more fuss than usual, which she does the faster she moves.

Breakfast of porridge, two bangers (sausages), baked beans, bread and marmalade with coffee. Alan called his wife on the RT, but she still had not reached home. He told me she worried when there were gale warnings about, as there are now.

I went to the quarter-deck to take my first turn at the wheel, and as I was a novice, Anderson-Bell (the only Scotsman on board) watched over me. He showed me how to recognize the king spoke by the two ridges cut into it, and to feel for it in the dark. He explained that a good helmsman had to anticipate what the ship was going to do next and try to meet her. *Mayflower* proved quite responsive to the rudder. When there was a drop or change in the wind, she was inclined to wander off course and you had to get back steady again before the officer of the watch noticed. Andy lectured me patiently: "The compass is divided into three hundred and sixty degrees, thirty-two points — each point eleven and one-fourth degrees; a quarter point is three degrees. If you can steer within three degrees on a sailing ship, you're doing well. To bring her toward the wind, ease her up a point, and fall off a point to bring her away from the wind." While I was receiving instruction, Jan paced the deck on the weather side of the ship so he could feel the wind on the back of his neck and his ears. Andy explained to me: "Jan is aware all the time of the wind and when it alters, he feels the change. That is why the helmsman also stands his trick on the weather side of the wheel, never on the more sheltered lee side as in steam. You notice he keeps looking at the sails and listening so that when he hears a sail flapping, he knows at once the wind has changed or we are off course." Jan had attached some boat lacing to the helm, weighted at one end and made fast at the other so that when you put the wheel to port or starboard, the lacing coiled round and you could see at a glance the number of turns you had made.

After my first hour at the wheel the Captain suggested I should hand over to Andy: "Conditions are too difficult for you to learn much," he explained. "Wait until we're in smoother waters." Anyway, it was nearly time to hand over the wheel to John Winslow, but Andy did it for me: he got the needle dead on course for John to take over. "Steering sou'west . . ." I went amidships to take my turn as porpoise. The reason for this description soon became apparent: whenever Jan whistled, I had to jump up, take a message, go down 'tween decks or up on the poop.

I took my duties very seriously and Andy and Stuart told me at 9:30 that it was time I rang the half hour by sounding the bell three times. I did so, only to be told off by Alan, who had a twinkle in his eyes: "Warwick, we don't ring the half hour on this ship!" I wondered if Andy would next tell me to get green oil for the starboard lamp and red oil for the port lamp. But I discovered there was even a knack to ringing the bell; you had to grip the bell rope below the hackle and bring it to the rim of the bell, clang, clang, two in quick succession, pause and then repeat so that the strikes were clearly sounded. I took a turn on the aft port hard-deck pump with Jumbo. I found it very tiring work. They had used the automatic pumps for six minutes to clear out the bilges and I looked over the port side and watched the brown water streaming out. She had shipped only about 1200 gallons of water since we left Plymouth on Sunday. Stuart remarked: "It is very little, only enough to keep her sweet." But 'tween decks in the stern, where the fifty-fifty club mess, a leak had been detected. Apparently it was only what is called "weeping," and nothing to worry about so long as it stayed that way.

The Voyage

Alan has an eye on everything that happens on board, even the small details. For example, today he wanted to know what was being done with the empty beer bottles, and checked with me to see if donors wanted them back, and then with the cook to see if he had any use for them. Then he called Jan over and asked him why the ensign was flying: "Take it down; don't want to wear out the bunting."

Alan took me into the fo'c'sle head and told me he was taking the southerly route. This means a longer voyage, over 5000 miles as against some 3000 miles. He gave several reasons for his decision: the ship was not galeworthy; the knight for the main lift was split and should have been strengthened with iron; the rigging was loose; the saddle of the main-topsail mast had jumped mast; and he wanted to get the ship there in one piece. We had had no trials, and a few days' more sailing was nothing against the unwarranted risk of ice, fog and gales on the more direct northerly course.

I think the main point was that Alan would have liked a couple of weeks to try her out, discover and correct the snags. After all, there were thirty-three lives on board and a valuable cargo.

Godfrey Wicksteed, the mate, clambered up onto the beak while I was there, on his way to the heads, and when he had finished, paused for a word to me: "I would rather we'd had some rough weather early on," he said. "We might have lost someone overboard, but at least the rest of us would have been tried and ready for anything that came our way." I was not sure I agreed, although I felt he had a point.

Wally, the cook, asked Dick to taste the soup and Dick told him frankly: "I'm afraid this stock has had it. It's too lively." "Don't worry," Wally replied, "get a bottle of Worcester sauce and we'll quieten it down."

At 11:30 we sighted two French trawlers off the port side, but there was no sign of life aboard.

I asked Joe Meany to whom he would like to send a message and he suggested his girl friend Anita, who lives in Waltham,

near Boston. Joe told me he is praying for the ship to reach
Plymouth in time for him to join his class for graduation on June
2. I hope so too. Joe spoke about his future. He wants to become
an electronics engineer. "There's great scope," he said, sure of
himself. Joe knows where he is going. Graham Nunn, our British
cabin boy, asked me to send a message to his brother Ronald,
who is serving in the R.A.F. in Boscombe Down, Wiltshire. "He
couldn't get to see me off; he tried compassionate leave, but they
wouldn't wear it. I'd like him to know I'm all right."

I have been thinking how to describe our wash at night. It
flashes with phosphorescent fire, as though we were churning
up spawn for the stars.

Adrian, the second mate, announced this afternoon that we
made 147 sea miles from noon till noon, which is reckoned good
going and at once started me off on a buzz of calculations about
when we would reach America. But I did not dare to speculate
when Alan was about. I know he considers such talk as tempting Providence.

Graham Nunn has fixed cloth to the table in the Great Cabin
to prevent plates, cups, knives, spoons and saucers sliding about
with the motion of the ship. Alan wanted to contact his wife
again today, the last chance he had of doing so on the radio telephone, which operates effectively for only three hundred miles
off shore. He asked Sparks to get through just after I sent our
position through to London and also a short press message.
Then the power started to give out. Apparently the set hadn't
been on charge today, although the generator was running. I
think that Jumbo, who had a tooth pulled this morning by Doc
Stevens without the benefit of a painkiller, had his mind on other
things. Doc gave him a shot of rum after the operation, an ob-
stinate back tooth. Gordon, the *Life* photographer, heard about
the operation after it was completed and asked for a repeat performance for the benefit of camera, specifying a front tooth for
the sake of composition.

We had a two-course tea: a kipper and then some meat, cold
lamb, and salad — lettuce, cucumber, tomatoes — bread and jam

and tea. Alan commented when this was followed by prunes and custard that Wally was giving us too much. He told the cook: "If you go on like this, we won't be able to get into our Pilgrim suits."

I discovered that none of our wrist watches tells the same time, so I asked Alan how we should synchronize them. The ship's clock showed Greenwich mean time, and some of us had that, but others were twenty minutes faster or slower. Alan answered my question, biting into his words so that they came out sharp: "Clock time is a function devised by landlubbers to run trains. When we pass under the meridian sun, that is eight bells and noon and that is ship's time. That's the only time to interest us."

I went on watch and took first wheel, with John Winslow this time standby. The black sea swarmed around us and the ship fairly scudded along, stretching out in front of me like a giant animal in the night. After a quarter of an hour Alan came into the chartroom and he reminisced about the big sailing ships and their spread of sails billowing like the wings of great birds flying into the incandescent night. I am so patently pleased with the progress we are making that Jan saw fit to temper my pleasure with some sound advice. First he told me our course: "We are west of the Bay of Biscay and crossing it until we find a Portuguese northerly which should bring us down to Madeira and into the trades." "Ah, the trades," I said as though I had gone to school with them. "Yes," said Jan, smiling, "the trades. We could reach the trades and nothing could happen."

"You're joking?"

"No," he said seriously, smothering a smile, "nothing is certain in a sailing ship. We could get force six or seven in the trades, but nothing could happen. We could be becalmed. That happened to me in 1947 and it could happen again."

I decided not to worry, which is a change for me, and when I turned in, I went off to sleep, rocked in the cradle of my cabin.

The Voyage

Sixth Day, April 25. During the night the wind freshened, and around midnight the sea began to rise. Beric Watson called me for the 8 to 12 watch and informed me: "We're running along with the swell. I went off course once and turned west, the sails flapping, but the Captain was on the bridge and he got her back." I forthwith made up my mind not to go on the helm, if the Captain agreed, until the sea was quieter. At breakfast he sat in what has become his accustomed place, the center of the table with his back to the stern. The Great Cabin window is always open and we crunch breakfast cereal to the sound of the wake bubbling and gurgling. Alan wants to smarten up the Great Cabin before we reach Plymouth. At present it is piled with cargo packages, film equipment, three chests and two typewriters. "We should have some cutlasses and pikes," he said. "You ought to have thought of that, Warwick." "This is not a pirate ship," I reminded him, "although we may need weapons to repel boarders at Provincetown." Jan was surprised to hear we had no weapons. "On my ship we have revolvers and rifles," he said. "Maybe you need them when your Eskimos get at the whisky," Alan said, and added with mock seriousness: "Anyway, we've got some handcuffs in case anyone gets frisky." Julian Lugren, our cine cameraman, reported a leak through the transom in the tiller flat; the water is slopping around and the fifty-fifty club are having to breakfast in their sea boots. I went out on deck to tell Stuart, but he was not disturbed, cocked a leg over the pin rail on the starboard side and said there was a more important leak requiring his attention. He and I put in some work on the hand pumps. We had to shift about four hundred gallons of water, and like every other job on board ship, there is a right way to do it: short continuous pulls on the pump, which keeps the water flowing and requires a minimum of effort. *Mayflower* can do no wrong in Stuart's eyes. She was bucking and swaying, but he commented: "She is sailing as neat as a pin."

Wally reported we had only two more days' fresh food. He showed me a pot on deck where some beef was salting down in brine. "That'll be good for boiled beef, carrots, pease pudding and some floaters," Wally said to me. I asked him what floaters were and he explained they were dumplings. By midmorning the whitecaps were more numerous. Edgar Mugridge and Stuart had to pack the base of the capstan with calking cotton and tallow to prevent water getting down 'tween decks. I still haven't had a shave and I am getting used to going barefoot.

Adrian Small, the second mate, told us at midday that the ship had logged 148 sea miles during the previous twenty-four hours. This provoked a discussion, the first of so many, on the possible duration of the voyage. I went right out on a limb as a thirty-day man and said I thought the ship would make her Plymouth, Massachusetts, landfall on May 26. I based my opinion on the belief that the ship would continue to make the same rate of knots as she was doing in a smoother sea (I suppose I should say lighter) and weaker wind force. We have put a chart in the Great Cabin to mark our daily progress. This is tantalizing, because although, for example, 148 sea miles sounds good for a day's sailing, it doesn't look like much when it is marked down on the chart.

In the late afternoon the sea mounted into a heavy swell and came washing over the scuppers, curling over the gunwales. The wind was blowing near gale strength. The Captain was standing on the poop deck, legs planted apart, eyes fixed on the sails. He shouted an order and Joe Lacey clambered up the mainmast ratlines while the ship bucked, bounced and swayed beneath him. Graham Nunn followed Joe, and Maitland Edey and old Ike Marsh shinned up the foremast ratlines. Maitland was thickly clothed under his oilskins. He had just been hauling on ropes and when he came to climb into the foretop, he faltered as the ship pitched and nearly fell. They furled the main-topsail and the fore-topsail and this seemed to ease the motion of the ship. When Beric Watson came off the wheel, he said the stern sea on our port quarter was putting the topsails under great strain. The ship had been doing seven knots and she maintained this after they brought in the topsails. While I was standing talking to Beric on the fo'c'sle, Dick Brennan, whose thick black beard and

thick brows over small close-set eyes make him look the old sea
dog, walked slap into a wave which came curling over the waist
of the ship. The seas began to throw the little ship around
heavily and the helmsman found it difficult to hold her on course
with the seas coming sideways on. The Captain ordered the
lateen yard lowered and made fast, and this, together with the
taking in of the topsails, made for a more settled motion.

At night I climbed up into the poop, looked down over the
ship and saw reflected in the lee bow wave, sparkling with whale
dust, the starboard light.

Seventh Day, April 26. There was a heavy quartering sea
throughout the day and night with the ship rolling and pitching
wildly. It was difficult to maintain a balance and I found myself
gripping the nearest rope; during the night sleep was impossible;
it was enough of a job to avoid being thrown out of my bunk.
Alan kept the ship running free under fore and mainsail courses
and the spritsail, but in case the weather worsened he took the
opportunity to exercise the watches at stations for taking in sail.
We were still heading west-southwest. Alan spoke to me again
about the matters which were causing him concern. He did not
like the way the fore and aft masts worked and the bowsprit. The
foremast was, in his opinion, little better than a knotty broom-
stick, and the cordage rigging allowed too much play. The mainmast moved laterally about ten inches or a foot at its head with
each roll of the ship causing the main yard to jump and the heavy
wooden saddle to dig into the pine; the foremast stumbled and
threw all its rigging forward like a hard-mouthed horse jerking
at its rider. All these things may not have alarmed Captain Jones
in 1620 but certainly alarmed our Captain! The after gun ports
leaked, the main deck leaked, there was seepage in the starboard
side near the main chains, and the chafe aloft on the rigging was
terrible. Alan had to put all hands aloft to fight this chafe and
fit rolling tackle. He said to me: "Make no mistake — if I had a
sou'wester, we should be in trouble, and we must expect a gale

or two." The wind was blowing force six and quite often force seven, which is near to gale strength, so I could understand and share Alan's anxiety. We looked out, for most of the day, on mountains of water and I should not have been surprised if one had crashed down upon us, sending us to the bottom. Even Felix found it difficult to keep his legs and suffered a greenstick fracture to his left foreleg, but Doc Stevens said there was no purpose in making a splint as it would probably heal itself.

In these heavy quartering seas you have to watch yourself, at least I know I do, against being pitched overboard. Jan Junker told me a true story of a man lost overboard from a ship in the Gulf Stream on Christmas Day and picked up the following day. "Of course, that wouldn't happen in this sea," he said with a wry smile. "You'd be gone for keeps."

Eighth Day, April 27. By noon today we will have been at sea for a week and we have made about 800 miles, which Stuart tells me is good, but we have over five thousand miles to go before we make our landfall at Plymouth. This means that if we average 100 miles a day, we take fifty days. The winds are now lighter, the sky clearer, and the ship seems to be settling down; at the same time we are naturally getting more accustomed every day to the motion of the ship. Last night a comet was visible off our port bow. I had overcome my fear of heights sufficiently to perch on the main yard of the foremast; the movement of the ship is, of course, exaggerated up there, and in the night with the wind in your face and the sway of the mast it is the closest thing to flying. We are quite alone in the ocean, making south for Madeira to get into the trades, where the wind should be constant, good and strong.

We have discovered that there is another Pilgrim descendant on board, other than John Winslow. He is Chief Petty Officer Charles Church from Nova Scotia, a descendant of Richard Warren, a signatory to the Mayflower Compact. He heard about the *Mayflower* from Chief of the Royal Canadian Naval Staff at

Ottawa, Admiral de Wolfe. He has signed on as a seaman for a token one shilling a month. Everyone calls him Canada and he has made himself assistant to our engineer, Jumbo Goddard, fixing everything that needs fixing, from a galley stove that won't light to a wireless aerial that has fouled the ropes. I asked Canada what he thought of the decision to go south. "I don't think it makes a heck of a lot of difference," he said, "which route we take, though a friend of mine who has a fleet running the northern route was very apprehensive when I told him we might go that way. Some of his vessels are over ten thousand tons and they were having a rougher passage than usual at this time of the year, meeting a lot of ice. It all depends on your luck. One thing is for sure: *Mayflower* will be a hell of a lot steadier this way. Right now we are scooting along."

Ninth Day, April 28. Our second Sunday at sea. It is four days since we sighted another ship, and although it is just over a week since we left Plymouth, the departure seems another world away. There is no doubt in the mind of the Captain — and his view is shared by Wicksteed, the first mate, Adrian Small, the second mate, and by Jan Junker — that we have every reason to feel pleased with ourselves. True, the ship is stiff because she is over-ballasted and she has yet to prove herself capable of a little over seven knots, but notwithstanding, we have come over a thousand miles in eight days, and this despite a day and a half when we were practically becalmed. Before the morning service at 10:30 Alan said to me: "The northerly wind has been very good to us. It funnels down, drawn by the trades, to the equator. Soon we should be far enough south to be assured of a westing." After the service he gave a little talk about the Pilgrims and told us that although no one was sure of the route they took, it was fairly certain they did not come south where the power of Spain ruled the seas but took the northern and more direct route. Alan has a gift for talking about the Pilgrims as though they were his next-door neighbors, and the crew are really interested and anxious that these talks should continue until we reach the other side. He introduced us to some points of view that would surely set some historians' ears burning: he confirmed that there were those who felt that the Pilgrims were not Puritans in the strictest sense, that the narrow puritanical strain had come afterwards and that in the main the Pilgrims were good, ordinary folk who wanted to worship as they wished and be left alone to do so. He also made the point that they were really bound for the Hudson River and were prevented from getting there through the duplicity of Captain Jones. He told the crew that he thought we could be fairly confident of sighting Nantucket Lighthouse in about thirty-eight days, and added: "But who knows, we may even be in time for Joe's graduation." This caused a melon of a grin to shine from Joe, our American cabin boy, who has missed all the important events of his class year and has his heart set on being with his class for graduation.

Everyone has been given permission to send one personal message during the voyage. But even this is difficult, as the radio set is playing tricks on us and, apart from a shortage of fuel for the generator, has twice been out of commission through breakdowns. The weather is becoming noticeably milder, although we do not often see the sun through the clouds.

This afternoon, after a party on deck — with Stuart, playing the banjo, and Beric Watson, on the guitar, serenading our chippy, Edgar Mugridge, who is celebrating his thirty-first wedding anniversary — there was a little light rain, but not enough to put out cans and rubber and plastic sheets we have ready to catch any quantity.

This evening I went out on the fo'c'sle with the lookout and took pleasure in the steady surge of the ship, going on her course like an old cart horse. I never tire of looking at the curve of the sails against the night sky and listening to the wash of water against the sides, and the sound of the ropes thumping against each other and the woodwork. At 8:30 we sighted a ship's light on the starboard beam and were reminded that there was a world beyond the universe of our horizon.

The Voyage

We are beginning to acquire a brand of humor peculiar to our own situation. Edgar Mugridge said to me as he emerged from 'tween decks: "I don't think I'll go ashore tonight," and Stuart Upham added: "I wouldn't if I were you, Edgar; it's dark as a cow's guts." Before I turned in I went into the Great Cabin and drank some cocoa, and on my way to my bunk paused to listen to the reassuring cry, the voice of the watch calling out boldly in our world of wood, rope and flax: "All clear ahead . . . the lights are bright."

Tenth Day, April 29. We are off the coast of northern Morocco, and will soon be far enough south to make our westing. The sea is now more friendly-looking, a lighter blue, and the air softer and warmer than it has been. We saw a ship balancing distantly on the horizon amidships on our starboard beam, but before we could make her out she was lost from sight as though she had dropped off the edge of the world. Our world has become such a desert of sea, broken only by the white horses and the monstrous patterns of the clouds, that our eyes seek out any sign of other life. Some porpoises were reported by the dog watch, but when I questioned them, they were vague as to details.

At breakfast there was an example of the sort of humor men cultivate when they are thrown together and insulated from the outside world: I noticed a saucer of glass marbles on the table, and when the mate sat down, he said: "Ah, at last we have them. I knew someone was hiding them. I've been done out of a bazooka, but I'm darned if I'm going to miss the marbles." When Graham served me, he said: "I really didn't take the marbles, Mr. Charlton, whatever Mr. Wicksteed may tell you." The marbles are a free gift given away with the breakfast cereal. The mate had noticed yesterday that the packet offered a free bazooka, and finding none, had insisted he was entitled by rank to the next free gift. He collected them, five glass marbles, with great solemnity and went on watch.

There is a report from 'tween decks of a leak in the main

strake on the starboard side, but Stuart assured me it was nothing to worry about as we must expect a few leaks in a new ship. I only hope it does not cause too much discomfort to the fifty-fifty club.

On deck today the crew enjoyed the change in weather; some of them wrote their journals, others worked on chafing gear and others read. Doc Stevens just lay full length, closed his eyes and murmured: "Isn't it bloody wonderful," over and over again. Jumbo was reading what I supposed to be an engrossing thriller until I looked over his shoulder and saw it was a book on investment procedure. Over tea Alan talked about his early days at sea and how he shipped on an English ship. "The ship was all right, but the master wasn't, although he taught me a lot about what not to do if you wanted to get the best out of men. He thought of men as chattels and when I asked him for leave to go home for Christmas he wouldn't give it. The fool thought I'd run away from his blasted ship. One of the troubles with the Englishman is that he can't forget his class distinction, a lot of foolishness, though I suppose they live in such a crowded island you can't blame them."

Later, I went up on the quarter-deck to see him about the regular press messages he has agreed to send out about our progress once weekly. The last one went out on Saturday and did not get to the newspapers until the following Monday. He agreed to send the next message on Friday and also to make it longer. He showed me the chart and the course we hope to take. "I'm glad I've come south," he confided. "She's a slow ship, a good four knots slower than Baker said, and I really wouldn't trust her masts and rigging in a gale. It might have been all right for the old ones, but it's not good enough for us. We've had a wonderful offing and we've missed all the bad weather." With that he walked out on deck into the night and told me to close my eyes for a few moments to get used to the light, and when I opened them I looked down at the ship swaying on her way. For the first time since we left Plymouth I did not have to reach for a rope to steady myself.

Eleventh Day, April 30. The wind and the sea have been dropping for the past two days. Jan Junker said to me this morning: "In two or three days' time we should be into the trades and make our westing. There are variable winds in between, but it looks as though we'll carry this wind until we get a northeasterly." He explained to me that the trades follow the sun, so that when the sun is north, the limit of the trades moves up, and when the sun goes south, in winter, the limit of the trades is not so far north. Dick listened to Jan telling me secrets of the winds and commented dryly: "Take my word for it, Warwick, we'll have to go so far south to pick up the trades we'll make our landfall at the Pole instead of Plymouth."

The ocean is a much lonelier place than I imagined. Everyone is on the lookout for fish or birds, but it is rarely that we sight anything. When we do, it is an occasion and we cry out to the rest of the ship's company. Today, for example, I had borrowed Dick's binoculars and was fortunate enough to see a pomarine jaeger, a brown long-tailed bird that lives in the ocean. It nests on rocky shores and eats what it can steal from other birds. I shouted for everyone to see and the glasses went from one hand to another as everyone on deck took turns at bird watching. It stayed with us for most of the morning, venturing short flights but never near enough to the ship to be seen clearly without the glasses.

At lunch today there was apple pie, which I enjoyed so much I had four helpings. After making a pig of myself I thought a gesture was indicated to the galley, so I sent Wally and Dick my bottle of beer. There is a free issue, one bottle per man every day, and I have been giving my bottle to whoever is sitting next to me, but in future I will give it to the galley; they work so hard and in such heat they need more liquids than anyone else.

In the evenings we have started a bridge school in the Great Cabin which consists of myself, Dick, John Winslow and Lee Israel, the photographer. I have made two rules: the first, that we do not play for money, and the second, that cheating is compulsory. We have many days at sea ahead of us and I felt it would be difficult enough for us to keep our tempers living in such a confined space without adding the possibility of a row over cards. Cheating consists of winks, nods and inflections of voice when you are bidding and, just to make sure, an occasional look at your opponents' cards. After the game we usually have a talk before going off to our bunks, and this evening was no exception. I was remarking about the scarcity of life at sea, at least life visible to us, when Wally came in with a jug of tea.

"Believe me," he said, setting down the jug and pouring as he spoke, "you never know what's in the sea. An octopus or phantom could come out of it and take the lot of us. All excepting me. They don't take stewards."

"How do they know who are the stewards, Wally?" I asked.

He pondered for a moment so that he forgot what he was doing and filled a mug to overflowing, then he exclaimed, his face creasing into a sly smile: "I know: the gulls tell them."

"Why should they do that?"

"Because the white gulls are stewards. Yes, that's what happens to us when we die. We become white gulls."

"And how about the black gulls?"

"Ah," he said, shaking with his own merriment, "those bastards are seamen and firemen."

Twelfth Day, May 1. Today we have reached the beginning of the most crucial phase of the voyage. It is only a fortnight since the ship did her first trials, three hours round Tor Bay, and back to Brixham, and yet we have come over a thousand miles across the Atlantic. But now the winds which have blown us thus far are petering to a whisper; the sea is a rich royal blue, swelling slowly and sinuously under an African sun, and we are beginning to see some signs of ocean life.

This morning we watched a flotilla of Portuguese men-of-war float helplessly in our wash and the Captain pointed out some golden weed from the Gulf Stream. "See," he said, "we are going in the right direction, and it doesn't take much to blow us along." Fortunately, this is no less than the truth. We are only getting a wind of about force one and it is pushing us through the water at about two knots. Mind you, to use the words *wind* and *force* to describe the breath of air we are getting seems an overstatement, but I find our continued and steady headway with light airs most reassuring; so did Jan, although he reminded me that it still *might* be days before we had the fine breeze we needed to take us west.

In the expectation that we would go the colder, more hazardous, but quicker northern route, I had come prepared for rain, fog and ice, but not for the sun. Not so my shipmates. They appeared of a sudden in tropical shirts and shorts, and I did my best to meet the weather by discarding my long woolen pants and going barefoot in jeans and a string shirt. There was plenty to do all day to occupy the crew: the chippy made a bench table for washing up outside the galley, put up shelves in the Captain's cabin, while I worked with the crew greasing shackles on the outside of the ship, greasing all ventilator screws and giving a coat of red oxide inside. We hoisted the main yard in the afternoon, probably because the Captain is going to put the bonnets on. These are additional sections of mainsail which may be added to increase the sail area in light weather.

In the afternoon I went up on the poop and Joe Lacey, who was up on the main yard, shouted that he had sighted a sea serpent. I looked astern to where he was pointing and for a moment thought he was right, but then the object, which was about a hundred yards away, began to move and I saw it was a humpbacked whale. It showed itself for a moment and then sounded, probably frightened by the hum of our generators. At four o'clock Wally served us a mug of lime, which was most welcome after the heat of the day. When Wally filled my mug, he said: "Board of Trade regulations, sir. Must give you lime after eleven days out. Do you the world of good, it will." His hooded eyes closed in silent merriment, and he added: "Nothing like a bit of lime to clip your corns and stop the sap from rising."

Our run from noon till noon was 107 miles. If we do a little over half that for the following period, we shall be doing well, and so long as we have a fine easterly within a day or so, then I feel there is little to worry about. Tonight we had a portable radio on deck and listened to opera. The night was so bright, the air so soft, the waters so smooth, the music so sweet, I half expected to see Aphrodite emerge from the undulating deep. Had she done so, I would have made her most welcome — despite the lime juice.

Thirteenth Day, May 2. Today we have been dodging along hoping to get the right slant to carry us across, but meanwhile the wind continues to carry us not only further south, but southeast.

This morning at about 8:30 we sighted a ship on the port quarter and we ran up our ensign, but they ignored us and continued on their way. We tried to find explanations for this indifference, a hurt to our vanity, and Alan suggested that everyone must have been working in the hold, so that the watch dare not disturb them even to admire us. But despite his explanation we felt rather like a woman who has woken up one day to find in the mirror that she has lost her looks.

The ship never fails to demand some service of us; we are her acolytes, and today we were busy as usual making chafing gear, oiling the topmast yard and shortening the mainstay. This is the stay that comes from the mainmast and keeps it from going aft. It had stretched and given us too much drift on the lanyards. I made my first ascent of the ratlines to oil the fore-topmast spar. I hate heights, and although the ship was moving sedately through the water so there was hardly any sway, I climbed slowly, holding on to the ropes as though I were following Hillary up Everest. They hauled up a bucket of linseed oil and a wad of waste, with which I treated the shakes, dabbing the oil into the longitudinal gashes to seal off the air.

Throughout the day Palma, one of the Canary Islands, has

been on our starboard beam. Anderson-Bell has been urging that we make a stop, saying that these islands are famous for the delights they have to offer visiting seamen. Sparks seconded this suggestion for different reasons: we could take on board some fruit, top up our water tanks and reset our rigging, which is working loose. He also added, by the way, that the sight of the island beauties would not come amiss. But Adrian Small stroked his trim red beard and said: "Not all the Canaries are worth stopping at unless you're interested in goats and tomatoes or both, believe me."

Adrian had gone to the Canaries to work on *Moby Dick* for John Huston. "After the last day's shooting," he told me, "there was a terrific party, but I packed my gear and did not say good-by. It was February and I did not fancy going home to snow and ice and a terrible winter. There was a lovely little two-masted schooner, the *Bella Lucia,* sailing on the tide." She was crewed by ten Spaniards, none of whom spoke a word of English, but Adrian managed to make them understand that if they could use an extra hand, he was ready and willing. Adrian had no work permit, so it was agreed he should be the official stowaway. Although he could speak only a few words of Spanish when he went aboard, a few weeks with them did more for his Spanish than a year of schooling. "We traded between the seven main islands that make up the Canaries," he explained, "and used to be at sea for about eighteen hours at a time. We'd get to some place and the skipper would go ashore and want to know where the cargo was, and if it wasn't ready, then we'd all go up to the factory and sit around waiting for them to pack enough tomatoes for us to carry. All the packing was done by girls and we didn't think much of them, I can tell you. They looked most unattractive in their thick woolen black stockings.

"Sometimes we carried passengers and a deck cargo of goats' fodder. The passengers, usually entire families moving from one island to another, had to fend for themselves on deck. They used to dig holes in the fodder for shelter. We only charged them a little per head, but they had to supply their own food and water

as well as shelter. Mind you, we lived rough ourselves. Outside
the galley there was a carcass of a goat and we'd eat goat's meat,
goat's cheese, drink goat's milk. Sometimes we'd have a bit of
rice and some wine. The wine was rough and cheap, but safer
than the water.

"My experience of the Canaries was goats and donkeys, no
grass, no trees — just scrub." I thanked Adrian for his information and related the essence of what he had told me to Andy
and Sparks. I noted that afterwards they looked less often and
longingly at the gray lump of land on our starboard beam. Perhaps I should have told them that Adrian spoke only of the barren
islands, and that Palma was as attractive as they had imagined.

There was an amusing incident during the afternoon when
Joe Lacey was aloft. He shouted with all the strength of his
lungs: "Land ho. Land ho." Alan was on the poop and he
looked wearily at Joe, who had just come on watch. "Land ho,"
Alan said, as if to himself, and then, raising his voice so that
Joe and all of us could hear: "I know, it's been there all bloody
day." But Joe's high spirits and quick Irish wit were not so
easily squashed. "Maybe," he said, "but it's the first time I've
seen it."

Alan could not control a smile.

Fourteenth Day, May 3. John cabled me to ask for our position
at noon today and anticipated position tomorrow and Sunday so
that he, and probably Felix Fenston, could come out on a launch
from Palma and collect Lee's pictures and Julian's film. This is
the last point at which they will be able to make contact with
us until we are near the United States. Alan does not want to
make any rendezvous, I suppose because he is fearful of delays.
I replied to the cable, giving our possible position at noon tomorrow as seventy miles southwest of Madeira. This, together with
our position at noon today, the weather reports and the known
speed of the ship (a maximum daily average of about six and a
half knots) should provide John with sufficient information to

find us. I wondered if he would use a seaplane if conditions were good enough, as I knew they ran them from Southampton to the Canaries.

I am beginning to think a fairly reliable picture of the next few weeks has at last emerged. It is true that we have been forced further south than we wished, until we are much nearer South America than North, but we are now through the Canaries and in the latitude where we may reasonably expect an easterly to take us west. This means we still have over three thousand miles of ocean to cross in our slow square-rigged ship. Jan, who, I find, does not express his views lightly, today volunteered his opinion that we have at least another forty days' sailing. We have been out of Plymouth fourteen days tomorrow, so if Jan is right — and I think he will not be far out — we shall be fifty-four days at sea before making our landfall at Plymouth, Massachusetts. This is longer than I had hoped. I think that forty-five days would have done us credit, but as things are, we will have taken just under a fortnight less than the Pilgrims, who did not have modern charts, weather reports and navigational aids. They also made their crossing during winter on an old, overcrowded ship and they went north about! I can see Alan's point of view: *Mayflower II* is untried; he does not want to risk lives; our ship is overballasted and therefore slow. But nothwithstanding these drawbacks and Alan's conviction that she would not stand up in really bad weather, I am naturally disappointed that we have had to come south, despite the dangers of the shorter northern passage.

If we had come through ice and fog, avoided collision and made a record crossing, what a wonderful way of showing that the spirit of adventure, the spirit that made England great, is not dead. Having said that, I do not underestimate the task ahead; this is not an easy ship to sail. Her shortness, combined with the breadth of beam, makes her difficult to maneuver and she is a bitch to steer. She switchbacks up and down the swell, sways, rolls and pitches. This morning, for example, Doc Stevens had to go up the mainmast, and when he came down, the motion had made him so sick that he was forced to retire to his bunk 'tween decks. Beric Watson, who was on watch during the early hours of the morning and who had also been aloft, was sick over the side. Both these men are good seamen in excellent physical condition and would not readily give way to sickness. In fact, everyone is giving his best, getting to know the ship more intimately every day. Godfrey Wicksteed, the first mate, sets an example and seems always to be on duty, so that no one is sure when he sleeps. He is either pacing the quarter-deck, checking the man at the wheel, watching the set of the sails, fitting extra chafing gear, or encouraging the crew to go aloft, attending to all the needs of the ship, and with such good humor he might be taking a party of boys for a day's sailing on the river. He has a great zest for his job and I suspect he would be happy if we did not touch land for two or three years. Sailing is the passion of his life and even his schoolmastering has been spent for a good part afloat. When he was a master at Gordonstoun, where he was in charge of sailing, one of his pupils was Prince Philip. I asked him what he thought of the Prince, knowing I would receive a frank reply: "Oh, he was a good lad," he reflected, "always ready to do the really necessary jobs. We could do a lot worse than to have him with us now."

The sea has been choppy and the motion of the ship erratic, but the sun has been shining and I saw my first porpoise and a solitary flying fish. I felt for the first time near the brink of seasickness, but I fought it off by an effort of will and without recourse to the tablets Doc gave me. When I went to the beak today, our bow was breaking into the short seas and I discovered that we have the only sanitary system in the world which flushes the user. Really, this *Mayflower* is quite unique!

Fifteenth Day, May 4. At last we have the trade winds and we are turning our bows towards the west. The Captain was quite openly pleased with life and gave the order "Splice the main brace," so that at eight bells there was a muster of all hands and the issue of lime juice was triggered with two bottles of rum. Beric Watson brought out his guitar, so did Graham Nunn, and they strummed and sang some new verses to the ship's song. We were all in festive mood because at the back of everyone's mind was, I think, Jan's warning that we might have several more days' run further south before we picked up the trades. The Captain, who naturally does not like to go on record with prophecies, stood watching and smiling as we gathered round our minstrels in the waist. He called to me and said: "You know, I think we may do a couple of thousand miles during the next fortnight," and he added with a smile his usual rider: "If the Lord is good to us, of course!" So here we are, heading in the right direction at last, a curving course towards Bermuda and then, with the help of the Gulf Stream, north towards the Nantucket Lighthouse.

I half expected to hear the sound of a fast launch approaching us all day or the drone of a seaplane engine, but there was no sight or sound of either, and then at about eleven o'clock at night Stuart and I both thought we heard the faint hum of an airplane engine, although the time seemed most inappropriate for an Atlantic caller. We looked out the stern window in the Great Cabin, but all we could hear and see was the wash of the ship foaming busily away under the star-pricked sky. We were walking out on deck when at last we traced the source of the sound we thought was an aircraft, and found it came from the galley. All our supplies of fresh food are finished, including wrapped bread, and Wally was busy baking fresh bread for the morning. The heat from the galley was enough to give many people a stroke, but Wally was busily folding blankets over the bread tins in a temperature of 120 degrees, rivers of sweat running down his face and soaking his shirt. I knew that he and Dick worked an average of fifteen hours a day and wondered why anyone would choose such a dirty, uncomfortable and often thankless task. Dick, I knew, would have done anything to be aboard. He was my friend and had set his heart upon making the voyage, whatsoever he was required to do, since some years ago when I had first mentioned the idea of building *Mayflower* to him. For that matter, everyone sailing in *Mayflower* was a volunteer and it is not difficult to understand why. After all, it is not every day the opportunity occurs of sailing a square-rigged ship across the Atlantic, and then, of course, there was the flame of adventure and romance inherent in the project. But I must admit I was puzzled as to Wally's motives for making the voyage. First of all, there is his age: he is fifty-four and first went to sea as a pantry boy at £3.10.0d. a month thirty-seven years ago. I should have thought he had had his bellyful of slaving in hot galleys cooking for ravenous crews; then there is his health: a few years ago he had half his stomach removed. He pulled up his shirt and showed me the neat needlework of the surgeons. "Forty-four stitches. I reckon they had to use a sewing machine . . . " And nine years ago he was stricken with cerebral hemorrhage. He thinks this was brought on by a fracas in the Hamburg docks. He stood in the doorway of the galley, a thin little man in a white apron, hands and arms dusted with flour and long streaks of perspiration, his heavy eyelids drooping with fatigue, looking in the thin yellow light a tired old tortoise of a man.

The ship swayed rhythmically as he spoke; the squish-squash of the sea and the occasional flip-flap of a sail could be heard in the background. "In those days after the war," he recalled, "Hamburg was a hotbed for black marketeers. You could buy the bloody place for a tin of fags and a pound of coffee. But I wouldn't have them around my ship. One night I found five of them on board; they put a proposition to me and I ordered them off. It was in February on a freezing cold night. About an hour later I went ashore to go aboard the ship docked next to us. But I no sooner set foot on the quayside than I went spark out. I never saw who hit me over the head, it was that dark and it happened so suddenly; and then I was pitched into the water. I suppose that the shock of the cold sea and instinct came to my rescue, because I was picked up swimming toward some steps. Well, after a few hours' rest I was walking about again, with a thick head, mind you, but on my feet. Five months later I went down with cerebral hemorrhage and I reckon it was that crack on the nut that did it. I can tell you, they thought I was done for, but I pulled through and was soon back working on the ships."

"Well, Wally," I said, "that still doesn't explain why you're here. Surely it's not for your health?" "Oh, no," he said, his thin lips curving into a faint smile, "it's not for me health. I have come on this ship with one object: I am getting on in years and I want one final burst so I have done something different from every other Tom, Dick and Harry. It wasn't an easy decision for me to make. I talked it over with the wife for a couple of days, and then it was my boy Tom that got the wife to agree. He's a bright lad, my Tom, twenty-six, an electronics engineer. He said to let the old man go: 'We'll all be proud of him,' that's what he said and that decided the issue."

All of us on board count that decision as fortunate. Food is what sustains us, relieves the monotony, keeps us happy. Wally's presence is our assurance that whatever else suffers on this voyage, it won't be our stomachs. He is, in his humble way, a perfectionist and philosopher of the saucepan. Not a day goes by without his preparing a tasty surprise. "Never let them know what they're going to get from one day to another," he explained. "If you know what you're going to get, it spoils your appetite. Then I believe that the meal has got to look good as well as taste good." Although our fresh food is finished, we have no complaints. How he produces thirty-three meals, three times a day, on one small range worked by diesel oil and an emergency primus, with heavy swells and a quartering sea seeming to make no difference, is a source of wonder to us. Dick Brennan regards him with something akin to awe. Dick has only one worry: that Wally will work too hard and be forced to give up. "Got to look after him," Dick says at least once a day, and we take the hint and invite Wally every evening to take a nip of whisky or rum in the Great Cabin. This he accepts with a certain ceremony. He brings us some cocoa and a snack at ten o'clock at night, sits down, and then we say: "How about a nip, Wally?" He considers the proposition for a moment, as though it were unexpected and as if it needed careful consideration, and answers: "I don't mind if I do," then produces a glass he has been carefully carrying.

While I was talking to Wally and the bread was baking, the watch was attracted by the smell and I left Wally as he was dishing out newly baked bread thick with melted butter, a slice of Cheddar cheese and cups of hot chocolate. He is essentially a thrifty man, whose years at sea have taught him to husband his stores. "On a sailing ship in particular you can never tell how long you'll be at sea," he reminded me, "so I'm making it my business to see we don't starve like those Pilgrims did, however long it takes us to get there."

I heard later from Beric Watson that he had found Wally at two in the morning, sitting on the edge of his bunk 'tween decks, fast asleep. Beric gently lifted up the legs of our little cook and made him comfortable.

Sixteenth Day, May 5. The order was for all hands to wear costume for the Captain's Sunday morning service. I heard Joe Lacey shouting down the aft ladder to 'tween decks: "Put your Pilgrim clothes on. Everyone in Pilgrim clothes. Captain's orders ..." This remark about Pilgrim clothes made me reflect on the not uncommon misconception about the Pilgrims: the idea that they dressed alike, obeying austerity rules regarding dress. I think that children's history books are to blame for spreading the impression that the Pilgrims all looked alike — the men, for example, wearing drab gray clothes and stiff hats. Actually it was a period when people liked color. Pilgrim women, for example, dipped their materials in saffron to get a bright orange color, or in indigo for rich blue shades. The year 1620 was an "in between" period for women. Earlier, during Queen Elizabeth's reign, the English people had been very fashion conscious. Later, when Charles I ascended the throne in 1625, his court brought a renewed interest in high fashion. At the time the Pilgrims left England, women of all classes wore fairly low necklines — frequently with an unrelated collar, choker-fashion, around the neck — and dressed in velvets and handsome satins if they could afford them, which few Pilgrim women could.

Some women aboard the *Mayflower* had lived in Holland for several years as religious refugees, and Dutch fashion was reflected in their caps and sleeves. Dorothy Bradford, who lived in Leyden and Amsterdam, would have worn a cap tied under her chin and full, rather elaborately trimmed sleeves. But eighteen-year-old Priscilla Mullins, from Surrey, would have pinned her cap in her hair and worn split sleeves.

The Pilgrim Fathers, however, inclined towards Lincoln green or russet brown in their everyday garb. For dressier occasions they chose a variety of colors. Ruling Elder Brewster, for example, took along a wardrobe which included a red cap, a violet coat and a pair of green drawers. We had no one on board impersonating the Pilgrims. Our two descendants, Winslow and Church, were seamen and I had provided them with seventeenth-century seamen's kits for wearing on ceremonial occasions, and similar costumes were provided for all the ship's company. Naval uniforms had not yet come into use when the *Mayflower* sailed, but most of them wore leather jerkins, loose breeches, long woolen stockings, buckle shoes and Monmouth caps, and this is how our crew were decked out when they assembled on the quarter-deck.

I had been in a quandary when it came to my costume: I could hardly pass myself off as a sailor, as this was my first voyage in a sailing ship of any rig, let alone square-rigged, and I did not think it either fitting or appropriate to dress in a costume which might be identified as that of a Pilgrim. I decided that as there were Saints and Strangers on the first *Mayflower*, and recognizing that I did not fall into the first category, I would adopt the military dress of the time. As I still held the rank of major in the Army, I did not think anyone could take this amiss, even Captain Standish. I wore a rust jerkin with buttoned fastenings tied with points. The sleeves had wings and were of a close-fitting material, trimmed with braid in circular longitudinal stripes. The cuffs were of white linen. I wore knee breeches, knitted stockings and buckle shoes.

Captain Jones wore no marks of rank, going to sea in the same garb he wore ashore. He could be distinguished from his crew only by the better quality of the clothes he wore, and he had more of them. It seemed appropriate to have Alan Villiers more readily recognizable, so he was dressed in black, in a costume of similar design to my own. He stood on the quarter-deck, all of us gathered around him, the ship pitching and swaying, the Union Jack fluttering from the lateen yard, as he read in his hearty voice from the Bible.

After the service he read Bradford's account of the voyage of the first *Mayflower*, and as it is the only reliable report we have, apart from *Mourt's Relation*, it seems fitting to include it here:*

> After they had enjoyed fair winds and weather for a season, they were encountered many times with cross winds and met with many fierce storms with which the ship was shroudly shaken, and her upper works made very leaky; and one of the main beams in the midships was bowed and cracked, which put them in some fear that the ship would not be able to perform the voyage. So some of the chief of the company, perceiving the mariners to fear the sufficiency of the ship as appeared by their mutterings, they entered into serious consultation with the master and other officers of the ship, to consider in time of the danger, and rather to return than to cast themselves into a desperate and inevitable peril. And truly there was great distraction and difference of opinion amongst the mariners themselves; fain would they do what could be done for their wages' sake (being now near half the seas over) and on the other hand they were loath to hazard their lives too desperately. But in examining of all opinions, the master and others affirmed they knew the ship to be strong and firm under water; and for the buckling of the main beam, there was a great iron screw the passengers brought out of Holland, which would raise the beam into his place; the which being done, the carpenter and master affirmed that with a post put under it, set firm in the

---

* This and subsequent quotations from *Of Plymouth Plantation 1620–1647* by William Bradford. Samuel E. Morison, editor. Alfred A. Knopf, New York, 1952.

lower deck and otherways bound, he would make it sufficient. And as for the decks and upper works, they would caulk them as well as they could, and though with the working of the ship they would not long keep staunch, yet there would otherwise be no great danger, if they did not overpress her with sails. So they committed themselves to the will of God and resolved to proceed.

When the Captain finished reading this extract from Bradford, there was a touch of incongruity as we queued for an issue of cigarettes and chocolates. Most of the crew went below to change out of their costumes, and Beric, Graham, Stuart and Scottie reappeared with white cowboy hats and colored scarves, and they climbed onto the fo'c'sle, which they used as a stage to give a rendering of the *Mayflower* song. This group, every one of whom had learned to play an instrument since joining the ship, had introduced the refinement of Scottie knocking out the beat on a fire bucket. What they lacked in skill they made up for in determination. We were all in high spirits, a little drunk with those nor'east trades they were singing about:

> Oh Blow ye nor'east trades, now blow the *Mayflower* on,
> Oh Blow ye nor'east trades, now blow the *Mayflower* on,
> Oh Blow ye nor'east trades, now blow the *Mayflower* on,
> At seven knots we won't be sailing long.
>
> We're bound for Massachusetts, that's in the Yew-es-ay,
> And when we get there, Lord, we will bless the day.

They sang a number of couplets, which they added to as and when the occasion demanded. Here are three of them:

> Please tell me, Mr. Maitland, oh what's our course and where,
> Said he, "I don't know, sir, just that li'l ol' point right there."
>
> We had a life raft on t'deck, stowed and ready loaded,
> When t'doctor pulled t'string, t'ex-ex thing exploded.
>
> Jack Scarr had some garbage, he kept it in a sack,
> He threw it to windward and promptly got it back.

Seventeenth Day, May 6. Edgar, Stuart and Canada spent the day checking up on the shakes and generally trying to make the ship more comfortable. First of all they checked minor deck leaks, of which there were half a dozen. These, unfortunately, were of a special nature, caused by a turpsy pocket in the timber. They had to be hardened down with a calking iron and packed with a thread of oakum and paid up with marine glue. In addition, some of the deck fastenings had to be reglued. These had been paid up when wet and the glue had not taken.

Edgar celebrated his birthday today. He wanted a bottle of rum and asked me to approach the Captain for him. I went up on the quarter-deck and did so, and the Captain naturally asked me why Edgar did not do his own asking. "He's scared of you," I said. "Is he?" said the Captain. "That's good. But tell him he'll have to get over his fear if he wants a bottle of rum." I relayed the message to Edgar and a few minutes later saw him all smiles descending 'tween decks clutching a bottle. Although I was not able to accept his invitation to "have one," I went below for a few minutes to see the fifty-fifty club toast him. I noted a new instruction in the tiller flat: GENTLEMEN, IN CASE OF FIRE, PLEASE YELL FIRE!

We have made 150 knots up to noon today. We hold rigidly to our course and our little ship endears herself more to us every day by the dogged manner of her progress across these vast seas.

Tonight I had a cup of water for the first time since we left Plymouth. I let it stand for about forty minutes while we were playing cards in the Great Cabin, and when I came to drink it, noticed a thick deposit at the bottom of the cup. Dick assured me: "It's only rust." In future I'm going to stick to tea and cocoa.

Eighteenth Day, May 7. We have broken our record! The run for the twenty-four-hour period which ended at noon today was 160 miles, and the Captain said we would have logged eight miles more if steering had been better. This run led inevitably to discussions as to the maximum possible performance of the ship. Stuart asserted: "You ain't seen nothing yet. Under ideal conditions this vesseel would do twelve knots. We're only just beginning to get to know her." I am far more interested in what she will do right now, so I pinned Stuart down to give his estimate for the maximum day's run during the voyage and he asserts she is capable of doing two hundred miles in a day. I hope he is right, but I also agreed with Jan, who says that the present rate of progress, if we can keep it up, is very satisfactory.

This has been a strange day with everyone half asleep. I think the tiredness that overtook us all has also something to do with the motion of the ship, which is like a pendulum. Alan thinks the motion excessive, but Jan does not agree with him. "I find it quiet," he said, "particularly compared to my ship, the *Kaskelot,* which is about the same size. Her motion is so bad that we no longer get any passengers. We used to have them, but the word got around and now people stipulate in their contracts that they are not to be carried on my ship." Jan says our present daily rate of progress is as good as that of the clippers, so we have plenty to be proud of.

Felix has now found his sea legs, which is not bad for seven weeks old. I am quite fascinated watching him adjust his little body to the sway of the ship. His greenstick is cured now. We nearly lost him this afternoon when a wave caught him, but Dick grabbed him as he was on his way over.

Wally has been sick all day, confined to quarters. This is hardly surprising. He has been putting in too many hours. Joe Meany helped Dick with the galley and so did Jack Scarr. I went aloft today, to help tighten up the sails. I hung on for dear life, but it was a most exciting experience, not so frightening as I expected. Jim Horrocks, the sparks, told me tonight that land was a lot nearer than any of us thought, so I took the hook. "How far away do you say it is?" "Never more than a mile away," he said, pointing down to the deck.

Nineteenth Day, May 8. Our run till noon today has broken yesterday's record: 164 miles! I thought the news so good all round that I could not keep it to myself and went 'tween decks to tell the fifty-fifty club. When I told them we were at the halfway mark, John Winslow called for three cheers for Warwick Charlton, which I thought very kind of him and of all of them for joining in, but a little misplaced as I had no part in bringing the ship safely to this stage.

Doc Stevens is going to celebrate the occasion tomorrow by feeding his leeches. "I have named one of them after you," he said, "so I think it only fair you should give him a feed." With the eyes of the fifty-fifty club upon me there was nothing to do but agree. "How much blood do they take before they are satisfied?" I asked. "Oh, any amount," said Doc. "You'll probably feel a little faint, but don't let that worry you. I've some blood plasma on board and I can always give you a transfusion." Andy Bell has to feed one named after him, but there is a third leech and I don't dare to ask its name.

Wally is still not well and Dick has, for the time being, taken over as first cook. He is making a good job of it, too, and is loud in the praises of Joe Meany, who seizes every possible opportunity to help out. The more we see of Joe the higher he goes in our estimation: quiet, almost self-effacing, but with an underlying self-confidence and willingness to do any job aboard ship, however menial.

Tonight we changed the set of our sails. Stuart came into the Great Cabin and reported: "The lateen is clewed up; the starboard clew garnet on the main is taken up so that we get the maximum amount of drive from the foresail. The reason for this is that the wind has come more aft." One thing is puzzling me: What has happened to all the sea life? I saw a couple of flying fish today but nothing else. I think we're going too fast to see much and this is all right by me and the rest of the ship's company.

We are over the brow of the hill. This evening Alan said to me casually, at teatime, that tonight, or by tomorrow morning at the latest, we should have passed the halfway mark. That really is very good for the ship to have done in nineteen days. With characteristic caution he said that we have had things so much our way thus far we must expect some setbacks before we reach our destination. But I was not in the mood to be cautious. I knew that the first half of the voyage was expected to be the most difficult. First of all we had to get clear of the approaches to the Channel, battling with westerly winds, which are dead muzzlers. The idea is to get a good offing so that you get clear of the Bay of Biscay. If you don't, you can be swept in towards Cape Villano, just north of Cape Finisterre. In the past, several naval ships have been wrecked there. Now they have a very powerful light as a warning and a sailing ship has to keep well away from it, as we did. Then we got a northerly which enabled us to keep a steady rate of progress, so we have averaged six knots and have not had to tack at all, but have sailed down with the wind on our starboard quarter or starboard beam. The only difficult stretch was just north of the Canaries when the wind backed to west and forced the ship through the Canary Islands. Although this was a pleasant diversion, it wasn't what Alan wanted. There is always an element of danger sailing through islands.

We sailed through the islands still on the starboard tack, and when we were between Teneriffe and Palma, the wind veered to the north and we were able to steer a sou'westerly course again and so clear the Canaries. Since then we've had favorable winds all the time. We made a good southing to make sure we were well in the trades to make our westing, and began the crossing proper. We'll keep on our westing as long as the trades last.

Twentieth Day, May 9. It really is no use counting your mileage on a sailing ship! Alan, Adrian and Jan have told me this often enough, but I am so anxious that we arrive in America in good time, as nearly as possible within the date bracket I gave them, that I am constantly working out possible ETA's. Yesterday, heartened by a record day's run, I was cock-a-hoop and so were the rest of the crew. Joe Meany was all smiles as he helped

out in the galley, confident he would make his graduation day;
the fifty-fifty club were talking about asking the Captain to
release some liquor for a party, and I secretly held the view
that we would be off Plymouth by May 25, to the surprise of
our hosts. Then in the evening the wind began to drop and
during Jan's watch only 14 miles were recorded. A punishment
for presuming on the benevolence of the wind gods!

All night the ship crept over the ocean like a heavy wooden
monster, waddling oh so slowly, heaving wearily from side to
side and her sails flapping like empty wings. No one gets much
sleep when this happens. This morning the wind freshened a
little, but by noon our run was only 116 miles. Not so bad as I
imagined, but with no sign of improvement it was cause for
concern for the future. As if to emphasize the uncertainty of our
progress, Wicksteed announced to me that we are not in fact
halfway! There was a miscalculation in the total distance — an
underestimate, of course! The correct distance is 5400 miles and
we have made only 2500, so we have at least another day's sailing
before we are halfway.

Today a flying fish landed on deck and Dick caught it and
cooked it and divided it among six of the crew. They said it
tasted just like mackerel. Doc Stevens is saving the leeches until
four o'clock tomorrow. This news put out Gordon, who had one
of his seven cameras ready to snap them feasting on one of my
limbs. This evening the radio set broke down. Sparks suspected
the vibrator; he fitted the spare, which is working, but he does
not consider it reliable. I hope we don't lose our only link with
the outside world.

Twenty-first Day, May 10. At six o'clock this morning they
were hosing down the decks and some of the water came into my
bunk from the quarter-deck, with the result that I was up and
about at once. I found that we were lolling along in a listless
sea, making no more than two knots. I decided to take my time
over the business of washing, put a canvas bucket over the side

and poured some tepid Atlantic water into my plastic pail, which serves the dual purpose of washbowl and washtub. I made a great business of brushing my teeth, reflecting that the salt content in the water would do them good, but wondering how much plankton I was swallowing in the process.

While I was shaving I noted that my mustache suggests some Tartar ancestry, and my beard promises to be dashing, but how dashing depends upon the duration of the voyage. At breakfast Alan remarked gruffly that he had not had a good night's sleep. "Never do when the ship stops moving," he added, but I made up my mind not to be depressed even if we were becalmed.

At nine-thirty everyone began gathering in the waist. Edgar Mugridge and Joe Lacey were using the adz to shape a spar for a studding sail they are going to hoist on the starboard side of the foreyard. It is small and won't make any appreciable difference to our speed, but Alan believes such activity is good for the morale of the ship's company. Scottie, Peter Padfield, John Winslow, Ted Edwards and David Cauvin were busy either sweeping the decks or making chafing gear, and Ike Marsh was parceling and serving a jack stay to be used on the main yard.

Then, at ten o'clock, Dick Brennan and Wally Godfrey came out of the galley and stood contemplating the scene as though they were waiting for something to happen. It soon did. Doc Stevens came up from 'tween decks wearing a surgical mask and white linen cap. He carried some surgical instrument, forceps, scalpels, stethoscope, and laid them out carefully upon a blanket which had been spread on deck. I asked him what he was doing and he replied: "Preparing for the patient." He disappeared 'tween decks and while he was gone Joe Meany asked me how I felt. I told him I had never felt better in my life and he accepted my assurance with considerable gravity and nodding of the head: "Then you won't have to worry about shock," he said. Before I could question this remark the doctor reappeared and handed me a bottle which contained the reason so many of the crew had found jobs to do in the waist: three leeches. "Your time has come, boy," said Doc. "Just lie down, and I'll give the poor blighters their feed." "They look quiet enough." I said, peering at the black wormlike creatures which wriggled round the bottle. "Maybe they do now, man," agreed the doctor. "They're quiet and thin, but how would you feel if you hadn't had a drop of decent blood to drink for twenty days?" I lay down on the blanket, my arms were seized by people I thought had become my friends, and Doc took the leeches with his forceps from the bottle and placed them on my stomach, which he had bared for the purpose. As they arched their slimy bodies, I felt sharp nips and they began to feed, amidst shouts of encouragement from the ship's company.

Doc then shook a liberal helping of tomato sauce onto my stomach, "just to help the flavor," but to the consternation of Julian, who was busy filming the scene. "Please, Doc," he remonstrated, "someone will have the film banned." He swabbed off the sauce, poured on some salt, removed the leeches, and the operation which formed the first part of the ceremonies to mark our reaching the halfway stage was over.

The second ceremony, which was performed by David Cauvin, consisted of a bottle drop. The bottle contained the names and signatures of all the ship's company and the finder was asked to forward the document to Dick's club, with the promise of a reward. Later, Alan told me there was little chance of the bottle's being found, because the ocean currents were not favorable, but that later, nearer Bermuda, we might drop some more bottles with greater expectations that they would be found.

At twelve-twenty we sighted our first ship for several days, a tanker probably bound for the West Indies. We signaled her and asked her to inform the gentlemen of Lloyds that she had sighted us. Alan thought this a wise precaution to take as our radio is still not working, despite the hours Jimmy Horrocks has spent taking it to pieces and putting it together again. Alan is not worried about our being unable to pick up weather reports, but rather by the possibility that wives and families might start to fret at the absence of a daily position report from us. The ship came in closer to identify us and then made off without wasting a moment longer than absolutely necessary. However, it was good to see evidence of other shipping. In the evening the wind freshened and blew astern of us, so that we began to bowl along. This makes up for the fact that we logged only 95 knots.

Twenty-second Day, May 11. Three weeks ago today we were becalmed within sight of our port of departure. Now we are bowling along in the northeast trades. The time passed quickly for all of us and so far without mishap. Apart from a few cases of seasickness, only Wally and Felix, our cat, have required medical attention. Both are now well again. Felix is growing up to be a real ship's cat, spending the day on deck, allowing most of us to stroke him, but always returning to Graham at night. Wally has recovered from his sudden collapse, which was brought on by overwork, and is now back and ruling over the galley.

By noon today we had logged 120 miles, a good enough run for Alan to radio Ronnie Forth in Plymouth, Massachusetts, that he could expect us during the first week in June. Alan said to me: "We have to do about another seventeen hundred miles in the trades and then about nine hundred to make our landfall." The experienced sailors consider we have been most fortunate in the weather, which, apart from a few days, has been kind to the ship. Of course, anything could happen during the next two or three weeks; we might run into a heavy storm or be becalmed. The first possibility is more probable than the second, but it is a comforting thought that if we do run into bad weather, the crew have had three weeks' practical experience and know their ship. They now feel confident of their ability to handle her during an emergency. This could not be said when we left England with a new ship and only three hours under sail in Tor Bay.

Everyone has settled down to the comfortable routine of life on board, which is punctuated by the watches and mealtimes. There is a great deal of talk about food, the sort of food we have enjoyed at home and hope to enjoy in America, but the meals Wally serves are plain, wholesome and filling. We have no complaints and there are still some apples and lemons left, although they will be finished within a few days.

This evening we decided to have a sing-song on deck and this resulted in nearly two hours of singing, under a full moon, songs of such sustained bawdyness that even the rough seamen who sailed with Captain Jones might have felt at home. But I would be giving a very wrong impression if I mentioned only the talk of good food and the singing of boisterous songs. Like the Pilgrims who sailed before us, we are deeply interested in the world we live in and the problems it poses.

Twenty-third Day, May 12. The day broke with fickle winds. The light airs held some promise of better breezes to come, but they petered out as the sun rose. Before the Sunday service I engaged in the routine of make-and-mend. Joe Meany and Joe Powell both stripped and had a bath on deck, pouring buckets of sea water over each other. Alan took the pram out on a line to take some film of the ship, and when he was coming back aboard, stumbled, lost his balance and was nearly pitched into the sea. Those of us who were looking over the side thought for a moment that we would have to dive in after him, but he recovered himself and surprisingly enough kept hold of all his equipment. Alan told me, just before we sailed, that he could not swim, but this does not prevent his putting the pram over the side whenever the opportunity arises.

After the morning service we sat on the quarter-deck. The ship rolled in the swell and Alan gave his last reading from Bradford:

> In sundry of these storms the winds were so fierce and the seas so high, as they could not bear a knot of sail, but were forced to hull for divers days together. And in one of them, as they thus lay at hull in a mighty storm, a lusty young man called John Howland, coming upon some occasion above the gratings was, with a seele of the ship, thrown into sea; but it pleased God that he caught hold of the topsail halyards which hung overboard and ran out at length. Yet he held his hold (though he was sundry fathoms under water) till he was hauled up

by the same rope to the brim of the water, and then with a boat
hook and other means got into the ship again and his life
saved. . . .

Being thus arrived in a good harbor, and brought safe to land,
they fell upon their knees and blessed the God of Heaven who
had brought them over the vast and furious ocean, and delivered
them from all the perils and miseries thereof, again to set their
feet on the firm and stable earth, their proper element. . . .

But here I cannot but stay and make a pause, and stand half
amazed at this poor people's present condition; and so I think
will the reader, too, when he well considers the same. Being
thus passed the vast ocean, and a sea of troubles before in their
preparation (as may be remembered by that which went before), they had now no friends to welcome them nor inns to
entertain or refresh their weatherbeaten bodies; no houses or
much less towns to repair to, to seek for succour.

At lunch Alan was in festive mood and produced a bottle of
Portuguese wine which had been given to him by his friend the
Portuguese Ambassador. First of all he toasted the Queen and
then the Portuguese, the latter "because they were fine sailors,
knew the Atlantic and taught the rest of the world a thing or two
about navigation in these parts." The other reason for his celebration is that we are nearly halfway. In the afternoon the ship
continued to roll and work her gear. Alan was on the poop scanning the horizon for a sign of the dark ripple of movement on the
water that was the forerunner of a wind when there was a snap
and the fore-topsail yard broke. Joe Lacey went aloft to inspect
the damage and reported that it had probably been caused by the
snatchlike motion of the ship caused by the swell. It seemed to
me that if the breathless calm and heavy swell persisted, all the
cordage and spars would be severely tested. The broken yard was
sent down, the sail unbent, and Edgar Mugridge and Joe worked
together repairing the spar, sweat pouring down both of them.
The spar had been dried out by the sun and was like matchwood.
Two hours later, at 6:30, the spar was ready to be sent aloft,
where conditions were anything but ideal, as the ship continued
to sway and roll violently. But as dusk approached, the wind
came and the fore-topsail was again helping us on our way
westward.

The Voyage

Twenty-fourth Day, May 13. Becalmed! Whenever I thought of sailing in *Mayflower*, I used to have a picture in my mind, a preview sponsored by my imagination, which was as clear as a newsreel: the little ship was always in the midst of mountainous seas; I stood on deck looking up, awed by the great waters, lashed by the wind and the rain; the sails strained at their masts; the rigging was drenched with the spray and taut to breaking point; and thus we rode the Atlantic. Never for one moment did I imagine that we would be crawling along as we have been today, sails drooping, and that far from feeling the rapier point of danger in my stomach, I would experience the ache of infinite boredom. I discussed this with Jan and he told me that the majority of voyages, even those most adventurous in retrospect, were made up in greater part of humdrum. We leaned over the side as we talked, staring at the water which slipped so idly by. "What is there in life that does not become boring?" he asked, and then went on to answer himself: "I have run before a storm for three weeks. Now, that sounds exciting, no doubt, and when you are working at the pumps, working for your life, it is exciting, but only at first. Even that can become monotonous, because pumping is monotonous whether or not your life is in danger." His thoughts went back to the war, to the time he, as a British agent, was dropped into occupied territory, only to be captured by the Germans and sent to a concentration camp outside Berlin to await execution. "Even waiting for death can become boring. Would you believe that? It is so. The Germans used to make me stand in the cold while they hanged my friends, the men who had been captured with me. Such a sight they thought would move me, make me talk. I remember one day they brought out a man whose face they had branded and whose back they had whipped and I had to stand there in the cold, waiting for them to put the rope round his neck and finish the job. Do you think I felt pity? Do you think I felt my time was nearer? I tell you I had seen so much, felt so much, I was bored and I only wanted them to get it over and done with." He stopped, turned, stared up at the sails, and I felt he was angry with himself for speaking about the past, so I changed the subject.

[159]

"You were pretty certain we were not going north about."

He laughed. "How so?"

"I have noticed that you only brought summer clothes."

"Well," he admitted, smiling, "I suppose I thought it most unlikely. Such a course was uncomfortable and uncertain and the prevailing winds were against us. You must count your blessings. We were lucky that the northerly wind which carried us away from Plymouth held. Every day it blew stronger and the seas were higher; it took us off to the southwest, so that in three days we were out of the Channel. After only four days we were off the coast of Spain, off Cape Finisterre. We went steadily southwest and the weather became warmer. Oh, I know you will say it's too warm, but believe me, it is better than the cold. We had one clear windy day after another, and when you look at our course on the chart, it is almost a straight line, no beating about."

"That's all very fine," I said, "but you're forgetting that it is over a week ago since the northerly that blew us southwest ran out."

"I am forgetting nothing," he said, "because six days ago we turned the corner and headed west towards America. You are forgetting the cross seas which made some of the boys so sick. It is in seas like that that we serve apricot soup in Danish ships. It tastes the same going both ways. Be happy there are no cross seas now."

I wanted to know how long he thought we would have to dawdle along before we found a good wind again. "Now," he said, "we are between one current of air and another, but we are moving all the time in the right direction. You will know soon enough when we are in the trades." He looked up at the blue void of the sky and gestured with his hand as though he were painting a vast picture. "When you see towering clouds, when the rain splashes down, when the flying fish come aboard during the night, then you know you are in the trades."

I decided I would try to contain myself and keep a watch upon the heavens for the signs given to me by Jan.

I also decided that I would not allow familiarity to rob me of

[160]

the flavor of our adventure. I listened to the sounds from below decks — the sound of voices coming up from the open hatches, the creaking and groaning of the timbers as the ship rolled with swelling sea — looked up at the crescent of our sails, and savored again the romance and drama of the situation: sailing day after day, over two thousand miles from home, a community of thirty-three men in a seventeenth-century ship, journeying in time, if you like, to the moments in history of Drake and Columbus. I thought of this when I stood high on the poop and I was no longer galled by our almost empty sails but watched proudly as her masts swayed majestically, and I looked westward to the horizon where we would make an old discovery anew.

Twenty-fifth Day, May 14. Now I am beginning to learn about the sea, to understand why Alan, and other experienced sailors on board, listen to me working out average speeds and arrival dates as though they were humoring a child. It seems that all the ocean charts, weather forecasts and past experience count for little: the sea has her own unpredictable moods. Take the past few hours as an example: early last night the air was heavy and charged with threat of storm, and then lightning zagged across the sky. Gordon Tenney hurried below decks and returned clothed in yellow oilskins and carrying his underwater camera. "Looks like we're going to get it at last," he said, peering into the black night. "Ah," I said knowingly, "the storm. The storm you have been waiting for." A flash of lightning lit the ship and I caught a glimpse of Gordon smiling, nodding. "Yes," he said, "looks like tonight's the night."

In the distance we heard the first muffled drum note of thunder rolling out of the skies and across the waters. I did not voice what was in my mind: that I did not really care if he did not get any storm pictures at all; that the ocean was big and our ark was small. But as though he sensed my thoughts, he said: "If a really big sea builds up, we'll float on the top, like a cork." The roll of thunder came closer, then there was a rush of cool air and we lifted our faces as the rain fell. Dick emerged on deck in oilskins. "Cost me twenty quid, oil impregnated silk," he said, "so I must give them a wetting." From the tiller flat I could hear the sound of voices raised, and the phrase repeated over and over: "It's raining, it's raining . . ." The crew began to run out on deck, those off watch who had been roused from their bunks by the news naked, carrying soap and towels, and drenched their bodies in the rain. I followed their example, took off my jeans and let the rain wash away the sweat, the stickiness of salt water from my body. The shower, for that is all it proved to be, lasted for only a quarter of an hour and was followed by a fresh breeze and a calm sea. The sails filled and the ship began to move more swiftly through the water, and then, with the wind coming right astern, to sail faster than she had done since we left Plymouth, at about nine knots.

Gordon, deprived of his longed-for storm, glumly retired to his bunk to get out of his oilskins. Stuart stood watching the bow waves in the moon and pronounced dramatically: "See how she goes. But I say we have seen nothing yet, seven knots, eight, nine; she's doing that now, but she'll do better. You just wait and see if she doesn't do twelve!" But we never found out, for three hours later, after she had logged 25 miles for the watch, her speed had dropped to about three knots. I stayed on deck talking to Joe Powell, delaying turning in, although I was physically tired, because the changing mood of the sea made me restless. Joe talked about the time he was filming in Ischia, doubling underwater work for the stars. "Those Italian girls are lovely when they are young, say about eighteen," he recalled. "I can tell you our eyes opened twice as wide as normal when we first arrived. They used to come to talk to us wearing a handkerchief round their loins and not much more round their breasts. They used to clack around us dressed like that in their wooden-soled beach shoes, but the boys found out it didn't pay to get too friendly. Before you knew where you were, the whole family appeared — mama, papa, brothers and sisters, uncles and aunts." Getting to sleep took longer than usual, and I wished I had not talked to Joe. My mind was nearer the Mediterranean than the Atlantic.

I slept late and it was nearly ten o'clock when I stumbled out on deck to find that the sails were flapping aimlessly and we were becalmed. For the first time I felt that Alan's usual calm was ruffled. He stood for hours on the highest part of the poop, scanning the skies, watching for a breath of air, and was twice tantalized as over on the horizon, to port, the wind blew and the white clouds moved impudently along. When a breath of air came our way, it took the ship about and we began to drift imperceptibly towards Africa. I heard Andy Lindsay mutter something bitterly about the wind missing us because we were in the valley, and Scottie, watching the slow drift of the current, remarked that we were a Kon-Tiki with sails. Nevertheless, most of the crew were in remarkably good humor and I found that some of my normal impatience had deserted me. One of the watch spotted a large fish astern. We thought it was a shark, as it swam a few feet below the surface right under our stern. We got Edgar to bend a nail into a hook, fitted it to a line, and David went up onto the poop. The fish took the hook, which was baited with a flying fish, but David struck too soon and the fish, which turned out to be a dolphin, twisted free when it was almost on board. I felt secretly pleased as it swam swiftly away to freedom.

During the afternoon we took the opportunity to stop some holes amidships. Canada went over the side and, with the help of Stuart and the mate, calked a seam. They used handfuls of porridge and cotton to fill a hole, and then sealed it with putty. A small brown bird flew in quite close to satisfy its curiosity and Maitland identified it for me as a common sea bird, Wilson's petrel. It had been following us for several days, he said, but had never before approached near enough for identification. Our run until noon was 89 miles logged. Today it cannot be more than a tenth of that, but who am I to say? During the night we may be carried along by wind that will prove Stuart made no idle boast about twelve knots.

The Voyage

Twenty-sixth Day, May 15. Becalmed. A burning sun, a lazy swelling sea and not a breath of wind. Almost at first light the Captain decided to use the ship's working boat, which has a two-cylinder diesel engine, and we swung it over the side, using the derrick. Jumbo, as chief engineer, was in charge. Canada went along as his assistant and Gordon, of course, was there with his camera. We fastened a tow line, because at least it would give us the feeling that we were making some reply to the unrelenting stillness of the skies. The decks were burning hot underfoot and I was tempted to wear some shoes, but instead I sat on the hatch cover with Ted Edwards and Doc Stevens and we worked together franking ship's mail. We are carrying about 100,000 envelopes with an illustration of the ship on the front and the words "*Mayflower* Ship's Mail." The Postmaster General issued us a special maiden-voyage cancellation mark to frank our mail, so each piece is a collector's item. We are sending them to all the people who have supported the project in England, to a list of nearly a thousand sent to me by Ronnie Forth of people actively associated with our welcome and to collectors from America and England who have written in and sent their addresses. The Captain appointed Peter Padfield Chief of Post Office and asked us to finish all franking in ten days so we would leave reasonable time to clean the ship up for arrival. There was one envelope over which I took particular care: it was addressed to the President of the United States and contained greetings from Sir Francis de Guingand and news of how the Mayflower Trust hoped to give practical expression to the fostering of Anglo-American relations. It was also a letter of introduction for me to the President. I was not sure whether I should send it through the mails or deliver it personally. If I took it myself, it would not need the stamp and cancellation, but I remembered seeing some drawings of *Mayflower* done by the President's grandson David, and I thought that the President might like it for him.

We worked on the franking until eleven o'clock and then the heat became too much for us and we decided to have a swim. The work boat was pulling as hard as she could, but the ship was not making more than about a mile an hour, moving imperceptibly through the sea. Everyone else seemed to have the same idea at the same time. Most of us got into our swimming trunks, but Joe Powell and Graham Nunn decided to dispense with such frivolities and dived naked off the fo'c'sle head. Before I had a chance to follow them, the mate appointed me shark lookout. I took this job seriously, scanning a circle of water round the ship for the sign of a fin while Joe Meany and John Winslow entered into a high-diving competition from the ratlines. Both Joe and John proved to be excellent divers and it was apparent that Joe was also a first-class swimmer. He told me afterwards that he took it very seriously. "It is the best all-round sport," he said, "one in which you use all the muscles in your body. I like diving, but I don't take it too seriously. I know I'd never make top form in diving, but in swimming I think I might." Joe likes to do everything well and his assessment of his own ability had not a touch of conceit but was a simple statement of fact.

After lunch, Ike Marsh, although he cannot swim, decided that the cool blue waters were too inviting to be missed. He went over the side and we tied some rope around him and played him like a big fish. He swallowed a lot of water, and as he had lungs instead of gills, was soon protesting he had had enough.

Just a whisper of wind stirred in the midafternoon and we took the work boat off tow and used her to take everyone in turn for a tour around the *Mayflower*. We had none of us seen her sailing from the fishes' point of view, and I was very proud of her as she nosed gently along in the swell. Edgar Mugridge was sitting beside me and he kept on repeating over and over again: "Her's a real beauty, I'll tell you."

Our noon run was only 25 miles, which is more than I estimated. In the evening the wind freshened and there seemed hope that we would begin to move again at a decent rate. The hot sun, the cool waters, the chance for a swim are all very well for a day or so, but if for any longer I think tempers might get a little frayed. Thirty-three men have been twenty-five days at sea, and no one minds another three weeks so long as we are getting somewhere. Even Jan said to me in the evening: "There was, of course, a reason for the invention of the steamship."

Twenty-seventh Day, May 16. Despite a weather forecast of an easterly force three or five wind, which would have done very nicely, we were becalmed again, the sea a sullen lake. I asked Jumbo Goddard, our engineer, a man who has sailed for twenty-five of his forty-nine years, how he accounted for the failure of the weather to live up to the forecasts now coming out of Washington. "Oh," he exclaimed, as though I had asked a surprisingly simple question, "they just look at the map and see that's where the trades are supposed to be and invent the forecast. They don't really expect anyone to be where we are, so they are usually safe whatever they say." During the morning we had a cloudburst and caught buckets of water, which we used to wash ourselves and our clothes. I ran out on deck with a bottle of shampoo and had a wonderful bath which was interrupted only once when I had to haul on the ropes. Jumbo is the most philosophical man on board, the least disturbed by the past three days when we have had to drift with the ocean current and accept the mean light airs which have taken us off course and further south.

"We've been terribly lucky so far," he assured me, "so you don't want to let a bit of fluky weather get you down. Two or three days more and you'll see. We'll be bowling along again." He is most favorably impressed with the ship and asserts that her only defects are those to be expected in a ship which is an honest attempt to reproduce seventeenth-century ship design. "Her beams are crying out for oil," he said, "and her paint is getting thin. Of course, this hot sun is bound to open her up, but though there are a few leaks, we've managed to seal most of them. We wouldn't have them if this ship was built of seasoned timber, but you just can't get the stuff these days. Another thing: all the fastenings are sealed with pitch and a lot of it is coming out; this wouldn't happen if you'd used dowls, but pitch is right for the period and wooden pegs are not."

[166]

The Voyage

There is one advantage in being becalmed: there is little to do
on watches, so we spend a good deal of the time talking, getting
to know each other, and it becomes more apparent every day
that this *Mayflower* has a life and personality of her own, inde-
pendent of her predecessor. Some of the crew are, after their
own fashion, Pilgrims. Nearly all the ship's company, I have
found, hold strong beliefs upon one subject or another, which
they are quite ready to proclaim and defend if necessary. Doc
Stevens, for example, is a fifth-generation South African, but he
could not stomach the Malan government's policy of *apartheid*
and rather than compromise he left his home, as the Pilgrims did,
to work where he could express his views in freedom. He has not
found life in England easy, at £700 a year with a wife and four
children to support. But he does not regret the material cost and
the emotional stress that leaving the land of his birth entailed.
We lay on deck, eyes half closed to the brazen sun, as he talked.
"It's no use, boy. They won't face up to the issue; and it is just
this: is the white man prepared to live in a bastard society? No?
Then he must get out. All the rest of the talk about bringing them
along until they're on our level culturally or economically just
won't wash. The black man doesn't want freedom in ten or
fifteen or twenty years' time. He wants it now, like they've got it
on the Gold Coast. And you can't blame him for that, because we
would want the same, for the same reasons. They must face up to
it, man. Make up their minds that that is the issue. Are they going
to live with the black man or not? There's no compromise and it
is the only issue. I suppose I should have stayed and become a
political martyr. But that's not for me; not with four children.
So I got out, and I live my life in a working-class practice, and
when I get time off, I do a bit of sailing."

"Like this?" I asked.

"Oh, no, this should go on forever. I don't mind how long it
takes for us to get there. But I'll tell you what . . ."

But he never did, for he remembered that Joe Lacey had a
corn to be removed, and he was off 'tween decks to fetch his
scalpel, some cotton wool and surgical spirit, and we gathered
round to watch the operation.

The Voyage

Our run until noon was 25 miles. I could not for the life of me believe we had made so much way, and when I marked our position on the map, I saw that drift and contrary breaths of air had taken us still further off course and to the south.

Twenty-eighth Day, May 17. After a poor week's progress of only 480 miles *Mayflower* stands dipping in her own blue image of calm and almost stagnant sea. Our days' runs of 120 miles, 95, 80, 93, 24, 49 and 19 miles make a depressing aggregate, and even Alan finds the behavior of the usually dependable trades a little puzzling. He looked quite serious when he said to me: "No doubt about it, Warwick, the trades are taking time off. Perhaps they don't find enough work to do these days and have grown tired."

Meanwhile, the crew continue to make the most of the calm and seize the opportunity for another swim overside in the beautifully warm and translucent waters. Once again we posted a shark lookout and also kept a watch for the long trailers of Portuguese men-of-war, which have a poisonous sting.

This morning we sighted a ship. David Thorpe, who was on lookout, first saw her breaking the fine circle of the horizon astern. Everyone came out on deck, and when she came nearer, we identified her as the Italian liner *Lucania*. Jimmy Horrocks said she must have wanted to surprise us, because, although he had been in touch with several ships in our vicinity, she was not one of them. Her passengers and crew crowded onto her decks, and even onto her bridge, to have a sight of us. While I was running up the Red Duster, Alan said: "There must be at least a thousand aboard her and all of them are taking a look at us." She came quite near and circled us twice, sounding blasts on her whistle as if she were exclaiming in wonder and delight at the ageless beauty of our sails. She circled us at what seemed tremendous speed. We were making no more than two knots at the time and lurched in her wash. Later I said to Fred Edwards: "Did you see that girl in the red sweater, aft?" "Yes," said Fred, "I certainly did." "It may interest you to know," I said confidentially, "that she was looking and waving straight at me." Fred considered this information carefully, and shook his head. "Not when I saw her," he insisted. "When I saw her, she was looking straight at me." I soon discovered that every member of the ship's company believed the girl in red was waving at him, all except our Captain and I forbore asking him.

Twenty-ninth Day, May 18. This morning I was out on deck at five o'clock ship's time to see the dawn, and I had what I believe to be a most unusual experience. The sky was almost cloudless, the sea a placid swell, the air cool and clear. Along the gentle curve of the horizon to the east there began a brilliant display of color as the sun's rays slanted over the edge of the world. First there was a light which was frosted blue, and this was followed by tints of red and orange. Then, for a fraction of time, there seemed to be no light in the sky until the eyes were dazzled by a flash of light, a green flash of such depth and purity of color it seemed as though we were witnessing Genesis. This green light flashed for about four or five seconds before the sun began its slow climb into the heavens, as if shining for the first time on the first day.

The morning brought smooth seas and calm to light airs. The ship made little progress and for most of the day we were busy finishing the franking of ship's mail. When the last envelope was done, there was a cheer from the party working on the fo'c'sle head; they descended to the waist and hoisted Peter Padfield, who was in charge of mail, shoulder high. For a moment I thought they were going to cast him overboard, they were in such high spirits that a tiresome task was completed. But an order from the Captain to splice the main brace diverted their attention, and they crowded round the galley while Wally made a rum punch.

We started discussing what had been done to alter the weather. First of all, five days ago, Adrian Small had looked up at the wind-thin sky, taken out his clasp knife and stuck it in a crack in the mainmast. There was, he explained, a belief among sailors that a knife in the mast brought the winds. This one didn't, so yesterday David Cauvin, the son of the senior pilot of Cape Town, had whistled. Whistling is, of course, forbidden, but the ship's officers pretended not to hear. They knew of another superstition: that whistling makes the winds blow. This time it didn't. "I can't understand it," David said. "The last time I whistled for the wind was when I was an A.B. in the Dutch period ship, the one-third-scale replica of the *Drommedaris*. That was five years ago." This evening, a third and final wind maker was tried. David climbed out onto the forestay and tied one of his sea boots there, and it worked. Within a few minutes the wind freshened sufficiently for the studsail to be hoisted and we were soon bowling along at four knots. I remonstrated with David, and demanded to know why he had not used the boot sooner. "No good, man," he said. "You can't use a boot until you've waited for seven days." They have an answer to everything, these sailors, but whether or not the boot has anything to do with it, the point is that the wind is now blowing from the northeast and my optimism has returned.

Thirtieth Day, May 19. We are no longer becalmed. There is now the suggestion that the trades are with us again. Not in any force, but sufficient, in the Captain's words, for the ship to "ghost along." Indeed, she has shown us time and again that it required the merest breath of air to keep her on the move. The days of being becalmed were beginning to pall; the sea looked like an oily blue jelly; the decks were weeping black tears of pitch and the rigging sagged with idleness, dried by the sun. The strakes in the masts and spars were dark wounds aggravated by the sapping heat.

I had almost forgotten it was Sunday — the days had begun to telescope one into the other — but at breakfast Jan said: "No need to wear fancy dress today." I said limply, trying to eat a month-old egg: "Oh, it's Sunday." "Yes," said Jan, "it's Sunday and you should be happy. We are really moving now. Listen, can't you hear?" So I listened and there it was, the muted but reassuring voice of our wake, bubbling and gurgling again. I was glad that it was not necessary to change into seventeenth-century rig, and so, I think, was everyone else. The thick woolen stockings, cambric shirts and breeches would have been trying to our tempers in the heat.

Alan took the usual service on the quarter-deck and radiated good humor and confidence. "We're on the last leg, going downhill," he said. "With all the usual reservations I expect us to cover the last two thousand miles in twenty days. We are taking the route Columbus took, and from now on you should see more and more gulfweed. Columbus saw this weed and thought he was near land. What he didn't know was that the gulfweed he saw was on its second time round and was traveling west with the surface current. But there is plenty of reason for believing that Columbus was preceded by other pioneers, fishermen sailing from Portugal and the Basque Biscayan ports to the Grand Banks of Newfoundland for cargoes of cod.

"None of these ships ran the downhill way before the trade winds as we are doing, because they knew where the cod were and they were not to be found in warm waters. It was Columbus's good fortune that he stumbled upon the outlying islands of a great continent. He thought he had reached the Indies, and he went on thinking he had reached the Indies for the rest of his life, for which reason and for many others he was a source of trial to those who had to work with him. Since he was so loath to cross the equator that he never once sailed south of the line, his westward voyage towards India brought him by chance upon the discovery of the Americas. Leaving the latitude of southern Portugal, going south for a little for the true trade wind and then running west before it, he could scarcely go wrong. This achievement was remarkable and its results incalculable, but it is no detraction from it to offer some honor to the courageous Portuguese mariners who first dared to cross the wild western ocean

[171   ]

regularly in small vessels to seek and find cargoes of homely cod."

All day we relaxed, sunning ourselves, confident that in the true trade winds we too, like Columbus, could scarcely go wrong.

This evening I took a mental snapshot of our ship and her company. Alan was on the poop, where on the aft side he had made a bench seat, and he sat there hatless, in his shirt sleeves, lost in thought, but coming now and then to the surface with a sailor's reflex to check the set of the sails. David Thorpe, bearded, in a white cloche hat and long shorts, was at the wheel, looking like a cut from a Victorian print illustrating "sailing at Cowes." Jan, in tropical kit and beret, was pacing up and down the deck with a stolid, measured pace like a London policeman's. It is interesting to me to see how the crew show respect for his seamanship, for although he is listed in the ship's articles as our third mate, they address him as Captain Junker.

All, except the previous watch, who were in their bunks 'tween decks, were on deck or in the fo'c'sle head.

Doc Stevens sat, his legs dangling over the edge of the ship's work boat, writing his journal. I thought that with his finely drawn bearded features, searching eyes topped with the white operating cap, he looked like a fakir. Edgar Mugridge, who seems always to be sawing wood, making shelves, so that I have rarely seen his dumpy blue-overalled figure relaxing, was surprisingly playing with Felix, using a cork suspended on a piece of string. "The way she prances about I reckon she is a tom," he said.

Wally, in his white cook's cap put on for Sundays, was seated on a packing case discussing the next day's menu with Dick. The latter, naked except for a tattered pair of green shorts, his beard thicker than ever, sipped a mug of beer, listened to Wally, nodded and grunted assent and smiled. Scottie was sprawled on the boat deck, lying on his stomach, his body tanned honey brown, talking to Lee, who was tanned so deeply he looked more like Othello every day, except he wears a tartan shirt. Adrian, bare-chested, stroking his red beard, was discussing with Harry Sowerby Nicholls's *Seamanship and Viva-Voce Guide,* published in 1907.

Harry, a Cape Horner who sailed with Alan on the *Conrad*, keeps to himself, making rare excursions into conversation and then only, as in this instance, when it concerns the sea and sailing ships. Beric Watson was strumming away on his guitar, leaning against the port rail for'ard. In the fo'c'sle head Joe Lacey and Ike Marsh were busy trimming the navigation lights ready for sunset. In the fast-fading light John Winslow and Graham Nunn were playing chess, and Stuart Upham was trying to finish a drawing of the mainsails before the sun bounced down out of sight over the horizon. In the Great Cabin Joe Meany was efficiently clearing away and tidying up, but some of the crew still lingered around the tea table. We had had tinned salmon, onions and beetroot, bread and jam, oatmeal biscuits and tea. Godfrey Wicksteed was telling how he had once taken a party of thirty schoolboys on a factory visit. When the time came to leave, the management gave each boy a sample of their product — a hacksaw. Wicksteed described his trepidation as he sat in the back of a bus on the way home with his thirty boys, all of them itching to use their hacksaws. "I had visions of the bus disintegrating before my eyes," he said, "and to tell you the truth, I had a powerful urge to use my hacksaw, too."

While he spoke, Jimmy Horrocks sat at the Marconi Trans-arctic set, headphones on for a message from the *National Unity*, his previous ship, two hundred miles NNE bound for Venezuela with a cargo of iron ore.

Gordon, for a rare moment, was not "taking a picture," but discussing the merits and demerits of electronic flash as compared with flash bulbs.

The ship swayed peacefully on her way, the sound of our voices and the noise of our wake broken only by the rich mellow note of the ship's bell.

Thirty-first Day, May 20. During the night Adrian saw a large black fish by our stern. He shone his flashlight from the quarter-deck, but the beam did not reach far enough, some twenty feet from eye level. The brief glimpse he had of the fish in the moonlight made him think it was a large shark, but upon reflection, he decided that he had seen a blackfish, a species of whale which grows to a length of forty feet.

Every so often I say to myself: "I must remember today, all the moments of today, because they are the best." This feeling is not prompted by any particular incident or spectacular sight, but rather by a heightened sense of well-being, of feeling especially alive. Today was such a day. We were making about four knots; the ship seemed almost to glide along with scarcely any movement, certainly no sway, through the flat blue waters. Dick said to me as he stood, arms folded, outside the galley, warming himself in the sun: "Warwick, this is millionaire living," and I, feeling the caress of wind, a feather's touch which kept us cool, nodded agreement. There was, of course, the normal ship's routine to carry out. We have begun painting the ship. I took a pot of white paint and a wonderfully pliable long brush and thoroughly enjoyed myself, tongue in cheek, lost somewhere between brush and paint and the surface of the wood, and thought that even ships' painters could feel as Gauguin did about the pleasures of painting.

John Winslow and Beric Watson went aloft with Godfrey Wicksteed to adjust the main-topsail saddle, which had slipped, and I noted how much at home they have become aloft. Lee Israel, who has disclosed a wide knowledge and interest in marine life, made a net and spent hours catching pieces of gulfweed floating near the ship. We put it in a pail of sea water and from time to time Lee proceeded to clamber back from his position on the channels to inspect his catch and to give a running commentary to his self-appointed aides, bucket holders, watchers and weed examiners, such as myself, Julian and Joe Meany. "This," said Lee in his deep brown voice to which there was now added professorial overtones, "is sargassum weed, otherwise known as gulfweed. It is, as you see, a light brown-yellow weed bearing air vessels containing spores." He paused while we nodded and grunted our interest, and continued: "It cannot increase unless it fastens itself on to something else. It originates in the Sargasso Sea and the specimens we have here have traveled round the Gulf Stream and back, and then back again. Lots of animal life rides along with the weed and that is what I am looking for, and in particular the sea horse." We did not find any sea horses, but we did find some pulsing, ugly, dun-colored mollusk from two inches to a quarter of an inch in length. These creatures had six appendages and a crude mouth, and when touched, contracted into a tight, fleshy ball. They moved by waving their appendages through the water and had the ability to attach themselves to the seaweed with any part of their bodies. We caught three fish: one of them an angler, which had protuberances on the head like a fishing rod and ragged fins which looked like weed. Lee explained that this species became invisible as it traveled along with the weed and caught its prey simply by opening its mouth and letting other fish swim to their doom. We caught two of these anglers and a pipefish. This latter, which was almost white, looked like a miniature swordfish and was only about half an inch in length. There were also two varieties of baby crab and a velella, which looks like a Portuguese man-o'-war, the difference being that it has a blue sail and is smaller.

"There's a wonderful world in the sea," said Lee and I nodded, with a mental reservation that there was nothing quite so wonderful as the world above it, especially our world of wood and billowing canvas. I thought for a long time about the mollusk; it seemed a cruel joke, a dark alley of creation. I wondered if I had seen a glimpse of hell, to be a mollusk, going along forever, drifting with the weed, round and round, the monotony broken only by a passing ship.

Thirty-second Day, May 21. We have logged over 100 miles for the day's run, 101 miles, to be exact. This enabled me to make a mark on the Great Cabin chart recording our run, a mark, for a change, which was visible to the naked eye!

Jumbo Goddard, whose mutton-chop whiskers increase his likeness to John Bull, gave me a can of boiled linseed oil this morning and put me to work painting the beams, masts and hanging knees. This is the second application of oil they have had, but the timber is so dried out it soaks up the oil. Jumbo and Canada spent the day cleaning out the galley, scraping the grease-blackened deck, cleaning the stove and sink. This meant the galley was out of commission and we had to have cold food, but I was not sorry and thought it a welcome change in view of the weather — 80 in the shade at midmorning.

In the evening I persuaded Jumbo to talk to me about himself, because of all the ship's company Jumbo has led a life most devoted to pure adventure. A heavily built man with a bellow of a laugh and a deep voice that is heard from one end of the ship to the other, he has been a sailor, gold prospector, flyer, engineer, racing yachtsman, old-car buff, traction driver and a shipbuilder.

Thirty-third Day, May 22. Although Dick Brennan looks and sometimes talks like a rough, tough pirate, underneath, and not far below the surface, he is a gentle, sentimental man. For the past few days he has been telling us all separately, and with attempted casualness, that he would be having his birthday on board. Not that he placed much importance on the event, mind you, but he thought you might like to know as a matter of small, insignificant and passing interest. "I never celebrate it myself," he said. "In fact, I often forget which day it is." He had obviously decided that on this occasion he should not be allowed to forget, and we quickly made up our minds to give him a party. At midnight, with Dick scarcely concealing an "I-wonder-if-they've-remembered" expression, we showed him we had not forgotten. I gave him a numbered and signed copy of Sir Winston Churchill's *History of the English-Speaking Peoples* which had been presented to the project by the publishers as a gift for worthy recipients. I felt sure that Sir Winston would have considered Dick in that category. Wally invited Dick to go 'tween decks and there they split a bottle of champagne. I reflected that Wally was nothing if not a practical man, as his gift quenched his own thirst as well as Dick's. Then Dick came back to the Great Cabin and polished off a bottle of Scotch with Jumbo, Canada, Julian, Stuart and Mait. I settled for some lime juice, which, incidentally, Wally tells me is running short and will not last out the voyage. Some of the crew are by no means sad at this news, for they really believe Wally when he tells them it stops the sap from rising and they are fearful the results may be permanent.

Stuart gave Dick a present of a water color of the ship in full sail which he had made on board. The celebration of Dick's birthday soon developed into an all-day event. Joe Meany gave him three bottles of beer, Doc Stevens two packets of boiled sweets, Graham Nunn two hundred cigarettes — he has stopped smoking — and Alan gave him three bottles of rum.

In the evening, at 7:30, the big party began. Wally had used the rum to make a fruit cup, and this was served with snacks, biscuits and sausage rolls. Then came the big surprise — a birthday cake complete with icing. But this was only a mock cake, built over a tin, so that when Dick tried to cut the cake, the knife bent and nearly broke. We sang "Happy Birthday" and "For He's a Jolly Good Fellow" and called for a speech, but we had almost rendered our old pirate speechless, and I know he was grateful that only those near him saw the moistness in his eyes. He managed to get out: "Thank you, and that's all the speech you're getting from me." We wound up the evening with a sing-song, with Dick croaking "Side by Side." We all sang a song in turn, including Joe Meany, who acted as caller for that charming Kentucky mountain song "On Top of Old Smoky."

Alan stood on the quarter-deck looking down at the scene; we were gathered on the starboard side of the waist, the only light that of the moon and a small torch which I shone on the young American leading the singing. Dick said to me afterwards: "I'll never forget this birthday." Neither will we, for it was all our birthdays.

The Voyage

Thirty-fourth Day, May 23. Despite my expectations of faster runs, we are dawdling along in poor trades. Our run today was only 61 miles, but Alan seemed confident that we would improve on this. He explained to me that our average since leaving Plymouth was 100 miles a day, and he sees no reason why we should fall below that. This morning the bonnet went on the foresail. This, of course, gives us a greater sail area, and means we shall make more of the wind we are getting.

There were some porpoises playing around our bow this morning, but they did not stay with us for long — I suppose we were too slow for them! Alan told me he has seen two more blackfish, the species of small whale Adrian thought he spotted the other night.

This evening the weather report gave a storm warning with force ten winds, about sixty-mile-an-hour gales, blowing north of us, but sufficiently far enough away for us not to be unduly concerned at present. This news naturally prompted a discussion as to how the ship would stand up to such weather. My own view is that we would be hard put to survive. Our superstructure is of soft wood and might not stand up to heavy seas, and I also wonder if there might not be a serious possibility of our masts being carried away. Of course, we might get through a bad storm by putting out a sea anchor and running before it, but this would take us hundreds of miles off course. At least we would live to tell the tale. Still, as I have said, there seems to be every likelihood by present indications that the storm is too far north to worry us. The forecast for elsewhere over the Atlantic and Caribbean generally is easterly winds, force three to five and occasionally six, and southwesterly winds, force three to five, over the Gulf of Mexico.

There was salt pork from the barrel for tea today, but I did not find it very appetizing. Alan had two helpings and so did Godfrey Wicksteed, but Mait, Gordon and Dick shared my opinion that so far as barreled pork was concerned, the square-rigged sailors could have all the helpings they wanted, barrel and all!

The Voyage

Thirty-fifth Day, May 24. This has been a very quiet week and we are now some 1800 miles from Nantucket Lightship. Despite weather forecasts from Washington about wind forces three, four, five and even six, the northeast trades steadfastly refuse to blow. The beautiful blue sea is more often marked by drifting golden weed than by the whitecaps of breaking water. Alan said this morning: "The Pilgrims should have come this way instead of by the boisterous and ice-littered northern route." The ship has been out thirty-four days today, has sailed just over 3400 miles, and we probably have another fifteen or sixteen days at sea. Steady, slow progress is all very well, but it can get on your nerves and it is beginning to get on mine. This wooden world becomes smaller as the number of days at sea increases. We live very much on top of one another; there is little privacy, so I have come to appreciate Alan's point about not taking women, although I miss their company. There is one crew member, Jumbo, who finds this life entirely to his liking and cannot hide his pleasure at every sign of calm. John Winslow, however, agrees with me that people are getting a little edgy and says that he has now reached the stage when he is counting the days to landfall. I asked him if he is going to make his career in the Royal Navy and he told me that he would consider the matter when he returned home from *Mayflower*. "There are one or two points I have to iron out with them," he said, then gave me some surprising information about the Navy's attitude to the *Mayflower*. About a year ago he told them he had been selected for a place in the crew and to represent the Winslow family who were aboard the first *Mayflower*. He explained that the project had the support of a number of public men and hoped to make a considerable contribution towards Anglo-American relations. Would they, he asked, give him six months' leave to sail on the ship and show the flag for the Royal Navy and for his family? He recalled a recent incident when some R.N. officers had sailed a junk home from Hong Kong and had been given leave to do so, part pay, and had retained their seniority. Surely, he reasoned, he could expect similar treatment for *Mayflower*. But, oh, dear, no! He was told that if he sailed on *Mayflower,* he must expect to receive no pay and to lose six months' seniority! The fact that the Prime Minister and other members of the government had sent messages of encouragement to the project did not alter the attitude of my Lords of the Admiralty.

While John was telling me about his troubles, Canada came into the Great Cabin and stood listening. When John finished, he said: "You should join the Royal Canadian Navy. They've given me six months' leave, full pay, and I keep my seniority." I don't think any Navy, even the British Navy, can afford to lose keen, efficient officers, young men with energy and imagination, like John Winslow, but they're going the right way about it. The trouble with the Lords of the Admiralty, of course, is that they are not sea-minded. Fortunately, not everyone shared their point of view. John showed me a letter which was evidence that at least one officer in the American Navy was interested in the project and prepared to help John when we arrived in America. The letter, personal and unofficial, was from Vice-Admiral Austin K. Doyle. He wrote:

I was interested to learn from your letter of 13th February that "Mayflower" is expected to arrive Plymouth by 1st June. It is a remarkable achievement for a group to devise this second voyage and I can assure you that all my countrymen will follow your course with great interest. My wife is a member of the Mayflower Society and of course has received a number of communications from their national headquarters on the progress of the preparations for the undertaking.

The nearest station of my command to Plymouth is at South Weymouth, Mass., just outside Boston. I will notify the commanding officer, Captain L. S. Melsom, U.S.N.R., of your expected arrival and will ask him to set up a "training flight" for you to bring you down here. We will be very glad to see you and even though the last British student was graduated at Corpus last month there are a considerable number of Canadians now in our training pipeline.

As an added reminder for me, please let me know when you can be free to start on a tour of the Training Command. I can assure you that you will receive a warm welcome everywhere.

The Voyage

Thirty-sixth Day, May 25. It was hot and sultry in the morning, with dark clouds to windward, and we were making only about one knot. I felt most depressed and after a quick turn round the deck and a wash in a bucket of tepid sea water, went back to my cabin and lay in my bunk and reflected upon the uncertainties of travel by sailing ship. It seemed to me that there was no end to our voyage and I imagined that the interest in *Mayflower* must be diminishing on both sides of the Atlantic. For a moment I played with the ridiculous thought that someone in England might have built another *Mayflower* and arrived in America before us. Then at eleven o'clock I heard shouts from on deck and ran out to see what was happening, expecting a ship had been sighted. But we had another sort of visitor; a school of dolphins was on our port side forward, swinging along, six of them, just under the surface of the water. They had green bodies, little white flippers and golden-brown tails. They stayed with us for the best part of an hour, swimming up and down and around the ship trying to make out what sort of queer fish had come into their midst. The entire ship stopped work to advise our fishermen, David Cauvin and Adrian Small, how to bait their line. At first they tried salt pork, but the dolphins had the same attitude to salt pork as I did, so a bit of white bunting was tried and then they progressed to a spinner made out of a tin. But there were no bites and the fish swam gaily away. After lunch we were becalmed and Alan put out the pram so he could take some photographs — a dolphin's eye view of the ship. There was a very heavy swell, almost certainly the result of the storm which has been blowing to our north, and the pram nearly capsized.

When Alan came back aboard, he let Gordon and then me go out in the pram, and I had been out for only a matter of minutes when Alan shouted for us to come in: dark ripples on the water from the northeast had signaled a blow. I was hardly aboard with my oarsman, Andy Bell, before the ship began to move, and it was soon apparent, with the appearance of whitecaps, that we were going to make up for lost time.

[181   ]

The Voyage

My mood changed as quickly as the weather and I was all smiles and renewed enthusiasm as I went up on the quarter-deck to help the mate put over the hand log line. We were making nearly six knots and as night came, there was no sign of the wind dropping or our speed slackening. The crew were put in such good humor by this improvement in the weather that they played a joke on the cook, a daring venture on any ship, let alone a sailing ship. They stole his rock cakes, which he calls tab nabs. When he found them missing, he went straight down to the mess deck in the tiller flat and demanded their return. "I don't mind giving anyone anything within reason," he said angrily, "but I won't stand for gannets. I know every single item in my galley and my store and I can feel if even a lump of sugar is missing. There are twelve tab nabs missing and you'll suffer if they are not found." Canada acted as spokesman. "Don't worry, Wally," he said. "If you're short of tab nabs, we have plenty. How many did you say were missing?" "Twelve," repeated Wally firmly, glaring at the occupants of the mess deck. "Well, here you are, Wally," said Canada, producing a plateful of tab nabs from under the table, "just count them." Wally counted them. There were twenty-four. This was too much for him. "Who," said Wally fiercely, "did it?" The crew pretended to misunderstand. "If you want tab nabs, Wally," they said, "you only have to come to us." "Come to you, you lot of blackguards! I'll have your lives!" "Please, Wally," Jumbo interjected, "what more can you want? You've lost twelve tab nabs and we've given you two dozen. If ever you're short of anything, you have only to come to us. This must be the best service you have ever had from a mess deck." But Wally did not stay to hear any more. He went back to his galley and began to check his stores, a puzzled man. I don't think he will ever be able to live the tab nabs down, although I'm sure he has ideas for reprisals which will be hard on the crew's bellies.

Our run today was 67 miles, so our average has fallen slightly below 100 miles. However, if the present blow continues, we shall not only maintain our average but improve upon it. You see what an optimist I am!

The Voyage

Thirty-seventh Day, May 26. The sun was almost directly overhead, our course west by north, a half north, our day's run 119 miles, which I find most satisfactory. Alan said: "If she would sail a bit to windward, we could come north a little bit, but anyway, in about three days I expect we'll get our northing." He is bubbling with confidence and I only hope that the winds are more constant than they have been. We are now about five hundred miles east of the Barbados, in latitude 21 and as far south as we shall have to go. We tuned in on the Transarctic and heard "the voice of the Caribbean," Radio Trinidad, which included a commercial (choral music and a syrupy voice) for a mortician.

This was our fifth Sunday at sea and Fred Edwards has been in a state of suspense, waiting for the reply to a cable he sent two days ago to his fiancée Jocelyn in Liverpool. The cable was the outcome of a talk he and I had last Sunday when the third and final reading of the banns for his marriage was given by Alan. "Why don't you marry Jocelyn aboard *Mayflower?*" I asked.

"For one thing, the master of a ship can't marry people," replied Fred. "There is a popular misconception that he can, but it isn't so."

"But you could get around that. Have a justice of the peace perform the ceremony on board, between Plymouth and New York. How about that? Would Jocelyn agree?"

He turned the idea over for a moment, smiled doubtfully and said: "She might, but you know how it is. A girl likes a wedding at home, a reception for her relations and friends. But that's not the whole of it. Jocelyn has set her heart on a church wedding and I don't think I could change her."

But I could see that the idea appealed to him. It would mean seeing her sooner than he could have hoped. "You could have a wedding on board, a civil ceremony, and then have a religious ceremony when you got home. That way you'd please everyone," I said.

So he sent her a cable asking her to fly out to meet the ship at Plymouth and to marry him on board. All week he has been waiting for her reply. Every evening when Sparks was on radio watch, Fred came into the Great Cabin to see if there was any news.

The ship's company was almost equally divided as to whether Jocelyn would say "Yes" or "No." Alan thought she would say "No"; so did Stuart, Jumbo, Adrian, Wally, Dick, Sparks, Mike Ford and Doc Stevens. Canada thought Fred would get a "No" and so did Scottie. Harry Sowerby expressed no opinion one way or the other, which was usual. Those who thought Jocelyn would refuse did so on the grounds that her parents would prevail upon her not to be married anywhere else than at home, whatever assurances Fred gave her about a subsequent religious ceremony. The rest of us, who thought Jocelyn would agree, did so because we could not see a girl in love turning down the chance of marriage under such romantic circumstances as aboard the ship *Mayflower II*. Julian told Fred that if he *were* turned down, it meant Jocelyn had changed her mind about him altogether.

Tonight we had the answer! It was "Yes," and the ship is hardly large enough to contain a smiling, joyful Fred. He sat on the foreyard during the last hour of his watch on lookout singing happily and tunelessly to himself.

The motor vessel *Barrister*, bound for Greenock from Barbados, called us and asked if she could do anything for us. Alan replied: "Many thanks. Everything okay." This put paid to any ideas we had had of fresh fruit, vegetables and soft drinks.

Thirty-eighth Day, May 27. Over 128 miles logged and every indication that the days of being becalmed are behind us. Given a modicum of good luck we should be in Plymouth by June 10 at the latest. This morning they finished painting the Great Cabin, white walls, light-blue shelf. The beams are a deep brown now that they have been oiled. After we get to America I am going to ask the New Zealand, Australian and Canadian governments to supply us with native timbers so we may have paneling throughout. Edgar Mugridge has made a locker with sliding doors, using packing cases — a good enough job, but it offends his craftsman's pride. When I complimented him, he said: "Her's all right for now, Mr. Charlton, but when I gets the timber, a bit of good oak, I'll make a proper job of her."

Not a day passes but some new work on the ship is put under way so that she will look her best when we arrive: this morning the day watch started scraping 'tween decks, and the waist has had a coating of oil. Doc was very pleased with himself today because some mustard and cress seeds he planted three days ago on some wet cotton wool in a cut-down biscuit tin were ready to be eaten. He gathered his crop with some ceremony, using a pair of surgical scissors. We all had a nibble for tea.

At four o'clock we sighted a ship creeping over the horizon astern on our starboard beam. Joe Lacey identified her through binoculars as an empty tanker. Soon she made straight towards us, flying a lot of bunting. She was the *Belgian Pride*, and circled us, blasting off her whistle, all her hands on deck waving and shouting. Then her master, Captain Sart, called over to us: "I'm dropping a parcel." We put out the pram with Doc Stevens and he returned after fifteen minutes' hard rowing with a lifebelt from the *Belgian Pride* to which was attached a metal box.

I took it up on the quarter-deck to Alan, who bellowed his thanks across the water, and they gave us a cheer before sailing on the course for the West Indies. The metal box contained a note from Captain Sart wishing us Godspeed, some chocolates, cigars, cigarettes, a bottle of eau de Cologne and a bottle of brandy. Alan dished out the chocolates to the nonsmokers and the rest of us got a cigar and a packet of cigarettes. The latter, a packet of twenty-five adorned with a picture of a red-haired girl wearing a black hat and yellow feather, tasted like a mild version of an American cigarette. Alan was most generous about the brandy, splicing the main brace, but the eau de Cologne disappeared into his cabin. I supposed he was keeping it as a present for his wife.

The sight of a ship turning off course to have a look at us, sending a message of goodwill and dropping a parcel of gifts into the sea, was a thrill to all of us, not only because it broke into the monotony of the day and relieved our loneliness, but because it was a reminder that *Mayflower* had caught the imagination of people of all nations. I think that they perceive in our little ship a glimpse of man before the atom age, when he was less complicated, had fewer doubts, both about himself and the world around him; an age of ignorance, perhaps, but also one of faith and courage.

Water, wind, sun and sail. They make you feel as though you are close to the beat of the pulse of life; the breath of the wind, the sway of the ship moving with the sea, the slow dignity of the sunrise and sunset. At first you look at these things apart and then you feel part of them. I was today and I felt what sailors have been trying to tell me, laughing "to see the sails conceive big-bellied with the wanton breeze."

Thirty-ninth Day, May 28. Our course is now northwest by west and the line on the chart is curving gently but firmly in the general direction of Nantucket Lightship. I have made a second bet with Mait. My first bet was that we would see Nantucket on or about midnight on June 2; now the bet is double or quits (I stand to lose $30) that we are west of Nantucket Lightship by midnight on the eighth. If we maintain our present rate of progress, another 135 knots today, I consider I have an excellent chance of winning. I also think Mait hopes I shall win; we have all been at sea quite long enough — thirty-nine days. I know we have experienced none of the privations of the Pilgrims; the weather has been kind to us, our diet has kept us fit. Nevertheless, we miss our families and the feel of solid earth underfoot. Most of us are sunburned and have benefited from the physical challenge of the voyage. The first two or three weeks also constituted a mental rest from the cares of life ashore, but now I feel, and most of us share this feeling, a sense of frustration from being out of touch too long. This feeling is probably accentuated by the fact that we have had to restrict the use of the radio to

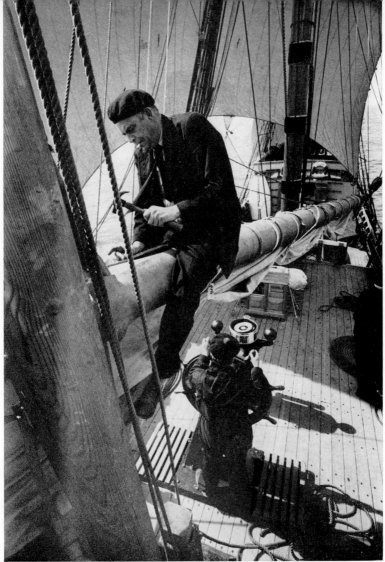

Jan Junker, third mate, at work on the lateen yard, with
Anderson-Bell, the only Scotsman aboard, at the wheel

Gordon Tenney from Black Star, reprinted by courtesy of Life maga

Postmasters for a day — the stamp collectors' mail

Working the capstan below decks

Gordon Tenney from Black Star, reprinted by courtesy of Life maga

Out on a limb — Joe Lacey

Transatlantic News Features

Transatlantic News Features

First Mate Wicksteed
"shoots the sun"

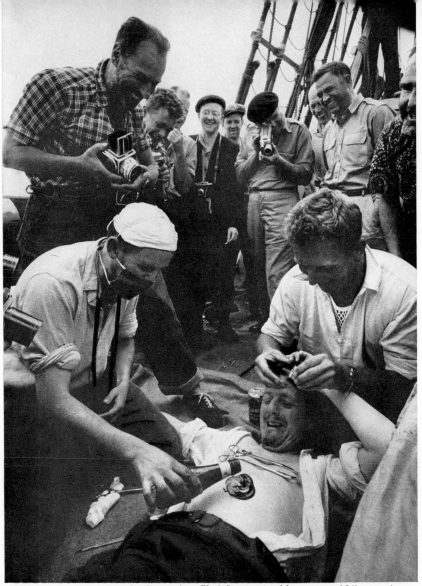

The author undergoes an "operation"

The ship and First Mate Wicksteed (with cap) in tow during
doldrums

Gordon Tenney from Black Star, reprinted by courtesy of Life magaz

Commander Villiers conducts a Sunday service at sea

Gordon Tenney from Black Star, reprinted
by courtesy of Life magazine

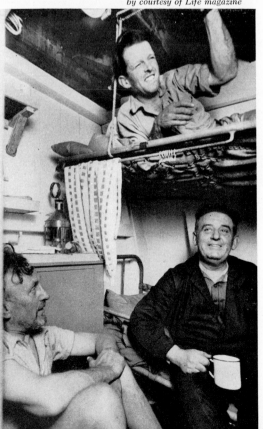

At ease in typical cabin. Charlie Church (*upper bunk*), Stuart Upham (*left*), Edgar Mugridge, ship's carpenter (*right*)

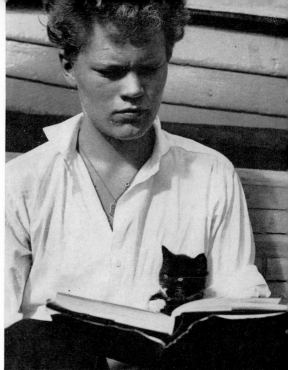

Graham Nunn, English cabin boy,
with Felix, the ship's cat

Joe Meany, of Waltham, Massachusetts, the American cabin boy

Commander Villiers speaks to his crew about Columbus

Singing for the trade
winds

Bringing in the spritsail in heavy weather

Rain squalls batter the crew

Gordon Tenney from Black Star, reprinted by courtesy of Life magazine

A hatful of wind

Crewmen fight gale winds on storm-lashed deck off New England

Gordon Tenney from Black Star, reprinted by courtesy of Life mag

Coast Guard training ship *Eagle* and Navy blimp greet *Mayflower*

At anchorage in Provincetown harbor with Pilgrim Monument
in background

Yale Joel, reprinted by courtesy of Life mag

Land ho! A wonderful ship and her splendid crew arrive in port

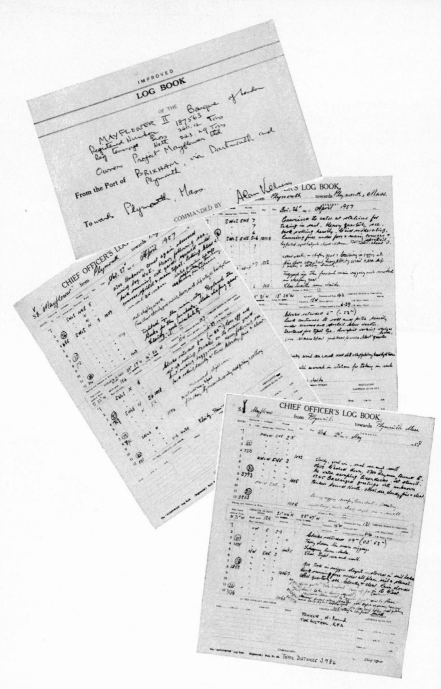

Reproductions of pages from
Mayflower log

Gordon Tenney from Black Star, reprinted by courtesy of Life magazine

Furling the sails in harbor of Plymouth, Massachusetts

The captain and crew go ashore in Plymouth in specially built shallop

Gordon Tenney from Black Star, reprinted by courtesy of Life magazine

"Being thus arrived in a good harbor, and brought safe to land . . ." The *Mayflower II* at her mooring, Plymouth, Massachusetts

ship's business in order to conserve fuel. This policy has been strictly followed, so that no one has sent more than one personal message home since we left Plymouth.

One of our most engaging members is Maitland Edey, a most likable and sensitive fellow altogether. He came on the voyage to write a story for *Life* magazine, but straightway let it be known he expected to take his turn on watch and work as an ordinary member of the crew. He has a courteous manner and a mellow voice with youthful flexibility. He is forty-seven but has looked after himself and has the physique and fitness of a man in his early thirties. I was surprised to learn he had four children, the eldest a son of twenty-one. Just before the voyage Mait went to Sweden for his son's marriage, and he told me about it with his usual dry humor. "My son lives on a barge on the Seine," said Mait. "He has been living in Paris for the past couple of years. He wants to be a writer and takes this seriously enough to go about dressed like a tramp. He met a very beautiful Swedish girl, they fell in love with one another and she took him to Sweden to meet her parents. They, not knowing he had a presentable father like me, did not like the idea of their lovely daughter marrying a young man who, apart from disdaining normal conventions of dress, did not go much into hair brushing either. They wrote to me and said as much. Whereupon I wrote back and explained that our son had been well brought up and indicated that there was every reason to hope for some improvement in the not too distant future. Anyway, when they did get to meet me and my wife, they saw that their daughter had two solid citizens for in-laws, so everyone was very happy." The man who told me this had a five weeks' growth of beard, was barefooted, wore jeans that had seen better days, and nothing else. His hair was unbrushed and it was then eleven in the morning. I know who Mait's son takes after!

We have had two more visitors today. The first, a French liner, the *Colombie,* was bound for Plymouth from the West Indies. I sighted her smokestack peeping over the horizon to the southwest. Then she made a line for us, circling close and fast, so that Alan looked anxiously at the mainmast. She tooted continuously, her decks lined with passengers who shouted and cheered: "Good luck, *Mayflower II*," and we called: "*Vive la France*." Later, her master, Robichon, sent us a signal: "Very happy having met you in such good condition. We will send you at your port arrival — indicate address — our ship's medal and pictures to commemorate this day. We should be glad to receive pictures of our ship taken in the rigging of your beautiful ship."

Our second visitor arrived at four in the afternoon. She came up on our weather quarter. Then, showing seamanlike consideration for a sailing ship, steamed on to our lee quarter and overhauled us. She was the *Olna*, a Royal Fleet Auxiliary tanker, bound for South America from Malta. She flew the blue ensign defaced with a horizontal device of an anchor in gold. It was the first time we had seen a ship of the Royal Navy. She spoke to us in Morse over the radio telephone and used flags to send international code and also visual Morse. Her first message was enough to make *Mayflower* blush: "You are very beautiful." Fred Edwards went onto the poop to read and reply. The second message from the *Olna* was: "Is there anything, repeat anything, I can possibly do for you?" Alan told Fred to reply: "No, thank you very much. We are okay." She replied by flags in international code: "WAY," which means: "Have a good voyage." She gave us three cheers, which we returned. But she had not finished. She semaphored: "You look like a lovely oil painting." On Alan's instructions Fred replied: "I bet you say that to all the girls," and then she sent her last message to us, by international code, before steaming away: "Godspeed." We were all very pleased to receive this attention from one of our own ships, as up to now, the foreigners have shown thmselves not only the most interested but the most gallant. But the *Olna* showed that the attention of a British ship is worth waiting for. When I was on the 4 to 8 watch, we were creaming along until we ran into a rain squall which lasted for about twenty minutes. After that the wind fell off a little, but we were still making about five knots.

The Voyage

Fortieth Day, May 29. We bowled steadily along in the warm sun, logging a comfortable 124 miles by noon. There was a short, low swell, a slight sea and northeast trades blowing force four. The sky was cloudless, except for a few white tufts of cumulus. We are having what sailors describe as "flying-fish weather." I saw over a score of them soaring gaily out of the water. The weather was broken only by a few welcome squalls which brought rain showers in the evening. These, as ever, turned the ship into a nudist colony.

During the morning Jimmy Horrocks was calling the Royal Auxiliary tanker, the *Tide Race,* one hundred miles southwest of us, and he was answered by another tanker, the *Tide Austral.* The latter exchanged positions with us, then during the afternoon called us again to exchange positions and to say they expected to sight us at eight o'clock. They kept radio contact all day and then, sure enough, just after eight we saw a light on our port beam, a long way away. We called up the *Austral* and told them that as they had come so far out of their way to see us, we would burn flares so they could have a good view of us. Alan set the first one off a few minutes later, but a rain squall came in between us. They signaled with their ten-inch lamp, but at that range (they were four miles away) we could not answer. When the *Austral* was two miles closer, she called again and sent us a message: "Good luck and good voyage from Royal Fleet Auxiliary *Tide Austral.*" Alan replied: "Thank you and good voyage to you, too." He ordered more white flares to be lit fore and aft and the mate played the deck searchlight on the maintop as the *Austral* steamed around on our weather quarter and used her deck lamps to light us. We gave her another flare display and I took over the searchlight from the mate, who climbed the ratlines with a flare and nearly gave them a brighter sight of us than we intended when his flare flickered round the ropes.

When our flare display was over, Jimmy Horrocks went aft to the Great Cabin and asked the *Austral* on the Transarctic what they thought of the show. They replied: "Very good, most impressive, but not to be seen after a few drinks. It was appreciated by all on board, except our Chinese crew members, who are most perplexed."

Forty-first Day, May 30. Although to outward appearances life aboard goes on as usual, there is a growing air of suspense and, so far as I personally am concerned, downright impatience to sight America. Mait shares my feelings. The ship's job now is to scrape the decks, a back-breaking, sweat-making, dirty job, done naked to the waist on the knees. The decks, which started out a clean light brown, are already black with use and we are removing the grime and surplus pitch by hand with iron scrapers.

Mait sat on the working boat with me, waiting his turn to scrape the 'tween decks, and we fell to discussing the different stages of the voyage. At the start we agreed that it was all we could do to find our feet, keep dry and warm. After the first few days, when there were heavy seas and we had skirted winds of gale force, we began to get to know our way about the ship and to take an interest in the men who shared our watch, to gain confidence in our ability to do a job aboard ship; and this was followed by a period of pure enjoyment of the voyage and the growing sense of comradeship, redolent of the Army and of school. When we had passed the Canaries, and progress was either very slow or we were becalmed, boredom began to sap the spirit. Finally, when the northeast trades began to blow with fresh consistency, our spirits billowed with hope. Above all, the voyage has been (see, I am talking as though it is over, although we still have to sail a thousand miles) an opportunity to relax for longer than any time before in our adult lives. Mait, for instance, is a man who retired because he was too busy to work. Since 1941, apart from his war service, he has been an executive on *Life* magazine, but as though that were not enough to occupy his interest, he is also vice-president of the New York Philharmonic Symphony Orchestra — a most painstaking and active vice-president, I am sure. He is an expert yachtsman and commodore of the yacht club at Edgartown on Martha's Vineyard, where he lives. He is also engaged in the civic life of Upper Brookville, a village thirty miles from New York. He is a member of the school board, a trustee of the village, deputy mayor and the Road Commissioner. Two years ago he retired so he could devote more time to these interests and also write some books. Then he was invited by *Life* to return to journalism on a special assignment. I think the Pilgrims would have approved his decision to sail in our replica of their ship. They would have had to overcome first misgivings prompted by his dry humor and slow, almost sly, smile, but then they would have judged him a most worthy representative of the great nation they helped to found.

And Joe Meany, a perfectionist in all he attempts, even the serving of meals on this swaying bark, would also have received the accolade of their approval. Joe — the decisive — made up his mind to go to Annapolis when he was eleven, and through his own ability and perseverance is going to get there. I think Joe has always known what he wants and liked what he knew, and that surely is a Pilgrim characteristic! Gordon Tenney, who has taken four thousand photographs in order to ensure that he has a complete photographic record of life aboard *Mayflower*, although he knows that only a small part of them will be used — Gordon Tenney, whose camera is always there if the topmast snaps or a flying fish lands on deck — Gordon has the stern application that would have viewed the stark New England coast in 1620 and decided to make a home there out of the wilderness. Yes, we are fortunate in our Americans aboard *Mayflower*, but there is one of them who would, I am sure, have puzzled the Pilgrims. Andy Lindsay is a man who scorns the convention which invests most Americans with the desire to earn a lot of money, own a new car, and become vice-president of the company. Andy wants enough to live, to live simply, to move around. He takes a job so long as his interest lasts and goes sailing whenever he can get a ship. That is how he came to be with us. He had sailed with Alan on the *Joseph Conrad* as a boy eighteen years ago and when he heard about *Mayflower*, took a ship for England and arrived at Brixham after cycling three hun-

dred miles from London. I saw him one day in the shipyard helping with the rigging — a silent man engrossed in what he was
doing. Most days, between watches, he has been weaving a
beautiful and intricate sailor's belt from fine cotton yarn, but
when I asked him today if he sold them, he said: "No. I make
them to give to people, one or two a year. People have offered
to buy them, but I like to make them when I want and I like to
give when I want." There is a remoteness about Andy Lindsay
which cannot easily be bridged. He is very near to being an
island, and the Pilgrims would have been surprised at that, for
they were a gregarious people and the millions who have come
after them are nothing if not that. Andy does not share his
thoughts. For example, I told Andy this afternoon that our
run was 143 miles, and added: "If we keep this up, I'm going to
win my bet with Mait." He said: "Good," without looking up
from his weaving, so that I did not know if he shared my enthusiasm for the nearness of journey's end or wished to sail on forever
to endless horizons. I felt he gave me his word of approval as a
present, as he does one of his sailors' belts.

Forty-second Day, May 31. During the midnight to four watch
I spent an hour talking to Mike Ford as the ship seemingly raced
along under ideal conditions. I thought we might pass our
previous record of 164 miles, but the wind dropped towards first
light and we had a run of 143 miles, which is still very good.
Mike, who is in his early twenties, has recently taken a job
straight from Oxford with the plastics division of Shell. He spoke
about the existence of a purposeful God. "I find it difficult to
believe in a purposeful God," he admitted. I told Mike that I
had asked all on board whether they believed in a purposeful
God and all had replied that they did. He said, looking out across
the waters and up to the starlit infinity of the heavens: "Well, I
am one who is not sure. I am inclined to the belief that man alone
has choice and responsibility and he cannot place responsibility
for rightness and wrongness on God." During the night watches
there have been many such discussions, and the sailors tell me

this is quite common at sea, where man is reminded of his own insignificance on earth and in the universe.

This week of good progress sees the ship beginning the last lap and heading directly towards Nantucket Lightship on a course passing some hundred miles inside Bermuda. In the past seven days we have made 850 miles. I spoke to Alan in the chartroom and asked him whether he had decided how we would enter Plymouth. "I should like to go in looking as though we had just been for a trip round the bay," I said.

Alan smiled wryly. "We're going to look pretty smart. That's why I've had the boys painting and scraping the decks, painting the chartroom and the Great Cabin, but we won't dress ship, if that's what you mean."

"No," I said, "I don't mean dress ship, but something after that fashion."

"We'll see what we can do, but I don't think we'll give anyone the impression we've only been for a trip round the bay, however smart the crew turn out. We'll have come over five thousand miles and that's caused a little wear and tear. Still, if the Lord continues to be good to us, we'll get the ship there in one piece, which is something. Not even a broken topmast. She'll look smart enough." He glanced up at the topmast as he spoke; it seemed to bend dangerously with the wind. "And if it does snap, then we'll mend it," he added.

This evening we had the first "arrival" message, and it came appropriately from Sir Alfred Bossom, who has been such a stanch supporter of the project from the beginning. He cabled: SINCEREST CONGRATULATIONS TO ALL UPON YOUR DISTINGUISHED ACHIEVEMENT. MAYFLOWER SYMBOLIC OF FRIENDLY RELATIONS BE-TWEEN TWO GREAT ENGLISH-SPEAKING NATIONS AND MAY THIS FRIENDSHIP GROW AND BE MORE DEEPLY ANCHORED IN HEIRS OF BOTH PEOPLE.

Forty-third Day, June 1. Since we left Plymouth, England, we have been in daily radio contact, apart from two days when there was a technical fault on our set, with Portishead Radio, near

Bristol. This is the long-distance radio communication station for the United Kingdom and is used by shipping throughout the world. It handles all marine communication to the United Kingdom and also relays traffic between ship and ship when they cannot for some technical reason communicate directly with one another.

At first we used Land's End Radio, but after two days out, Jimmy established daily communication with Portishead. Today, as we are nearing the American coast, he established communication with South Chatham Radio Station, Massachusetts, which is operated by the Radio Marine Corporation of America. They told him they had some traffic waiting for us and I was naturally curious to know what it would be — perhaps greetings from the governor of a state? It was, however, from a Brooklyn laundry and addressed to the Captain — an offer to collect, launder and deliver all our dirty washing free of charge and return it "immaculate as the souls of the Pilgrim Fathers." Alan politely refused the offer, and remarked to me: "But if they could do the washing right now, darn it, I'd be grateful." I got off a message for Joe Meany to St. Mary's High School, Waltham, Massachusetts. CONGRATULATIONS SUCCESS TO CLASS OF 57 STOP HOPED TO MAKE LANDFALL IN TIME TO BE PRESENT GRADUATION BUT POOR NORTHEAST TRADES DELAYED US STOP NOW HEADING NANTUCKET LIGHTSHIP LAST STAGE OF FIVE-THOUSAND-MILE VOYAGE STOP FOUND MY SEA LEGS AFTER THREE DAYS OUT NOW LOOKING FORWARD TO FINDING LAND LEGS.

We logged 110 miles, which was reassuring as the wind had dropped off several times during the day. I was getting myself worked up into a state of tension for fear that we would be becalmed within sight of America. During the past three days I have had a total of not much more than six hours' sleep. I make attempts to turn in, but no sooner do I put my head down than I feel the ship has come to a stop, so I get up and go on deck to make sure we are still moving. Once up, I stay talking to the different watches and waiting for the dawn to break. Felix, who has recently made his home with me, keeps me company on these vigils, whiling away the time pretending to be a ferocious tiger. His game consists of hiding behind a coil of rope or a night head and stalking me. I am supposed always to be surprised but to put up a strong resistance until the beast of prey is repelled.

Forty-fourth Day, June 2. We are moving from one wind belt into another, and last night and early this morning the wind was all over the place. But Alan made the best of what there was by anticipating the direction of each squall, so that by the time each hit us, he had the yards already braced to take advantage of it. By noon today we have covered 85 miles. This is, we hope, believe, expect, our last Sunday at sea.

At nine o'clock, an hour before the morning service, Alan announced that he would keep the service on the quarter-deck to a minimum as we were in the midst of one rain squall and might run into another if it ceased.

Wally was not present after the service to issue the cigarettes and the sweets for nonsmokers. He was evidently feeling out of sorts and confined to his bunk. Dick took over and we had tinned ham, mashed potatoes and peas, followed by tinned pears with condensed milk and some Cheddar cheese. After lunch I was talking to Stuart about Joe Meany, how this was to have been his graduation day and how disappointed he was to miss it. "Well," said Stuart, "what are we waiting for?" I went up to the chartroom and had a word with Alan. I asked if he would officiate at Joe's substitute graduation aboard ship, and he agreed. Stuart undertook to make a mortarboard from one of his own cloth caps, a square of cardboard painted black and a tassel made from a rope's end. We made a gown from an oilskin turned inside out and a blue sheet for a cope. I wrote his certificate of graduation:

> Know ye, all men, by virtue of these letters patent, that on this day, Sunday, the second day of June, nineteen fifty-seven, on board the barque *Mayflower II*, commanded by our beloved master Alan Villiers, we do hereby grant, by virtue of our sov-

The Voyage

ereignty of the seas, to Joe Meany, a citizen of Waltham, situate
in the Commonwealth of Massachusetts, that from this day forth
he be a graduate mariner in these our domains, having regard
to his diligence in making of baggy wrinkles, scraping of decks
and other divers duties of the seaman, and that he henceforth
be accorded such rights and privileges due under the honourable and ancient customs of the seven seas.

Signed: NEPTUNE REX

ALAN VILLIERS, MASTER

Andy Bell inscribed this declaration on a large sheet of cartridge paper and Jimmy Horrocks supplied an illuminated first
letter and a painting of the ship between the British and American flags. We also made a seal, to which was attached some
blue ribbon, stuck the cartridge paper to a sawed-off piece of
painted broom handle and rolled it up. Andy Bell and Peter Padfield made themselves beards from baggy wrinkles and carried
an oar each as Neptune's mariners. Stuart and I carried the
mortarboard, certificate of graduation and gown on cushions to
the chartroom. Alan told the mate on watch to blow the whistle
for all hands to muster on the quarter-deck. When they had
assembled, he called to Neptune's mariners: "Bring forth Joe
Meany." Joe looked quite worried as he was hustled forward,
and then Alan told him that as he had missed one graduation
we had devised another for him. He then read out the declaration with great solemnity, and dressed Joe in the mortarboard,
gown and cope. Joe thanked us for what we had done and I think
he was moved that we should have tried to make up for the
graduation he had missed. In some measure I think we succeeded.

This evening I was invited to a party on the fo'c'sle head given
by the first mate's watch. They produced a number of delicacies
saved for the party: some bottles of chicken breasts, honey,
canned fruit juice, bottles of beer, some whisky and rum. We
sang and chattered away like schoolboys celebrating the end of
term, but there was the catch of sadness to our laughter, for we
knew that the happiness we felt, the feeling of comradeship, our

shared love for the ship would at best be a memory within a few days.

Forty-fifth Day, June 3. Today we nearly lost a crew member through strangulation. At seven this morning Alan gave the order "Let down the main tack." We were doing four knots and there was a nice light breeze which could fill the mainsail. Fred Edwards jumped to obey the Captain's order, threw off the starboard clew garnet, and, as normally happens, it ran up into the air. But unbeknown to Fred, the cat had caught itself in the turning rope, and we watched helplessly as Felix went up into the air like a department store elevator, looking very sorry for himself. Fortunately, he landed back on deck unharmed, but his confidence in ropes was shattered!

Our course is north-northeast. We are two hundred miles south of Bermuda and the wind is moderate, southeasterly, force three to four. We were making about five knots under ideal conditions; there was only a slight swell and a sunny, almost cloudless sky. Early in the afternoon we heard the sound of an airplane engine and soon sighted a distant speck which proved to be a seaplane of the United States Navy; John Winslow identified it as a Glenn Martin Mariner. It flew over us for nearly an hour, swooping to make passes from stem to stern. We waved to its crew and Alan ordered the red ensign hoisted on the lateen yard, the Stars and Stripes on the foremast, the latter in honor of our first visitor from the United States. Through the open hatch of the plane they took pictures and we, from the deck of a seventeenth-century bark, returned the compliment. I was happy they should see us under such good conditions, the sails filled with wind and the ship rising and falling with the swell as though she were curtsying. Our spirits were lifted by the American plane circling our little ship, which sailed on alone in the blue circle of the distant horizon.

We made 120 miles, which obviously disappointed Alan but pleasantly surprised me. I found Godfrey Wicksteed busy writing letters when he came off watch. Before the voyage began he had gone around talking to schools about *Mayflower,* nearly three hundred of them in a year, and he is writing a letter to each one. He let me read a typical letter, written painstakingly in longhand, as they all are:

Mayflower II,
NORTH ATLANTIC,
LAT. 22 NORTH, LONG. 40 WEST

TO ALL THE CHILDREN, THE TEACHERS, AND OTHER STAFF AT DEDWORTH GREEN COUNTY PRIMARY SCHOOLS, WINDSOR

DEAR FRIENDS OF *Mayflower II,*

I am trying to write you a letter as I sit in my very small cabin, full of all sorts of things, pump handles, anchor cable clips, water funnels, boxes of soap and candles and all sorts of ship's stores that I am supposed to look after. Also there are various parcels that I am taking to special people in America and, of course, the Album which has all your names in it. There is just a little room left for me and my own things — my bunk takes up more than half the floor space and there are two deck brushes, a compass, a life jacket and a kitten on that. Though we very seldom have any fresh water to wash in (except when it rains) I have a tiny stand for a basin and if I put the basin outside the door that leaves me a place to write, but I have to sit on a paint drum as there is no chair. In the old days, it would have been a barrel I would be sitting on. Perhaps you will excuse me if the writing is not at all good — the ship is rolling and the paint drum is not very steady.

We are now in the tropics (where it is very warm) having come a very long way round to get good winds; the Captain says nobody knows for certain what way the Pilgrims went, but he wants to go the best way and this is it. Even though it is thousands of miles longer it may still be quicker than by a straight way. We are already halfway in three and one half weeks and the Pilgrims took nine weeks. By the time you get this letter you will know all about how long it has taken us, but this is how long it is now. The winds so far are in the right direction but not always strong enough and the other day it was so calm that the Captain let us bathe and even put the ship's boat out so that we could take photographs. Everybody had a turn. I hope you will see some of the pictures.

The Voyage

I have just been looking again at yours and reading your accounts of visits and sports, and your nice poems. Please keep thinking of us. Best wishes to all of you,

Yours sincerely,
GODFREY WICKSTEED

Forty-sixth Day, June 4. John Lowe sent me a cable saying he was coming out with a movie cameraman from Bermuda to intercept us and expected to land alongside and discuss all the details of the arrangements for our reception. I signaled Captain Long, the commanding officer of the naval station at Hamilton, giving our position, course and speed. I was anxious to hear all the news, and to get off the cine record of the voyage so that it would be processed and edited for the television networks to coincide with our arrival. Early in the morning I heard the sound of an aeroengine and soon it appeared, a flying boat coming from the northeast. It was a United States Coast Guard aircraft, and Alan ordered the James I flag to be hoisted to the mainmast and Old Glory to the foremast.

The plane flew over us, swooping low, making passes from stem to stern. Through the open hatch of the plane cameramen were taking pictures. After a few minutes the Coast Guard plane was joined by two United States Navy aircraft, both of them seaplanes. One of them lost altitude to see if conditions were suitable for landing, and I tried to catch sight of John as they flew low within a hundred feet of the water, but I could not be sure if he was one of those waving to us through the hatch. Apparently the swell, gentle though it appeared from the ship, was too heavy for a safe landing and take-off, and one by one the aircraft flew back towards Bermuda. One of the Navy aircraft dropped a canister for us before joining the others. We lowered the pram with Beric Watson aboard and he had a fifteen-minute pull before he picked up the canister. "My, you feel alone out there," he exclaimed as he climbed back over the side. The canister, which was attached to an unexploded smoke bomb, contained a message from the crew of the aircraft:

[199]

Crew 8 VP-89 — Salutations. Hope these papers will make your voyage a little more enjoyable. Good luck and God's speed.

There was a two-day-old copy of the New York *Times* inside, and the rest of the day it was passed round the ship. We have made 131 miles, and as anything over a hundred improves on our average, I am well pleased. I am sorry John could not make it. Our course is NNW, about 150 miles southwest of Bermuda. Maybe he will try again tomorrow.

Forty-seventh Day, June 5. At six this morning I was roused by Joe Meany shaking me and shouting: "They're here, Mr. Charlton, they're here." He was away before I had a chance to collect my thoughts enough to ask him who. I pulled on a pair of trousers and rushed out on deck to find that the reason for the commotion lay each side of our ship, only half a cable's length away to port and starboard; two Italian battleships, the cruisers *San Georgio* and *San Marco*. Both ships' companies manned the sides. We heard orders being shouted in Italian — "Off caps" — and then they gave us three mighty cheers. The *San Marco* lowered a launch; we put a ladder over; and as they came alongside, an officer shouted: "Permission to come aboard, sir." Then he stood looking up at the ship, threw wide his arms and exclaimed: "*Magnifico! Magnifico!*" We escorted him to Alan, together with one other officer and three ratings. The latter carried gifts of wine, and they also sent us up from the launch oranges and fresh vegetables. The officer saluted Alan on the quarter-deck and introduced himself: "Capitano Mario Casardi, sir."

"Welcome aboard," said Alan.

"Am I the first?" inquired Capitano Casardi.

"Yes," said Alan, smiling, "you are the first."

Whereupon Capitano Casardi proudly planted an Italian naval pennant on the binnacle as though he had reached the summit of Everest.

"I have a message for you from the Admiral," said the Capitano. He gave Alan a letter which he read at once. It was from Rear

The Voyage

Admiral Ernesto Giuriate, commanding the Italian Second Naval Division:

> The Italian Navy, which still endears at their full value the sailing traditions, follows your gallant enterprise with keen attention and great admiration.
>
> *San Georgio* and *San Marco*, on their way to the Jamestown Festival, were glad to alter their course in order to have the privilege of bringing you personally the salute of our Navy.
>
> Accept our three cheers in the same spirit in which they are given, from sailor to sailor and as the most hearty wishes for the success of your mission.

Alan asked the Capitano to convey his profound thanks to the Admiral for the signal honor he had accorded *Mayflower,* and for his message of encouragement and goodwill.

"Sailing ships, they are beautiful," said the Capitano, looking up at our curving canvas. "I was two years in sail myself. Please accept this photograph as a memento of our meeting," and he handed Alan a mounted photograph of the *San Marco* inscribed: "To the gallant hearts of oak of *Mayflower II* with all good wishes from *San Marco* ship's company."

"Please accept this as a small token of our appreciation," said Alan, indicating a box in which he had placed some Scotch whisky, champagne and sherry. *Mayflower* could do no wrong, for the Capitano noted the whisky, exclaimed: "Ah — Scotch — *magnifico,*" stepped back to take some photographs of the ship, saluted, thanked Alan once again and returned to the *San Marco.* All thirty-three of us gave the Italians as loud a cheer as lungs and throats were capable. They steamed off at furious speed, the *San Marco* crossing our bows only forty feet away, to the north. They had hardly gone on their way when we sighted four more warships steaming towards us out of the morning sun. Jimmy Horrocks told me they were a squadron of American destroyers and that their commodore was aboard one of them, the *Ault,* which had been asking for our position yesterday.

While the American ships were approaching, I spoke to Alan about the Italians. He had first seen their lights at two in the morning. They kept close to us all night, ready to pounce should any other ships attempt to get to us before they did. Then, both ships' companies dressed in whites and manning the sides, they had in a matter of minutes come alongside at first light to rouse us with their cheers. I thought it a wonderful gesture, showing how swiftly time can heal wounds, for it was only a little over a decade ago that we had been enemies. It was, if I may borrow a word from Capitano Casardi, *magnifico!*

The American destroyers steamed off our starboard quarter until they were some three miles away. The *Ault* detached herself from the others, which hove to, and came up on our lee side, about three cables away. They asked us on the radio telephone if there was anything we wanted, and we decided to add to our recently acquired supplies of oranges and fresh vegetables. They put off a whaler, which we secured alongside while we took off the supplies. Their officer presented the compliments of his commodore and asked for our ETA.

"What's that?" Alan boomed from the quarter-deck.

"Expected time of arrival, sir," said the officer.

Alan gestured towards the heavens and our sails. "We don't know things like that on sailing ships," he rasped, "but we could get there on Monday or Tuesday." This was the first indication Alan had given that our progress since Sunday had fallen below his expectations. Today, for example, we logged only 91 miles.

Mait and Gordon were given permission to go aboard the *Ault*. They took some gifts, a bottle of Italian wine, some whisky, sherry and champagne, and arranged for the delivery of Mait's story and Gordon's photographs to *Life* magazine.

They came back aboard after about fifteen minutes, their mission successfully accomplished.

There was a squall coming up astern and I went up on the poop to try to see through glasses what was happening to the other destroyers in the squadron. Suddenly they began to move towards us, sailing at half speed, until they passed us line abreast, all three ships with their sides manned. I had the honor of dipping to them and hauled the Red Duster to return the salute of these ships of gray steel, moving in perfect formation, honoring the replica of the ship which had helped to found their great country. When they had passed us, they broke formation and one by one sailed round us, each warship making a personal tribute to the little wooden ship sailing northwest through gray sheets of rain to New England as the Pilgrim Fathers had done.

This evening we seem to have found a good southwesterly blow; the wind is aft, with practically no sea and no swell. Jan said that during his watch, the 8 to 12, we made 26 miles, which seems to be about her maximum. At noon today we had 540 miles to go, so we need four days of wind force five blowing steadily if we are to arrive on Sunday. I don't expect we shall have that much luck, although we should pick up a couple of knots from the current when we get into the Gulf Stream.

Forty-eighth Day, June 6. Just before midnight Canada patted my hand to wake me and said: "One bell, rainin' hard, ship's rolling right along." I got into my bright yellow oilskins and rubber boots, the latter because I have found climbing the ratlines barefoot hard on the soles. The rain had stopped, but there were strong gusts blowing. David Thorpe was at the wheel in black oilskins, hard to see before my eyes became accustomed to the light, except for the white of his now familiar cloche hat.

Our course was north by west, the wheel was amidships, and it had been taking about two turns to starboard. We were right on course at that moment, but every time she rolled you had to put about one fourth to one half on the compass to steady her back. The Captain was standing there all the time looking at the compass. She was hard to steer, because the wind and the swells kept kicking her around. The moon was sometimes curtained behind dark clouds, but most of the time it was clear enough to steer by the stars. During the next hour I sat on the main hatch and talked to David Cauvin. He spoke about the time he sailed a third-size model of the *Van Riebeck,* which was roughly the same vintage as *Mayflower* and was built for the *Van Riebeck* tercentenary in 1952. We broke into our nattering to climb onto the fo'c'sle head and sought out the ropes which had been draped round the wrong pins. At four bells I went up the rigging to relieve the lookout. The wind was beginning to blow really hard and I could look down with satisfaction at the tremendous bow wave we were making. I was so anxious to see a light that my eyes began to play tricks on me and once or twice I was nearly caught out but stopped myself in time when I realized it was a setting star. There was a squall coming towards us and I was torn between my curiosity to experience a storm aloft and my fear of the mast's going. The sky became heavy and black, blotting out the stars; the sea, too, became black and menacing. Although there were deep rolls of thunder and the ship was twice lit by lightning, the wind from the southwest took the squall past us on the port side. For the second time on this voyage I had the feeling I was flying, the physical feeling of flying, and for a moment it was so real I shared the ecstasy of the birds.

After breakfast I turned in, but at eleven o'clock I was woken by the motion of the ship as she pitched and rolled heavily. I heard the sound of running feet on the quarter-deck, shouts, and the unmistakable sound of rain beating down upon the decks. I ran out to the waist to find we were caught in a wind of gale force and a confused, angry sea with waves like the crude hands of some prehistoric monster reaching out to clutch at us. The Captain was on the quarter-deck, his beret incongruous with his oilskins, the rain streaming down over his eyes. He stood, legs apart, quite calm, glancing round unhurriedly, taking in the situation, deciding upon action. Then he bellowed an order in his powerful seasaw voice which carried through the wind: "Take in the fore-topsails, lads." We had all subconsciously turned to him, waiting to see what he would do, and we responded to the command as though we had been drilled to meet such a situation. Jan gave the orders, telling which ropes to handle, and all hands hauled away, lashed by the rain, struggling to maintain balance as the ship fought with the wind and the seas. I hauled away at the greasy ropes, sandwiched between two half-naked seamen,

David Cauvin and Scottie, who had hoped the first rainfall would be a shower.

When we hauled on the main yard, the topsail yard was stuck. Three of us, Joe Powell, who had the most powerful shoulders on the ship, Graham Nunn and I, pulled until our arms and back ached. The quarter-deck was slippery underneath; and the ship swayed so that she came up to meet us and there was a real danger of our falling overboard. Joe Lacey went aloft to try to ease the yard and old Ike went with him. The wind was strong enough to snap the topmast and it must have occurred to Ike and Joe, but they were laughing aloft in the driving rain. While all this was going on, and until the storm had passed, the Captain did not change his position just behind and to the left of the helmsman. He sometimes smiled encouragement, but he spoke only to give an order, and then he used only the words absolutely necessary, except that he called us "lads." When the danger to our topsails was averted, we saw that the visibility had lessened. The Captain had put David Thorpe to sound the mournful blast of the Norwegian foghorn, one blast every minute.

When I lay back, my feet up on a bench, relaxing in the Great Cabin, I reflected that we might be within three days' sailing of our journey's end, but the Atlantic had reminded us that we were not finished with it yet. Alan came in and sat down. He said: "We're out of it now. Thank you for your help." Then he added: "The ship behaved well just now. I was pleased with the way she came through that. There was a moment when we could have been in trouble." I did not say what was in my mind, that I thought we had been in trouble for more than a moment and that most of our faces, had we been able to see them through the rain, would have expressed as much.

Forty-ninth Day, June 7. This has been John Winslow's day. It began with our sighting two Daring-class destroyers in the morning. John was delighted. He slapped himself on the chest and borrowed Dick's binoculars to make quite sure his eyes had not played him false. "I knew it," he said with delight. "I knew the Royal Navy would come up trumps in the end. We've had the Italian and American navies and now it's about time you all saw the real thing." The real thing was approaching us on the port side and we caught some of John's enthusiasm as they drew nearer.

We were so absorbed by the destroyers, we did not notice the squat shape creeping over the horizon. Ike Marsh, who was aloft, was the first to call out the news. "It's the *Ark Royal*," he shouted. This was almost too much for John, who nearly fell over the side as he used the glasses again. "Good Lord," he exclaimed, "I do believe Ike is right. I know a few of the chaps on board. Excuse me." He pushed the glasses into my hands and ran below and returned a few minutes later wearing his uniform and Royal Navy cap but still in shorts.

Ike *was* right. It was the giant aircraft carrier and she made her approach to us with ceremony befitting her majesty. First we were inspected by the two destroyers, which circled us one at a time, their crews shouting cheers which mingled with our own. The destroyers were followed by helicopters, three of them, which hovered over us so close to our topmasts I think we could have carried on a conversation had it not been for the sound of their engine. As it was, the pilots and cameramen smiled and waved to us and made signals for us to wave back and go aloft for their pictures. The presence of the destroyers and the helicopters, an indication of our own countrymen's regard for our enterprise, made me share in John's rising excitement. When the *Ark Royal* herself drew near, so that we could make out several hundred of her crew manning the sides, we were awed by the size of her and fell silent. She came to within three cable lengths, and although we were dwarfed by her, we did not feel humbled. Our sails were filled and we were making about seven knots, nearly our top speed. The *Ark Royal* had grace of line, despite her size, but I could see the wonder in their eyes as they passed us; our sturdy wooden ship, her masts webbed with rigging, sails curving with the wind, had a breath-taking beauty of her own, a beauty we had glimpsed for ourselves when we put out the working boat, a beauty they saw now for the first time.

John said, when the *Ark Royal*, her destroyers and helicopters had disappeared over the horizon whence they had come: "Say what you like, you can't beat the Navy."

"Even when they won't give you leave to sail on *Mayflower?*" I asked.

"They make you feel proud," he replied almost to himself. "That great ship coming out of her way to wish us Godspeed. I'm so glad they saw us under such ideal conditions."

But the conditions were not to remain ideal for long. The moderate sea turned into a rough beam sea and swell. The skies became cloudy and their lowness and density signaled squalls. *Mayflower* began to roll and pitch heavily. We were under courses, spritsail and main-topsail when there was a sudden shift in the wind and the vessel veered three points off course. This was followed, an hour later, by a cascade of rain and another shift of the wind. Alan clewed up the fore- and main-topsails. I went up in the quarter-deck to speak to him and found him watching the gathering clouds and mounting sea.

He saw me standing beside him, smiled grimly and said: "We're not there yet, you know." He turned and went into the chart-room, and I decided there was no purpose in troubling him further. All his life he had done battle with the sea and now I sensed he was preparing himself to do battle again.

Fiftieth Day, June 8. In the morning when the upper and the 'tween decks were washed down, some of the water trickled into my cabin. If I could have known what was going to happen later on in the day, I would have saved myself the trouble of drying it out. But every morning the decks are washed and nearly every morning some of the water comes through to my cabin. I have chided Stuart about this, especially as his is the only cabin in the ship which does not leak. Even the chartroom leaks, and

Alan has tarpaulin rigged over the poop deck whenever it looks like rain. "I think it not without significance that the builder has the only dry bunk on the ship," I told Stuart today, but as usual he had a reply which at least satisfied him. He pointed out that during our days in the tropics the sun had dried out the timbers and let in the sky and that he had used matches in his cabin to plug the holes. Finally he came up with a new one — historical accuracy! He ignored his own immunity from the morning hose-down and rain and said: "I shouldn't think there was a dry bone on the first *Mayflower*."

"If we are going to be so accurate, then you should have put in a weak main beam, so it could break during a storm," I replied.

"Had you reminded me of that I might have obliged," Stuart replied, laughing. "But make no mistake; the bit of water that comes in on this ship is nothing to what they had. In their days the superstructure was additional to the ship's main hull, a sort of house stuck on with vertical timbers along the ship's sides. The wonder is they weren't washed away."

I decided not to pursue the matter further. I did not wish to be forced to thank Stuart for making our superstructure part of the ship, even if it did leak.

After lunch we hit a squall and it began to rain hard. The wind was increasing in strength and the sea looked dirty. Alan ordered the fore- and main-topsails clewed up and he had the lateen bonnet taken in and stowed below. I looked out the Great Cabin window and saw six stormy petrels. When I reported this to Wally, he commented: "That's a sure sign we're in for it. Mark my words, those bloody birds can smell a storm."

Alan called for the four mates, told them in a matter-of-fact tone that he was expecting the weather to worsen and that they were to prepare to meet any emergency. He then defined the duties of each mate should we be overtaken by a storm. The word was passed round that there was to be no shouting on deck, so that every order could be heard.

The ship started to pitch heavily, and every time she thudded into the sea the bowsprit whipped in and out like a giant fishing pole. The hum of the wind in the rigging, the pounding of the seas against the ship's sides, the splash of rain across the decks were the voice of the gale blowing with increasing fury from the east. I asked Godfrey Wicksteed to estimate the wind force and he replied: "Force eight or nine." This meant a wind of over forty miles an hour. By six o'clock there was no doubt whatsoever that we had been hit by a storm and were going to have to make a fight of it to bring the ship through intact. Thick green fingers of water swam over the sides and soon the decks were awash.

Alan ordered all hands on deck and into life jackets; life lines were rigged fore and aft. I discovered my life jacket, which usually hung behind my cabin door, was missing, but David Cauvin went below and found one for me. We joined the others on deck. Jumbo and Canada poured oil into the tin urinal fitted halfway up on the starboard side of the fo'c'sle. The oil seeped through cotton waste placed over the drainage hole and out through rubber hosing onto the sea. Thus a film of calm was spread — miraculously, it seemed to me — which contained the waves, now some twenty feet high. Alan took over the wheel and began issuing orders to take in all sail. The bowsprit was taking a terrible beating. The ship was first carried high on the waves and then plunged down into the depths of the green walls of water. The spritsail had to be taken in to prevent the bowsprit from being carried away. Somehow, despite the confusion, we hastened to obey his orders and pulled at the hard, drenched ropes. But the sail stuck. There was not a moment to be spared to prevent the spritsail, and in all probability the bowsprit, from being carried away. Four of the crew, led by Joe Lacey, did what they knew they had to do. In that sea they crawled up the bowsprit and out onto the yard, first Joe and then Beric Watson, followed by Andy Lindsay and Adrian Small. Alan shouted to me and gestured that I was to come at once to the quarter-deck. "Look. Look at that," he shouted to me as he pointed to the four men risking their lives out on the yard, struggling to clear the sail. "See what I mean about sailing ships and character? This is what makes men. You don't get this on steam."

When all the sail was in and the wheel lashed, the ship lurched and rolled under bare poles.

At seven o'clock we sighted a ship's light abeam on our port side. Visibility had now so deteriorated that John Winslow was turning the handle of the foghorn. I thought its mournful note would be lost in the storm and that a ship would be upon us, unable to alter course, before she heard our warning.

Alan was calm, decisive, smiling at those near him and nodding approval when an order was carried out. The crew began to assume their several versions of his mood. Some of them began to make jokes. Joe Powell said: "Things must be bad. See, Ike has got his raincoat on." Indeed, there was something comical about Ike. He was not wearing oilskins like the rest of us but an ordinary raincoat and his cloth cap.

Stuart and Jumbo carried out a check below decks and reported that the bilges were pretty well dry. They took up the flooring to see if there was any water in the bulkhead compartment and found it also dry. Jumbo told me that while they were below, there was little indication of anything untoward going on.

Soon, Alan had done everything that could be done for the safety of the ship. When the tugging and straining at the ropes were over, he called all hands to the quarter-deck to splice the main brace and poured the rum himself as each man stepped forward for his portion.

He said to me: "Is the radio working?" I told him that Jimmy Horrocks was below in the Great Cabin on radio watch. We went below and Alan borrowed my notebook, scribbled a message, handed it back to me and said, smiling: "I've sent it to the gentlemen who are carrying our insurance. I think they ought to be more interested in our situation than anyone else." The message read:

LUTIDINE, NEW YORK
HAD TO HEAVE TO IN STINKING GALE

The Voyage

STOP WILL GET GOING AGAIN WHENEVER
POSSIBLE STOP ALL WELL REGARDS ALAN
VILLIERS

While Jimmy tapped out the message, Alan sat back and relaxed. I stood up and looked out the stern window and saw we now had fifty or more stormy petrels to keep us company. The ship lurched down a black hill of water and I was forced to sit down.

Alan was expansive, a rare mood for him.

"Well," he said, "all we can do is what it says in the book. Foresight is the job. Now we just hold on until things get better. At any time during the past twenty-four hours I was prepared for this: the weather was worsening: we were taking a chance running on; the spritsail is too big, but the foresail is all right and so is the mainsail." He fell silent for a moment and then said: "Warwick, do you understand what I mean about sail? It requires moral and physical courage. You win out together and you get a lift. It's a different outlook towards life." He hesitated, laughed and added: "Of course, some of them take to drink."

I asked him what he would do if the wind dropped enough, but just enough, to get under way again, and he said that he might run for New York. "I'll take reasonable risks, but I am not going to lose any lives. Anyway, you know I don't like to make forecasts. The only thing certain about the sea is that it can give you a kick in the behind and that kick can be permanent." With that, Alan remarked that he must get some rest even though he would not sleep, and went back up to the chartroom.

Dick brought us some hot tea and announced that Wally had been thrown off his feet in the galley and had hurt his arm, which was cut and bleeding. "Doc has had a look at it," he said, "and given him a dressing."

Then Dick clutched at me to keep from falling as the ship went over on her side at what seemed an impossible angle of recovery. He missed, landed on the deck, roared with laughter

[211]

and exclaimed: "This is the real Pilgrim spirit, living danger-ously."

"I know," I said, "but I am sure that when they lived danger-ously, they wished it would stop, and so do I."

Before I turned in I ventured out on deck, holding fast to the life lines and waiting for my eyes to become accustomed to the dark. Try as I might, I could not penetrate the black night, though I felt and heard what I could not see — the abandon of the gale, the tumult of the angry waters breaking about us and the spray dashed into my face. We were hove to on the star-board tack, heading north-nor'west and making leeway in a westerly direction at about one and a half knots, about 160 miles from Nantucket.

Bradford might almost have been writing an entry in our log when he wrote: "In sundry of these storms, the winds were so fierce and the seas so high, as they could not bear a knot of sail, but were forced to hull . . ."

Fifty-first Day, June 9. Nobody slept much during the night and the rain continued until early morning. The water seeped through into my bunk, and although I covered myself with oil-skins, it was so damp and uncomfortable I retreated to the haven of the Great Cabin. Before I could stretch out there I had to move Felix, who had found the driest and most com-fortable place in the ship. Sometime during the night, when I was halfway between sleeping and waking, I was conscious of someone else in the cabin, although it was dark and I had not, or so I thought, been disturbed by any sound. I played with the idea of asking who was there, but the emotional strain of the storm and the sheer physical tiredness occasioned by lack of sleep for the past three nights seemed to have robbed me of the power of decision. The ship was lifted by the waves. She shuddered, began to rock, and a voice called out softly: "Hold on . . ." I recognized Jan's voice. He told me later that he had come off watch, gone into his cabin to sleep and found it flooded out. I held on, as he had suggested, and the ship went over at a startling angle, then recovered herself. The watch reported in the morning that we had gone over nearly forty degrees.

"Jan," I said, "what did you think of the storm?"

There was a long pause before he answered, as though he were measuring our storm against all the storms he had known in a lifetime at sea. Finally he said: "It was enough. Yes, for this ship it was enough."

Throughout the night we continued to lie ahull to a heavy beam swell, the dark skies overcast, drifting through squalls of rain. Alan had the wheel lashed and the ship was pitching and rolling heavily. At five in the morning there was a break in the weather and he set the foresail and lateen.

At breakfast Stuart was loud in his praise of the ship and I think he has completely identified himself with her. He did not share Jan's view that the storm had been enough. "She could ride out that sort of weather for as long as you like," he said to me.

"It was for as long as *I* liked," I told him and I could see he was quite put out.

"You don't realize what a fine ship she is," he said, but I did not reply.

It was Jan's turn to speak. "Stuart," he said, his expression most solemn, "I had a strange dream last night."

"Oh," said Stuart, "was it about the storm?"

"No," Jan replied, "not about the storm. My dream was a vivid one and concerned you."

Stuart's interest was excited. "Please tell me about it."

Everyone at the breakfast table fell silent as Jan spoke. "In my dream I was presenting you with a book."

"How nice of you," said Stuart lightly, "and what was the title?"

"Oh, a long title," said Jan. *"How to Build a Ship That Doesn't Leak."*

Stuart was speechless and I explained to him: "Jan had practically no sleep when he came off watch; the water was pouring into his cabin."

Stuart ignored my remarks and switched to a subject that was sure to claim our attention: "How many days before we make landfall?"

Of course I was hooked. "We have just over two hundred miles to go," I said, "and I should think, if we have luck . . ."

Of one thing I felt certain: this was our last Sunday at sea. When we mustered for prayers, Alan kept the service short. The crew were tired and the anger of the sea was still sufficient to make the ship uncomfortable. At ten o'clock I sighted a freighter eastbound off our starboard bow. I watched her as she buried her nose in the seas that came flooding over her sides, and reflected that it was probably far more comfortable on *Mayflower* than on the freighter. I heard Alan's voice behind me. "You see what I meant when I told you that a steamship fights the sea," he said. "But not us. Not a sailing ship. We go with the sea. We don't fight, we are part of it."

At eleven o'clock a civil airline came over us and circled low ten times, so that I could read NORTHEAST AIRLINES on her side. We were cheered to think our position was so well known that an aircraft could find us easily. We had not been in radio contact with them, as we did not work on their frequency. (I discovered later that the visit of the Northeast airliner was a combination of fine navigation and good fortune. The United States Coast Guard service had sent out a tug to locate us and render any assistance if we were in trouble, but failed to find us, as the storm had caused us to drift some sixty miles off course. However, the Northeast pilot had accurately estimated from the strength of the gale and the probable rate of our drift where we would be. Had I known this at the time, I would have dipped the Red Duster in salute every time he circled us. He sent back a message to Plymouth giving the first news that we were all in one piece, and added: "In that sea, rather them than me.")

The Voyage

Fifty-second Day, June 10. Becalmed. I had hoped that I would not have to write that word again on this voyage, but when I went on deck this morning at 6 A.M., the sun was shining down on a listless sea and I could not be quite sure whether we were holding our own or drifting westwards.

The day began and ended with visitors: our first was the fishing vessel *Captain Deebold* out of New Bedford; she came alongside and gave us six enormous lobsters, which we handed over to Wally. Later in the morning we sighted the periscope of a submarine which surfaced and came within two cable lengths of us. Alan shouted to them: "How about a tow?" and they shouted back: "O.K." This set off a furious argument on the waist deck. Edgar Mugridge was shocked. "Never heard such a thing in my life," he asserted. "We have made it this far and I don't care how long it takes, so long as we get there under our own sail." There was heated discussion on both sides of the question, with Maitland Edey, Adrian Small and others all entering energetically into the discussion. I was in a difficult position. I thought Alan had been joking when he shouted to the submarine, but I could not be certain, so I said: "If Alan wants a tow, it is up to him, and there is nothing we can do about it." Privately I thought that if there was any likelihood of our being becalmed for more than a day or two, we would have to be towed. I felt that more than our feelings had to be considered. What about the many thousands who had been patiently awaiting the ship's arrival, the officials at Plymouth and Provincetown and newspapermen who had already been on the lookout for days for the sight of our sails over the horizon?

Fortunately, we did not pursue the discussion any further. We were interrupted by an aircraft which flew low and dropped some packages in the sea. They were scattered over a fairly wide area and Beric volunteered to swim off for the nearest, while Adrian Small put out in the pram for the others. Beric was the first to return with a parcel which contained two dozen cans of ice-cold beer. Adrian rowed back to the ship, the pram laden with a similar cargo.

The Voyage

This evening there was a clear moon and a calm sea and the ship rolled in a low southeast swell. Soon after dark a launch, the *Sheila Ann,* hailed us and came alongside. Joe Meany recognized the voice of Frank Kelly of the Boston *Traveler,* who had interviewed him before he left to join the crew. I went up on the quarter-deck with Joe and he and I posed with Alan for some photographs. Frank Kelly gave us newspapers, fruit and milk and departed into the night.

We were about sixty miles from the Nantucket Lightship.

Fifty-third Day, June 11. Providentially, a good breeze came up during the night and there was only a slight swell.

From first light there began a welcome which during the day included every possible kind of vessel that floats. Our first salute came, appropriately enough, from the mighty *Queen Elizabeth.* Alan said, as the great ship sounded off her whistles: "If only there were a photograph of the two together — the *Elizabeth,* which has done so much for Anglo-American relations, and our little ship, which is contributing to the same cause." He was very touched by the mark of respect from the *Elizabeth* and I, for my part, lost all restraint and jumped up and down with excitement, cheering and shouting. But even in my excitement I noticed the *Elizabeth* was leaving less wake than we were. I could not help mentioning this to Stuart, who replied: "What do you expect? They have had over three hundred years to improve on hull design."

An armada of ships followed during the day. There were two destroyers, tugs, fishing boats, private launches and the three-masted bark *Eagle,* a Coast Guard training vessel from New England bound for Bergen. Overhead, jet fighters and bombers turned, swooped and circled us. Two Navy blimps stayed with us for most of the day and helicopters came so near that it was difficult to hear the sound of orders being shouted on deck.

The *Eagle* sailed near enough for her captain to shout anonymously: "What ship?" Alan replied: "The *Mayflower,* three hun-

dred and fifty years out from England, sir." Then he addressed
the captain of the *Eagle* by name. "Karl, where in the hell is
Nantucket Lightship?" The rest of their exchange was drowned
by the thunder of aircraft diving low.

I was on deck shaving the side of my face, carefully avoiding
the beard which I had cultivated, when I spotted Bill Brewster
in a launch. I shouted greetings to him and he shouted back that
John Lowe was looking for us in the Coast Guard tug *Yankton*.
He said that Alan's wife had arrived and was staying with the
Hornblowers, and then he began to ask me about the voyage. I
was so engrossed listening to him and bawling replies that suddenly, with one absent-minded sweep of the razor, I cut into my
beard. With this damage done, there was only one thing to do.
I shaved it all off.

Bill Brewster's launch had to leave us, as it ran low on gas.
Soon afterwards our official escort, the Coast Guard tug *Yankton*,
hove in sight. There stood John on her deck, the unmistakable
Englishman in a severely cut gray tweed suit and green porkpie
hat, looking as though he had stepped out of the pages of *Bull-
dog Drummond* and was bound for an off-shore meeting with
the agent of some foreign power.

He passed over a letter giving me details of the plans for our
arrival and also the information that we were expected in New
York by July 1, where we would receive a twenty-one-gun salute,
the traditional welcome from the fireboats, followed by a ticker-
tape parade down Broadway and finally a reception from Mayor
Wagner at the City Hall. I mentioned this latter information to
the crew, but they accepted it almost nonchalantly. I suppose
that after blimps, helicopters, tugs, fishing boats and destroyers,
a ticker-tape welcome falls easily into place.

In the early afternoon Joe Lacey sighted Nantucket Lightship
and shortly afterwards we passed her at a distance of three cables
on our port beam. As the lightship sounded off her whistle, Alan
said to me: "Now at last we can say we have made the crossing."

That night Beric Watson told me that it was the mate's birthday; he was fifty-eight years old. I decided to surprise him and

at one in the morning got together his watch on the quarter-deck with some presents. When he came out of the chartroom, we sang "Happy Birthday to You." Alan told me he had never heard the like in all his sea-faring days. A lime-juice Western ocean packet and the crew singing birthday greetings to the mate under the moonlit sky!

When I went below decks, I did not turn in at once but sat up in the Great Cabin. This was almost certainly our last night at sea. Doc Stevens said: "I think it rather sad that *Mayflower's* sailing days will soon be over." I knew that he expressed the sorrow shared by many of the crew that the ship would never sail again, that she was destined to spend the rest of her days made fast to a wharf at Plimoth Plantation. "Well, that was how the voyage was planned," I reminded him, just as though it were already over. Fred Edwards said: "Well, at least we have shown people that Britain can build and sail square-rigged ships in these days, and that we have the seamen to man them. But when she is dry-docked, it will mean that Britain will be left with no real sailing ship at all."

"Don't you be so sure," I said. "I may build the *Golden Hind* and sail her round the world." Then I turned in and tried to get some sleep, but I was restless, fearful that an agonizing calm would humiliate us in sight of the American shore. I went on deck and paced out the remaining hours until dawn. The ship was now under all plain sail on the port tack, continuously escorted by the *Yankton*. We were making over seven knots and I said proudly to the first mate: "See, she is showing off."

Fifty-fourth Day, June 12. At daybreak we were sailing up the seaward side of Cape Cod when the hitherto mild weather suddenly turned to lowering skies, rain squalls and a 30-knot southwesterly breeze. We were approaching the dangerous tidal currents around Peaked Hill Bar, a graveyard for many a sailing ship, when we sighted the red triangular warning signal for small craft at Highland Coast Guard Station.

The Voyage

The sea was becoming more choppy and the wind increasing in strength, blowing against us. In this sort of weather we could have beaten about for days, and Alan made the only decision he could under the circumstances. He accepted a tow from the *Yankton*. She took us round Race Point and into Provincetown harbor, where, at 3 P.M., the ship was secured to a buoy.

Joe Lacey looked at the bare poles ruefully and said: "Maybe we have set the sails for the last time, Warwick." But I reminded him that if the wind was right we would sail across the bay into Plymouth on the morrow.

Despite the Coast Guard warning to small craft, many ventured out to meet us. They bounced and bucked among the whitecaps, reeling out of the water, showing half their keels. On our fore-topmast we had hoisted the Stars and Stripes and on our main-mast the flag of King James I, and the Red Duster on our lateen. We also flew a yellow quarantine flag to signal the health officer, Dr. E. Heibert, to come aboard. He was followed by the customs officials, all of which formalities lasted about ninety minutes. Meanwhile, Coast Guard launches patrolled around the ship to keep anyone else from boarding us until we had been cleared. I sighted one launch on which there was a familiar face, Bill Connor of the London *Daily Mirror*. He had done a great deal to encourage and support us before we left England and John had arranged for a Coast Guard launch to pick him up and bring him alongside. Dr. Heibert could see we were fit enough, but he had to make sure that we were not bringing the plague or any other infectious diseases into the U.S.A. While I took Bill Connor round the ship, a press launch came along our port side. There must have been nearly two hundred newspapermen and women, many of them with cameras, and there was also a party of Red Indians, wearing feathered headdresses. I shouted that they could come aboard as soon as the official ceremonies were over.

In fact, the moment we were cleared, we were boarded from both sides. There were press, radio and newsreel men and a host of men and women reporters. Mr. Horace Hallett, the chairman of the Provincetown Reception Committee, shook my hand and went up onto the quarter-deck. Harry Kemp, the eighty-two-year-old poet of the sand dunes, the one who had threatened to organize a boarding party if we failed to stop at Provincetown, looking frail and white in his black Pilgrim costume, was assisted up the companionway. I caught sight of Nancy Villiers, embracing her husband and surrounded by news and cameramen.

Mr. Hallett presented a handsome bronze plaque commemorative medallion to each of us. Then we re-enacted the signing of the Mayflower Compact. I got a moment to speak to Alan and he told me that he would remain at Provincetown until early the following morning, as we had missed the afternoon tide. Fresh vegetables, fruit, milk, water and bread came aboard, and we were invited to use the showers on the *Yankton*, which was tied up on our starboard side.

If ever there had been any question in my mind as to whether the first *Mayflower* could have held 102 Pilgrims in addition to her crew, it was now answered. Our poop deck, quarter-deck, waist deck and 'tween decks were thick with people; there must have been over 300 of them.

When I had a few moments respite from answering questions and shaking hands, I went into the Great Cabin to greet Felix Fenston, who had flown out from England for our arrival. We had scarcely exchanged greetings, however, before the immigration officers asked if they could use the Great Cabin to check our passports.

Somehow amidst the enthusiasm of the welcome, the jostling crowds, the handshakes, the back slaps and the questions about the voyage, Wally and Dick managed to produce cups of hot tea and an evening meal.

When darkness fell, all was quiet. The wind had dropped. The waters were calm.

Fifty-fifth Day, June 13. We left Provincetown at five the following morning with the pilot on board. An hour later we let go the tow and set all sail, as an east wind took us across Cape

Cod Bay. There was a dreamlike quality to our progress. The early morning mist lifted in gray ribbons, revealing the placid harbor with its gulls, a setting so formal it seemed to me an example of nature imitating art.

Our trip was marked by the noisy accompaniment of cannon going off, whistles blowing and jets swooping overhead and around us. We attracted a gay armada of several hundred boats of all sizes — steam yachts, motor skiffs, power cruisers and trawlers. Even a canoe and a houseboat with an outboard motor joined the throng. They spread out fanlike around us. Along the shore I could see people running, some of them children.

By 10:30 we were off Saquish Neck and surrounded by a forest of masts. Up in the ratlines and on the yardarms the crew, in their billowing sleeves, woolen caps and buckle shoes, reefed her sails.

We had to pick up our tow again to get into Plymouth because of the narrowness of the channel. The tug came alongside at too sharp an angle and its superstructure, radar equipment, mast and searchlight began to crash against our spritsail yard. I was watching from the quarter-deck and saw one of the crew of the tug apparently crushed between the yard and the tug's mast. Joe Lacey, always the first to react, hurled himself out on the yard, straining at the canvas and braces, which had been let go. Then Joe fell himself. He came back holding his sides, and we discovered later that he had cracked a rib. Miraculously the ship sustained no damage from her tangle with the tug, and the crewman who seemed in danger of being crushed was apparently unhurt.

Overhead, helicopter passengers peered out from plastic bubbles and Alan asked the Coast Guard to shoo them away. "They make it impossible to pass orders," he said. The closer we came to land, the surer we felt that everything in Plymouth that could float was out there to welcome us.

A few minutes before noon we made fast at the buoy and swung around in the harbor so that the thousands of spectators on the shore could see us.

A thousand terns swarmed over the tip of Long Beach and

turned sharply towards the harbor. The sun peeped through the clouds as though it did not want to miss the spectacle.

After about an hour, while we waited for the signal of a cannon, the shallop which had been built by Plimoth Plantation for the occasion started out to meet us. I was among those who went with Alan on the first landing party to the ramp at the side of Plymouth Rock.

As we rowed towards the shore I noted two Indians, and one of the shallop's crew told me they were chiefs, Red Feather and Yellow Feather, both direct descendants of Massasoit, who had shown such kindness to the early Pilgrims.

I glanced at Alan, with whom I had been so proud to sail, sitting beside me holding his black Pilgrim hat in his hand, and thought how like a young Churchill he looked, with his air of imperious determination.

We walked up the steps to be greeted by Ellis Brewster, the descendant of William.

Dozens of television and motion-picture cameras whirred. I stood with my feet planted apart, wondering if I would still feel the motion of the ship underneath. A man dressed as a Pilgrim beat out a roll on the drums. Ellis Brewster stretched out his hand and said: "Welcome."

The voyage of the second *Mayflower* was over.

APPENDIX

Design for *Mayflower*

THE following is a condensation of articles by William A. Baker which appeared in *The American Neptune*.

❊   ❊   ❊

The generally accepted reliable source of information on the voyage is Bradford's *Of Plymouth Plantation*. Yet Bradford does not name or give the dimensions of the vessel, for although the voyage to North America was a decisive move for the colonists, it was but another in a long series of fishing and trading voyages for the seamen involved, not worthy of special note.

Because of references to leaky topsides and the cracking of a beam during a storm, it is generally assumed that the Pilgrims' *Mayflower* was an old vessel when she made her now famous voyage in 1620. Considering the resources of those involved, it is possible that the chartering of a newer vessel might have been beyond them. It seems unlikely at this late date that any definite information regarding her age will ever be found, but a few assumptions and deductions have led to some interesting data on a vessel that might have been "the" *Mayflower*.

From Bradford's journal and a certified copy of William Mullins's* will it has been deduced that the master of *Mayflower* on her voyage was one Christopher Jones. Through the records of the Port of London it has been possible to trace the voyages of a *Mayflower*, Christopher Jones, Master, from August 1609 to

---

* William Mullins sailed in *Mayflower* with his family. All but his daughter "dyed the first winter." His will is filed in Somerset House. File reference 68 Dale ff68, 69.

[223   ]

Appendix

October 1621, during which period there is a gap that would allow for a round-trip voyage to North America.

The last entry in the London Port Books relating to the Christopher Jones *Mayflower* is dated October 31, 1621, when she unloaded salt from Rochelle; the last record of her master is in the register of St. Mary's, Rotherhithe, for 1621–1622: "Christopher Jones, buried 5 March." He left no will and his widow, Joan, was granted a commission of administration. In 1624, acting on a petition by Mrs. Jones and two of three other part owners that described *Mayflower* as "in ruinis," the High Court of Admiralty appointed four surveyors who valued the vessel at £128 8s. 4d. Her ultimate fate is unknown.

None of the investigators to date has found any record of *Mayflower's* dimensions. The only indications of her size are the burden of "9. score" stated by Bradford and similar figures which have been assumed to apply to the same vessel as given by other writers. A published note by the Earl of Southampton* listing the vessels sent to America in 1620 by the Virginia Company mentions a *Mayflower* of 140 tons. Next in size is Captain John Smith's reference to a ship of "a hundred and three score tunnes."†

Bradford's figure of nine score is open to two interpretations. Since he was writing about a vessel chartered in England it would seem logical that he was referring to the English unit of measure — the ton. On the other hand, it has been suggested that his residence in Holland might have led to his use of the Dutch unit — the "last," which roughly equaled two English tons. However, the consensus is that the nine score was the burden of *Mayflower* in English tons. While many have marveled that so small a ship could have transported the 102 passengers plus crew, the records of similar voyages during the early seventeenth century indicate that she was not unduly crowded. For example, *Margaret and*

---

* Earl of Southampton, *A Note of Shipping Provided for Virginia*, 1620 (Duke of Manchester's Papers, No. 121).

† Captain John Smith, *The Generall Historie of Virginia, New England and the Summer Isles.*

John of 150 tons carried eighty-five passengers, and *Abigail,* 350 tons, had two hundred and thirty passengers.

Such a variation in tonnage is slightly confusing, but tonnage always has been confusing. A record in the London Port Books helps a little to clarify the problem, assuming, of course, that the Christopher Jones *Mayflower* is the one in which we are interested. In January 1620, she unloaded 153 "tonnes of French wynes," 4 "tonnes redd wyne" and 16 hogsheads of French wines. With 4 hogsheads equaling one ton, this lading adds to 161 tons, which seems to check Captain John Smith's 160 tons but, as will be seen, rules out the 140 in the Earl of Southampton's notes. On the other hand, it seems reasonable to assume that a prudent skipper would not cram his vessel full for a midwinter voyage, hence Bradford's 180 is acceptable.

Since the burden is the only information regarding size, a study of the English tonnage rule and proportions of ships of the period will lead to a range of possible sizes if nothing more. The English tonnage rule of 1582, which was in use during the assumed life of the Pilgrims' *Mayflower,* was formulated by a master shipwright of the first Queen Elizabeth, one Mathew Baker. The purpose of the rule was to set up a formula based on the basic dimensions of a ship which would give a figure equal to the number of tons of wine that a ship was able to stow. One statement of the rule is as follows:

> By the proportion of breadth, depth and length of any ship to judge what burden she may be of in merchant's goods and how much deadweight of tons and tonnage. The *Ascension* of London being in breadth 24 feet, depth 12 feet from that breadth to the hold, and by the keel 54 feet in length doth carry in burden of merchant's goods (in pipes of oil or Bordeaux wine) 160 tons, but to accompt her in deadweight, or her ton and tonnage may be added one third part of the same burden which maketh her tonnage 213⅓.

Here we must resort to mathematics to boil the above down to a simple formula. To arrive at *Ascension's* burden of 160 tons the product of her three dimensions $54 \times 24 \times 12$, which in round numbers is 15,500, must be divided by 97. So, representing the length of keel, breadth and depth by the letters K, B and D, the formula for the burden becomes

$$\frac{K \times B \times D}{97} \text{ or } \frac{54 \times 24 \times 12}{97} = 160$$

But Mathew Baker's own notebook indicates that the division should be 100, so we have as the official rule

$$\frac{K \times B \times D}{100} \text{ or } \frac{54 \times 24 \times 12}{100} = 155$$

The discrepancy of five tons may be caused by the omission of odd inches when setting down the dimensions of *Ascension,* or it may be that she actually stowed 160 tons.

Now it is necessary to determine just how the three basic dimensions were measured. The length of the keel was the straight portion that would lie on keel blocks or touch on the ground measured from the afterside of the main sternpost to the intersection of the stem and the keel. Inasmuch as the lower stem of Elizabethan ships was usually an arc of a circle coming in tangent to the keel, the exact forward end of the keel would have been difficult to determine. The breadth was measured at the widest part of the hull to the inside of the planking, i.e., the maximum molded breadth, and the depth was measured from this point to the top of the keel. Because of the difficulties in reaching these points of measurement after a ship was completed, it became more or less common practice to measure the maximum breadth to the outside of the planking and the depth to the bottom of the keel.

A single thickness of planking on the breadth might not have made too much difference in calculating the burden, but if a ship proved to have insufficient stability, the shipwrights added one or more layers of planking on the outside in way of the waterline. This was termed "furring" or "girdling," and during the period in question the English had the reputation of having more furred ships than any other nation. By measuring to the outside of this furring the value for the burden was such that a charterer was getting far less usable volume in a ship than the burden indicated. The situation became so bad, particularly with ships hired for royal service, that in 1627 a commission was appointed to investigate tonnage measurement and to devise a satisfactory rule. The commissioners were not equal to the task of accurately calculating the actual internal volume of a ship and, after considering various methods used in taking the measurements, finally confirmed the use of Mathew Baker's rule of 1582.

It is interesting to note that the depth was not measured from a deck line as became the practice later. This is a result of the fact that during the late sixteenth and early seventeenth centuries shipbuilders had no tradition of a continuous deck running fore and aft to hamper their arrangements of a ship. The hull was usually considered in three sections, bow, waist and stern, with the deck levels in each arranged as necessary to suit the space requirements.

As for the proportions of ships, the reign of Queen Elizabeth I saw the first ships being built specifically for merchant service. Merchant vessels were still armed for protection against pirates and others on the high seas but carried fewer cannon than similar-sized vessels of the Royal Navy. Up to this time there had been little difference between vessels of the merchant and royal navies except that perhaps the men-of-war were constructed somewhat stronger.

It is a common fallacy to consider ships of this period quite tubby. This comes from comparing published dimensions listing the keel length of these ships with the length on the gun deck that was commonly used for later vessels. To obtain a better comparison the sum of the forward rake of the stem and the after rake of the sternpost, usually equal to the breadth, should be added to the keel length. Actually, naval vessels of a century later were fuller than those of the Elizabethan era because the increase in armament required more displacement in the ends.

William Borough, Comptroller of the Navy from 1589 to 1598, listed the following proportions for the vessels of his time:

Appendix

1. The shortest, broadest and deepest order — to have the length by the keel double the breadth amidships and the depth in hold half that breadth. This order is used in some merchant ships for most profit.
2. The mean and best proportion for shipping for merchandise likewise very serviceable for all purposes. Length of keel two or two and a quarter that of beam. Depth of hold eleven-twenty-fourths that of beam.
3. The largest order for galleons or ships for the wars made for the most advantage of sailing. Length of keel three times the beam. Depth of hold two-fifths of beam.

Unfortunately, the only tables of dimensions for ships of the period are concerned largely with vessels of the Royal Navy, but by eliminating the larger vessels and known galleys from consideration the proportion of the remaining ships should be typical of the average merchantman-warship combination. Table I* lists the three basic dimensions, the length-breadth ratio, the depth-breadth ratio and the burden, calculated under Mathew Baker's rule for a number of moderate-sized ships of about the 180 tons burden of *Mayflower*.

TABLE I

	Name	Date	Length of Keel — Feet	Breadth — Feet	Depth — Feet	L/B	D/B	Burden
1.	*Prudence*	c. 1582	51.5	24	12	2.14	.500	148
2.	*Ascension*	c. 1582	54	24	12	2.25	.500	156
3.	*Crane*	1590	60	26	13	2.31	.500	202
4.	*Quittance*	1590	64	26	13	2.46	.500	217
5.	*Answer*	1590	65	26	13	2.50	.500	219
6.	*Advantage*	1590	60	24	12	2.50	.500	173
7.	*Tremontana*	1596	60	22	10	2.73	.454	132
8.	*Phoenix*	1612	70	24	11	2.92	.458	185
9.	*Mary Rose*	1623	83	27	13	3.07	.482	291
10.	*Adventure*	c. 1627	63.6	26.2	11	2.42	4.20	183

* From M. Oppenheim, *A History of the Administration of the Royal Navy and Merchant Shipping in Relation to the Navy.*

Since the statement of the 1582 tonnage rule used *Ascension* as an example it may safely be assumed that she was a merchant vessel — note that her proportions are nearly those of Borough's second order. Although *Crane* was built by R. Chapman, her exact dimensions are used by Mathew Baker in demonstrating a problem of comparative burdens. *Adventure* was definitely a merchant vessel and she was used as an example for the 1627 tonnage survey previously mentioned.

Table II lists the dimensions and proportions of certain unnamed vessels taken from manuscript sources, three from Baker's notebook* and two from an anonymous treatise on shipbuilding compiled about 1600.†

TABLE II

Source	Length of Keel — Feet	Breadth — Feet	Depth Feet	L/B	D/B	Burden
1. M. Baker (A)	45	20	10	2.25	.500	90
2. M. Baker (B)	48	20	10	2.40	.500	96
3. M. Baker (C)	60	24	12	2.50	.500	173
4. Anon. MS. (A)	72	24	10	3.00	.417	173
5. Anon. MS. (B)	85	25	9	3.40	.360	191

From the context of the material in Mathew Baker's notebook it is assumed that the three vessels listed in Table II are merchantmen. Items 4 and 5 taken from the anonymous manuscript are respectively a "marchauntt man" and a "man of warr."

To give a range of possible sizes for *Mayflower*, Table III has been compiled for a ship of 180 tons burden based on the data given by Borough and the proportions of the vessels listed in Tables I and II, omitting those which would produce duplicate sizes.

* Mathew Baker's Notebook, Pepys 2820, Magdalene College Library. By courtesy of the Masters and Fellows of Magdalene College, Cambridge.
† Anonymous MS., "A Most Excellent Mannor for the Building of Shippes," Scott Collection Institution of Naval Architects, London. By courtesy of the Institution of Naval Architects, London.

Appendix

TABLE III

Source	L/B	D/B	Length of Keel — Feet	Breadth — Feet	Depth — Feet
Borough—1st order	2.00	.500	52.4	26.2	13.1
2nd order	2.00	.458	54.0	27.0	12.4
2nd order	2.25	.458	58.4	26.0	11.9
3rd order	3.00	.400	74.1	24.7	9.9
Prudence	2.14	.500	54.8	25.6	12.8
Ascension	2.25	.500	56.7	25.2	12.6
Crane	2.31	.500	57.7	25.0	12.5
Quittance	2.46	.500	60.2	24.3	12.3
Answer	2.50	.500	60.8	24.3	12.2
Tremontana	2.73	.454	66.6	24.4	11.1
Phoenix	2.92	.458	69.5	23.8	10.9
Mary Rose	3.07	.482	70.6	23.0	11.1
Adventure	2.42	.420	63.1	26.1	11.0
M. Baker (B)	2.40	.500	59.2	24.7	12.4
Anon. MS. (A)	3.00	.417	73.0	24.3	10.1
Anon. MS. (B)	3.40	.360	83.3	24.5	8.8

Thus we see that, considering the known merchant vessels, *Mayflower* could have had a keel length anywhere between 52.4 feet and 73.0 feet, a breadth from 24.3 feet to 27.0 feet and a depth of 10.1 feet to 13.1 feet. The reader may make his choice.

Turning now to a consideration of the appearance of *Mayflower*, one finds little agreement among marine archaeologists. A survey of the many etchings, engravings, paintings and what-have-you purporting to be this vessel reveals some startling representations — one etching depicts the square sails set on the after sides of the masts! Bradford is of little help; the only concrete item is the inference that she carried a main-topsail: ". . . he caught hould of ye top-saile halliards, which hunge over board . . ."

Using Bradford's 180 tons as a basis for size, the late Professor James R. Jack designed and built in about the year 1925 the model that is now in the Francis Russell Hart Nautical Museum at the Massachusetts Institute of Technology. In 1928, Professor F. Alexander Magoun published plans for a model that is essentially Professor Jack's but with certain features modified by the work of Dr. Anderson noted below. The model in the Science Museum in Boston appears to have been built from these plans.

At about the same time that Professor Jack was designing his model of *Mayflower* and using the 180 tons as a basis, Dr. R. C. Anderson and Mr. L. A. Pritchard were designing and building in England the model that is now on display in Pilgrim Hall, Plymouth, Massachusetts.

Metro-Goldwyn-Mayer produced a version of *Mayflower* in two sizes for the film *Plymouth Adventure*. A large sailing model was built for scenes showing the vessel at sea and a full-size partial reconstruction for the deck shots. This version appears to have been largely based on Dr. Anderson's work.

As for Dr. Anderson's model, it is best to use his own words as published in the *Mariner's Mirror* for 1926:

> When I was asked to prepare a design for a model of the *Mayflower* I was obliged to say that to the best of my knowledge such a thing is impossible, though I could produce a model of a ship of about the right size and type. This I hope I have managed to do, but it must be clearly understood that the model makes no claim to be more than it is called on its label, an "English merchantman of the size and date of the *Mayflower*."
>
> For dimensions the *Adventure* of Ipswich was a perfect godsend. She was used in 1627 to illustrate the results of various methods of tonnage measurement. . . . On "Mr. Baker's Old Way" she was 182 tons, while her dimensions were: length of keel 63 feet 6 inches, greatest breadth within the plank 26 feet 2 inches, depth from the breadth to the top of the keel 11 feet. Avoiding odd inches I made the ship 64 feet by 26 feet by 11 feet, and by giving her a total rake forward and aft of the same amount as her beam, 26 feet, I got a nice round number of 90 feet for her length from stem to sternpost. It is possible that the 180 tons of the *Mayflower* was a "tons and tonnage" figure; in that case her "burthen" would have been 25 per cent less, or about 135, and her dimensions would have been about 56 feet by 23½ feet by 10 feet. I think it is more probable that the larger figures are nearer the mark; they give a "burthen" of 183 tons and a "tons and tonnage" of 244.
>
> As to rig; there was little doubt that it should be the ordinary

three-masted rig of the time. The only question was whether to give such recent additions as a square mizzen topsail and a spritsail topsail. On the whole it seemed probable that a small and unimportant merchantman would not have had these extra sails. We therefore gave a spritsail, foresail and fore-topsail, mainsail and main-topsail, and lateen mizzen.

The primary question to be settled in drawing up plans for the second *Mayflower* was that of dimensions. Using Bradford's tonnage of 180, there is the range shown in Table III. It was tempting to follow Dr. Anderson and accept those of *Adventure* of Ipswich, but two statements made in connection with the tonnage investigation of 1627 raise some doubts as to the reasonableness of such action.

In the body of the tonnage report is the following statement of its purpose: ". . . to measure the *Adventure* of Ipswich, the greatest bilged ship in the river, and from her dimensions to frame a rule that in our best judgments might be indifferently applicable to all kinds of frames." The masters of Trinity House made the following comment: "The old rule is less true for lately built ships, which have great floors, but true for old ships with small floors." From these two statements it can be assumed that the reason for the use of *Adventure* as an example was that she was a new and an unusual ship. Hence, the use of her proportions to represent a merchant ship of some twenty or more years earlier is questionable.

If *Mayflower*, Christopher Jones, Master, of the London Port Books is accepted as the Pilgrims' *Mayflower*, it is known that she was afloat in 1609. A few reasonable assumptions push this date back to February 1606. If she was new at that time, her probable trade and builder would have to be considered when discussing proportions — if old, perhaps, as has been suggested, one of the anti-Armada fleet, there is no way of knowing how far back proportions should be investigated. A common merchant vessel for the lumber and wine trades, in both of which the Christopher Jones *Mayflower* was employed from time to time, would have required as much stowage space as possible. This points toward short length and relatively large breadth and depth for a given tonnage as the internal structure occupies a smaller percentage of the usable space as compared with a longer, narrower, and shallower vessel.

Changes in the proportions and appearance of ships are usually noted first in the larger, more important vessels: in the early seventeenth century these would have been the royal ships. *Mayflower's* builder would probably have been working in a small yard, building to conservative proportions that had proved successful over a period of years. Assuming *Mayflower* to have been built around the turn of the century, the general increase to the length-breadth ratio of the royal ships might have led him to improve somewhat on Borough's ratios of 2 to 2.25 for merchant ships.

The fact that the dimensions of *Crane*, built by R. Chapman in 1590, are duplicated by an example in Mathew Baker's notebook is an indication that at least two builders of the period were thinking along the same lines. Both these men built royal ships, and it is probable that their examples would be followed by the common builders within a decade. *Crane's* burden of 202 indicates that she was of the same general size as *Mayflower*, hence it has been concluded that her proportions are more suitable than those of *Adventure* for a replica of an English merchant vessel of the early seventeenth century.

Crane's proportions — length-breadth ratio of 2.31 with a depth equal to half the breadth — indicate a conservative design of good capacity yet an improvement on Borough. Therefore, for the second *Mayflower*, eliminating odd inches, I proposed the following dimensions: length of keel 58 feet, breadth 25 feet, and depth 12 feet 6 inches, which, by the tonnage rule of 1582, gives a burden of 181 tons.

✿　　✿　　✿

The so-called "lines" of a ship are the plan that delineates the form of the vessel. It may look quite complicated to the uninitiated, but, in reality, it is quite simple, as it merely represents a ship cut by planes in three directions. The ship is shown in three views — the side view or profile, the end view or body plan, and the bottom or plan view.

Perhaps the simplest description of "lines" may be to liken a ship to a loaf of bread — say a loaf of French bread well pointed at the ends. The outline of the loaf as seen from its side is its profile. Assuming this loaf of bread to have been purchased ready sliced, the cuts show only as vertical lines on the side or profile of the loaf. If, however, one looks at an end of the loaf and peels off slice after slice in succession, the change in shape from the pointed end to the largest slice is readily apparent. Similarly, the sections of a ship are vertical lines on the profile, while the body plan shows one half of these sections as seen from the end — from the bow on the right side and from the stern on the left. For convenience the body plan is usually drawn on the profile or side view using the maximum section as the center line.

If, however, the loaf of bread was purchased unsliced, it can be sliced in two other directions. First, let it be cut in layers parallel to the bottom. These will show as horizontal lines in the profile, but as they are peeled off, each shows the characteristic double-pointed shape of the loaf. On the ship such horizontal planes are called waterlines and represent different levels at which the ship may float. On a lines plan, the waterlines are usually drawn below the profile.

Instead of being cut parallel to the bottom, the loaf could have been sliced lengthwise parallel to the center line. Such slices would appear as straight lines in both the end and bottom views but would have shapes similar to the profile when seen from the side. On the ship these are commonly called buttocks and are long, sweeping curves drawn on the profile.

When the drawing of the lines plan for the second *Mayflower* was started, it was apparent that modern methods of drafting would not properly produce the characteristic shape of vessels of the period. Too many models have been built whose designers have assumed that any round and chunky-looking set of lines would do. To determine and understand the methods employed by the Elizabethan shipbuilders it was necessary to survey ship-building data over a considerable period of time. Study showed that much of the design procedure was closely allied with the construction and, generally speaking, ships' lines of the period were drawn with no other tools than a straightedge and a compass. Figure 1 shows an Elizabethan shipwright and his apprentice at work on the design of a new ship.

From the straddled-log to the shaped-log canoe, from that point to the Mediterranean galleys was a process that took centuries of slow development. As time passed and builders gained experience, rules of thumb were formulated for the proportions of vessels for various services, for structural parts, and for various fittings. These rules were passed along from master builder to apprentice until they were finally set down in writing. Ultimately they appeared in printed form, but the first really useful books did not appear until the latter half of the sixteenth century, and even then many details were taken for granted. It is impossible today to comprehend some of the design procedure and to know what is meant by certain terms.

It has been said that sailing ships of 1485 differed less from sailing ships of 1785 than they did from those of 1425. Hence, works of about 1450 are as early as need be considered and perhaps those of 1700 are as late as are useful. Standing apart from the mass of background material of these two and a half centuries, and falling roughly in the middle of the survey range, are the two English manuscripts mentioned in the previous discussions of the dimensions of *Mayflower*: they are of the utmost value in this particular study. The first, "A Most Excellent Mannor for the Building of Shippes,"* an anonymous work of about 1600, gives several outline drawings of mid-sections differentiating between "men of warr" and "marchauntt men." The second, attributed to Mathew Baker, and from which the basic data for the form of the second *Mayflower* was taken, was preserved by Pepys and was titled by him "Fragments of Ancient English Shipwrightry." It has been dated circa 1586 by English authorities.

* Hereinafter referred to as the I.N.A. manuscript.

Appendix

From a study of this manuscript I believe it to be of the note-book variety compiled over a period of time. The original author did not use all the pages for data pertaining to ships, for there is much mathematical material in another hand dated 1615.

While the "Fragments of Ancient English Shipwrightry" is written in English, the spelling and letter forms are such as to make its reading something of an exercise in cryptography. There are references to the Greeks and the Venetians, and one authority believes that the well-known profile of a large four-masted ship of the period represents a Mediterranean vessel rather than an English one. Yet notes on certain diagrams show that they were used in designing some of the Queen's ships, par-ticularly *Foresight*, 1570, and *Vanguard*, 1586; hence it is a reasonable source of design data.

Ships of the early seventeenth century, indeed long before and for long after, had definite shape characteristics quite apart from the decorative features so apparent in old prints. The upper works were most noticeable as they tumbled home to high, nar-row decks: that is, the sides sloped or curved inward from the waterline. The upper decks which carried the guns were kept narrow for several reasons. The weight and recoil of the guns put a severe strain on the structure and it was difficult to obtain long beams of suitable size; joints in beams were a source of weakness.

Of great importance in the design were the shape of the largest section and its location in respect to the length of the vessel. The widest part of this section was just above the load waterline to keep the ship from heeling too far under the wind pressure on the sails. This breadth was raised towards the ends to improve seaworthiness in heavy weather by providing extra buoyancy and to give fine sections below for easy passage through the water.

The largest section was located somewhat forward of the mid-length of the vessel to give a full bow and a fine stern. One draw-ing in the Baker manuscript shows a fish's profile on the under-body of a ship — an early example of the long-held theory that a good ship should have a "cod's head and a mackerel's tail."

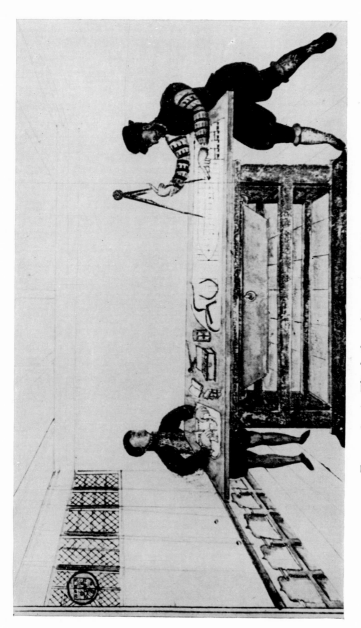

Figure 1. An Elizabethan shipwright and his apprentice

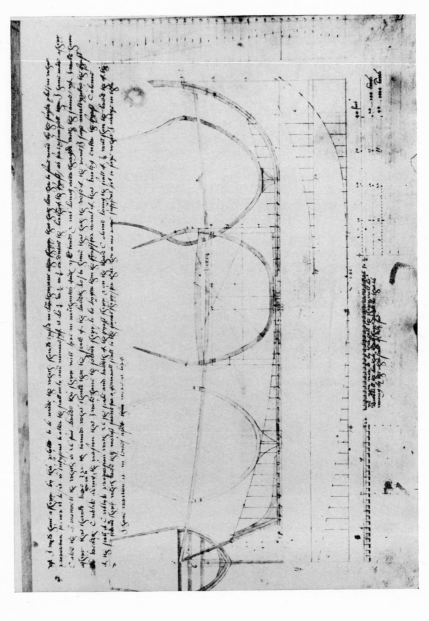

FIGURE 2. A drawing from the Mathew Baker manuscript

An attempt to describe ship-design procedure of the sixteenth and seventeenth centuries in any space less than a full-fledged textbook would be foolhardy to say the least. And to all except the technically minded such a description would be boring. But by reference to Figure 2, a drawing from the Baker manuscript, and Figure 3, the lines for the second *Mayflower*, some interesting details can be noted.

Briefly, the process of hull design consisted of setting down on paper a profile showing the keel, stem, and sternpost, the outline of the maximum section, a maximum breadth line in plan and profile, and the breadth and rise of floor lines. The curved lines are true arcs of circles, combinations of arcs, or lines derived from circles. Using the above basic lines as guides, the transverse sections through the ship were drawn in with a compass and straightedge. Available data indicates that these were transferred directly to the timbers, the shipwrights having no knowledge of fairing the sections by waterlines and buttocks.

The first step is to set out the length of the keel and to draw in the stem and sternpost. The overhangs of the stem and sternpost were termed the "rakes," and while there does not seem to be any specific data for the amount of rake at each end, the sum of the two usually equaled the maximum breadth. Published data indicates that in actual ships the forward rake was often greater and the stern rake less than shown on the drawings in the Baker manuscript. Figure 2 shows a stem profile composed of two arcs tangent to each other on a diagonal with the lower arc tangent to the keel. Other drawings show but one arc with a definite knuckle at the junction with the keel. The profile of *Mayflower* has a keel length of fifty-eight feet and uses the two-arc type of stem. The stern rake is greater than would be indicated by the published data for similar-sized vessels but not as great as the drawings in the Baker manuscript.

The next step is to delineate the maximum section, usually termed the midship section although it is not always located at mid-length, and in this there is a considerable choice of method. The available examples generally follow that shown in Figure 2, which on each side of the center line is composed of four arcs of circles and two straight lines — in a few the upper portion is a reverse curve rather than a straight line. The Baker manuscript notes that a four-arc section with straight lines is in the Venetian manner. A section having a curved floor, noted as the Greek method, and another flat-floored section, marked as Lyntton's system, are also shown. The I.N.A. manuscript gives detailed dimensions for both curved-floor and flat-floor sections. This curved-floor detail, coupled with the fact that this manuscript contains rules for the proportions of galleys, suggests that it may be a translation of a Mediterranean shipbuilder's notebook.

The best described section in either manuscript is a three-arc and straight-line section given in the Baker manuscript. One of the design problems for *Mayflower* was the determination of a reasonable method for the progressive reduction of the various radii from the maximum section to the ends. By choosing this type of section, there were a minimum number of arcs to worry about. Figure 4 shows the outline of the midship section of *Mayflower*. Mathew Baker starts his description "Fyrst ther most be maed with the bredth and depth of the shipp a paralillogram whose half shall souffyes for this works," but it is better to continue the description in modern English and the dimensions of *Mayflower*.

In Figure 4 the basic rectangle made with the breadth of 25 feet and the depth of 12 feet 6 inches is ABCD and the half "that shall suffice" is CDEF. One fifth of the half-breadth ED — 2 feet 6 inches — is subtracted from the depth CD, thus locating point G. The line HG is drawn parallel to ED. A line drawn from E to C intersects HG at point J and a perpendicular KM is erected from the base line to this point. The half-breadth of the floor is then EK and as the depth of the vessel is equal to half the breadth, half the floor is the same as DG, or 2 feet 6 inches.

The distance HL is set out as two thirds of ED. Now with a compass the center N is found on KM so that an arc tangent to the base line at K will pass through L. The second center O is found in the same manner on the projection of the line LN, while

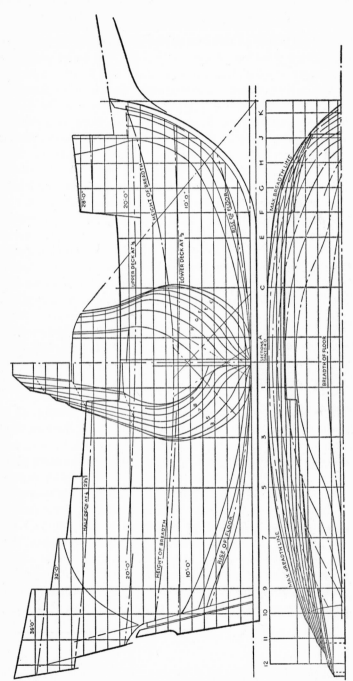

FIGURE 3. The lines of the second *Mayflower*

the third center is at Q, found by projecting a line from P through N. Point R is the same distance above Q that Q is above the base line AD. The total breadth at R is two thirds of the breadth of the ship AD.

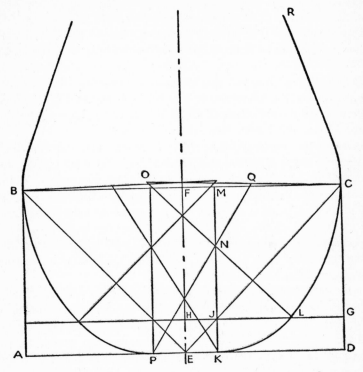

FIGURE 4. Outline of the midship section of the second *Mayflower*

In the earlier discussions of dimensions for *Mayflower* one of the reasons for the rejection of the dimensions and proportions of *Adventure* of Ipswich as a basis was a comment on the tonnage rule of 1582 by the masters of Trinity House: "The old rule is less true for lately built ships, which have great floors, but true for old ships with small floors." The floor is defined in an old dictionary of about 1620 as "so much of the bottom of her as she doth rest upon when she is aground." The widths of floor have been measured on ten of the sections shown in the Baker manuscript and these range from one sixth to one third of the maximum breadths; that shown in Figure 2 is about three sixteenths. Two sections in the I.N.A. manuscript have breadths of floor equal to three tenths and four tenths of the maximum. In 1670, Deane set out the breadth of floor as one third of the breadth of the ship. The above instructions for delineating the midship section result in a floor breadth of but two tenths of the maximum breadth. In view of this, the tonnage rule of 1582 that was used in the derivation of the dimensions of *Mayflower* is particularly applicable considering the Trinity House comment above.

As for the proper location of the maximum section on the keel, Mathew Baker gives the rule used by the "Ciscilianes and Candians" but modifies this in the light of his own experience. Without needless details and involved explanations, the rule as modified gives a location equal to 0.362 of the keel length abaft the forward end of the keel — for *Mayflower* this is 27 feet. This percentage is used on three of six profiles in the Baker manuscript: the remaining three are 0.308, 0.368, and 0.388, showing that he was not set in his ways.

In 1666 Pepys stated that Sir Anthony Deane was the first to be able to foretell the draft of a ship before it was launched. Mathew Baker was part of the way to this knowledge, for he discusses the effect of the location of the midship section on the trim of the vessel, trim being the difference in draft between the bow and the stern. He stated that "yf the same senter hade ben set on the myedest of the kell then the shipp wold have draw ase much water afore at the forefoot as abaft at the tuke [tuck]. now foreasmuch as the sentur is moved forod . . . the shipp will hange astarne as all shipp doth hose flower lyeth before the mydest of the kell. nowe to know what this shipp will draw abaft more than afore, work by the ruell of proportion. . . ." This "ruell of proportion" relates the position of the midship section to the height of the tuck (the junction of the flat stern with the sternpost). Working this out for *Mayflower* indicates that she would trim twenty-three inches by the stern.

For the drawing of the profile, the shape of the mid-section, and locating the position of this section, there have been definite instructions or good drawings plus definite dimensions. For much of the remainder of the work in drawing the lines, the design procedure is less clear. To shape the bottom of the ship, the breadth of floor, EK in Figure 4, and the lowest radius, KN, must be progressively reduced at each section towards the ends of the vessel, and at the same time the floor line must rise. Similarly, the body of the ship is shaped by suitable variations of the remaining arcs and their centers. The lines that guide these progressive variations for shaping the floor and body of the vessel are termed the rising and narrowing lines. Figure 2 shows only the rising line for the floor and the narrowing line for the body, but, fortunately, the three sections shown in addition to the midship section make it possible to develop the narrowing of the floor and the rising of the body.

From the midship section aft it can be seen that the breadth of floor has been reduced to zero at roughly half the distance to the stern but the lowest radius has been kept the same at that point. From there to the stern this radius is also reduced to zero. Working forward from the midship section, the breadth of floor becomes zero at the forward end of the keel while the radius is held as in working aft. The above pattern was followed in shaping the floor of *Mayflower* and, in the absence of definite information, it was assumed that the radius forward would be reduced to zero where the rising line intersects the stem.

By 1670, when Deane prepared his "Doctrine of Naval Architecture" of Pepys, the tapering of the breadth of floor was carried out over the entire length of the vessel instead of to the intermediate points described above. There are indications in the Baker manuscript that this was proposed if not actually done in some instances before 1600.

An indication of the rising line for the maximum breadth can be obtained by plotting the heights of the maximum breadth on each of the four sections shown on Figure 2. In keeping with the general method of design this should be an arc of a circle. Based on the measurements from Figure 2 it was so drawn for *Mayflower.*

The narrowing line that determines the maximum breadth at each section is clearly shown in Figure 2 as a combination of two arcs. There is a long radius arc from the stern to about the forward end of the keel and a shorter radius arc shaping the bow. Similar narrowing lines are indicated on other drawings in the Baker manuscript, a few being somewhat bluffer in the bow. By use of one of the diagrams in the manuscript the sections towards the stern may be made somewhat wider than a true arc would indicate. This particular diagram has been cited as the basis for dating the Baker manuscript as circa 1586 for it has the note "The firste that wase mad by this wase the *Vanguard.*" She was a large vessel of 449 tons' burden built by Mathew Baker in 1586. In keeping with the premise that *Mayflower* should represent a burdensome carrier, the bluffest of the bow lines in the Baker manuscript and the above-noted diagram were used in drawing the breadth narrowing line.

While the shape of the rising and narrowing lines of the floor have a considerable effect on the shape of the ship, those for the breadth have even more, particularly at the bow. The high rising line forward, as derived from Figure 2 and used in developing the lines for *Mayflower,* produced relatively fine lines in the forebody. The armament of warships was greatly increased during the sixteenth century, particularly in the ends of the vessels. Since the fastenings of the ship's structure were relatively poor, the whole fabric was quite elastic and this additional weight in the ends caused them to droop, a condition termed "hogging." Shipbuilders had to struggle with this hogging tendency until the end of the days of the large wooden ship. In the late sixteenth century it was partially overcome by increasing the displacement at the ends of the vessels.

To increase the displacement aft, the narrowing line for the breadth was pushed out, but the rising line was held in about the same position as on Elizabethan ships. Forward, the breadth was increased and the bow arc made bluffer, but the important change was the lowering of the rising line to a position nearer the load waterline of the ship. This position is shown very clearly on one of the plans in Deane's manuscript. It is a mistake to use this type of bow on an early sixteenth-century vessel.

In Figure 2 the curved shaded band running the length of the profile, like many of the other lines an arc of a circle of large radius, affects the external appearance of the ship rather than its shape. It represents one of the heavy timbers called "wales" which serve to strengthen the vessel and to give the apparent sheer line. Many old prints and paintings show decks following the sheer of the wales — a common error, but one wonders how an artist expected sailors to stand on such decks. Actually, there was little relation between the interior deck lines and the exterior appearance of an Elizabethan ship.

With the rising and narrowing lines for the floor and for the maximum breadth at each section determined, all the sections forward and aft of the midship section can be drawn in by progressive changes of the three arcs, or "sweeps," used in delineating the midship section. Two problems remain, the first being the reverse curve from the floor down to the keel where the floor rises towards the ends of the vessel. It is obvious from Figure 2 that in working aft from the midship section, this reverse curve reduces to zero at the stern. In working forward, the reverse at the quarter length is shown, but the ending is unknown. Again recourse was made to Deane's work and some reasonable-looking sections were derived.

The second problem is the determination of the shape of the upper works, which again were settled by reference to Figure 2, with some guesswork at the forward end. The sections aft are all straight lines with progressively decreased slopes from the midship section to the stern. Forward, the slope of the midship section was gradually worked into a reverse curve. Thus, the body plan for the proposed replica as shown in the center of Figure 4 was drawn. As a check on the sections and to make the lines more intelligible to the eye of a modern naval architect, the waterlines and buttocks were drawn.

Considering the drafting methods employed, the proposed lines as a whole are surprisingly good and indicate that a vessel built to them should be reasonably fast. The original *Mayflower's* return voyage to England of thirty-one days proved that she was no slouch. The poor windward sailing abilities of ships of the period can be attributed more to the sails and rigging than to hull form. If modern methods had been used in drafting the lines, some of the sharp reverses in the waterlines and the local bumps would have been smoothed out, but many characteristics of early sixteenth-century ships would have been lost. The lines shown in Figure 3 are the fourth set drawn for *Mayflower* and it is believed that they are as typical of the period as reasonable study and effort can produce at this time.

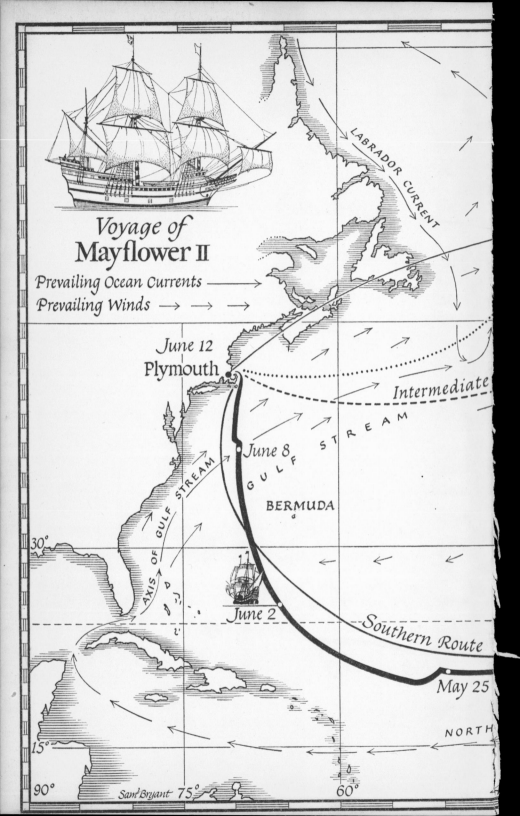

Voyage of
Mayflower II

Prevailing Ocean Currents ⟶

Prevailing Winds ⟶ ⟶ ⟶

LABRADOR CURRENT

June 12
Plymouth

Intermediate

June 8

GULF STREAM

BERMUDA

AXIS OF GULF STREAM

30°

June 2

Southern Route

May 25

15°

NORTH

90°   Sam¹Bryant 75°   60°